CW00858199

CALLED TO ADVENTURE

In Southern Sudan

Best wishes

JAN KING

Jan King

Map of South Sudan, showing the locations where I worked.

ACKNOWLEDGEMENTS

I would like to express my thanks to all those who have helped me on my journey. Firstly to my three grown-up 'children' who were happy for me to set off into the unknown and supported me in so many ways.

Alison thankfully kept all the personal airmail letters that I sent home and also helped with the editing. Murray looked after all my financial matters, including my income tax while I was away.

Peter Graystone lived in my little house, enjoyed it and made sure it stayed in good repair. Later he proof read this book and made invaluable suggestions. Pat and Keith Kingston gave me hospitality in their home several times when I was on leave in England.

My church, Emmanuel South Croydon supported me both in prayer and in giving. Several other churches also 'adopted' me while I was away, including Selhurst Evangelical Church, and St. Peter's South Croydon. Over 130 individuals gave me money to carry out to give to the pastors and their wives.

My thanks to Africa Inland Mission for being my sending body and sending my support money (from gifts from donors), so I had no financial worries during my years.

As I was writing I had friends who edited my work and made helpful suggestion: Gordon Thynne, David Huntley, Peter Graystone, and the members of my Reading Group.

Thanks too to ACROSS who found so many useful occupations for me during my years with them.

Special thanks too to Ian Chrystie and Hellen Riebold who gave me so much help with formatting and making the book and cover.

My greatest thanks are to the Sudanese themselves, so many of them. They prayed with me, helped me, encouraged me and cared for me in so many ways. I really miss their wonderful smiles and their deep, living faith in God.

CONTENTS

CHAPTER 1 HOW IT ALL BEGAN

A RUDE INTRODUCTION TO MY NEW LIFE

It was the children who heard it first, the throbbing sound of a high flying Antonov bomber, used by the Government of Sudan (GOS) to subdue the so-called 'rebel' south. The children cried out urgently, everyone looked up, dropped what they were doing and ran quickly to the nearest hole in the ground. The two Sudanese ladies who were showing us around the village, quickly led us to a large hole. The five of us tumbled in, three whites and two blacks, arms and legs tangled, lying trembling, our arms shielding our faces. The sound grew stronger and the tiny silver shape of the bomber came into view, actually looking rather beautiful, glinting in the bright sun. But it was carrying a deadly cargo that was in no way beautiful. It was fully armed with bombs sent by the GOS to subdue and crush those living in the south, who refused to accept the idea of Sudan being an Islamic republic.

The plane flew over our heads and then disappeared from sight. I got up and dusted myself down, feeling immensely relieved, but one of them gently touched my arm. "It will return," she said sadly – and it did. On its second circuit it again passed over but on the third it tipped up its nose and dropped a bomb. As it dropped we could hear the eerie whistling sound, but it fell harmlessly two hundred metres away. Now we all struggled to our feet and hugged one another in our relief. As we were visitors, newly arrived, many of the villagers gathered around us, showing their sympathy by signs, not being able to communicate in English.

One of the small boys was speaking urgently to his mother, who in turn spoke to the compound where we were to stay, many thoughts were revolving one of our guides, who translated for us. "Why were you afraid?" he asked. "Between us and the plane there was a bright light. Our God was protecting us!"

As we made our way back, many thoughts were going round in my head. First was a sincere thankfulness that nobody had been hurt, then a sense of wonder at what the small boy had just said. The predominant thought was a mixture of fear and of excitement. If this was the new life to which God had called me, what further dangers and adventures lay ahead?

We later heard that the same plane had travelled on to our other location, called Yomciir (Yomcheer) There, everyone had heard the approaching plane and it was directly overhead when it disgorged its load, they could hear it coming down with its whirring sound, when suddenly a huge gust of wind arose and swept the bomb into waste ground just outside our compound. How they praised God for this deliverance.

Back in the compound, my colleagues Russ and Lyn called for some of our workers to start digging a bomb shelter against any future unwelcome visitors. It would be a large, fairly deep hole, but without the benefit of any roof, as suitable materials were not available in this remote area.

We ate a simple meal together and retired to our huts. These huts, or tukuls as they are called, are made of mud walls on a framework of branches. The grass thatched roofs were amazingly waterproof. I lay on my back, under the essential mosquito net, gave thanks to God for the day, committed the night to His care and fell into a dreamless sleep.

CALLED TO ADVENTURE

So what was I doing, newly arrived in a war situation in southern Sudan? I was a westerner who had always lived in cities, not a youngster out for adventure, but a mature lady of sixty-two. This is part of my story that I love to relate.

In 1993 I found myself living alone for the first time, in a small house in south London. Sadly I had felt I had to divorce my husband, after 35 years together. God had brought me through the miseries of divorce, but I was 60 and now for the first time in my life, I found myself alone. I cried out to God and was aware of His presence in a new way. I had always read the Bible daily, but now I began to find new meaning and special comfort from it. I had heard other Christians say that a verse 'jumped out at them' and they knew it was directly from God. I had always felt a little sceptical about it, but now it seemed to be happening to me. The first such verse was:

"For your Maker is your husband – the Lord Almighty is his name." What lovely words of comfort, written by Isaiah the prophet of God, hundreds of years ago. Prophets in those days received messages from God, which they wrote down. Sometimes they were for their present situation, but they were often looking well into the future. I felt sure that this verse was telling me that I was not alone! But I also read, "Enlarge the place of your tent, stretch your tent curtains wide, do not hold back." How on earth could I do that, in my small house, I wondered?" Once again I became rather sceptical, but not for long, for it happened again.

The next morning I read, "Forget the former things, do not dwell on the past. See, I am doing a new thing!" Easier said than done, I thought to myself. Only God can choose to forget. But at least I must try not to dwell on the past. But what on earth is this new thing that God is doing?

Yet again Isaiah 'spoke' to me. "For I am the Lord your God, who takes hold of your right hand and says to you, 'Do not fear, I will help you. Small and weak as you are, do not be afraid, for I myself will help you.'" I really began to ask God what He was actually trying to say to me.

Over the next days, more verses from Isaiah seemed to be speaking to me. I somehow knew that this was not just for me to read for interest, but was directed straight to my heart, into my life. Then came the verse that completely changed my life.

"The Lord will guide you continually; He will satisfy your needs in a sun-scorched land and will strengthen your frame. You will be like a well-watered garden, like a spring whose waters never fail." I sat in my bed and took the verse to pieces. Firstly I realised that the 'sun-scorched land' was certainly not that dark gloomy November day in south London! Next I took great comfort in the promise that God would strengthen my frame, for I was suffering from ever-increasing arthritis in one knee. The bit about the well-watered garden was a great encouragement for me, as a Senior Citizen.

It was then that my mind went back to a huge tent at the Keswick Convention in the Lake District in N.W. England. This Convention has been going on since 1875, when 400 people attended. Today more like 4,000 may attend to hear Bible teaching.

It was in 1955 when I was a new Christian that I attended, with my mother who had also recently become a Christian. We were enjoying the meetings with all the wonderful Bible teaching. I had dropped into a Missionary Meeting merely out of curiosity and listened with some interest to missionaries from many countries telling their stories. The leader then gave the invitation to anyone who felt God's call on their life to stand – and suddenly, to my own surprise, I found myself on my feet. I was at that time a University student, so after talking with my friends, I made a tentative offer to a missionary society, but was quite rightly refused. God knew that I was in no way ready for such a calling. Gradually my sense of call dimmed and was very nearly forgotten

THE CAMBRIDGE SEVEN – OR SEVENTY

In 1885 seven young students felt the call to mission in China. One was C.T. Studd, a famous England cricketer. They all gave up their promising careers to travel to the depth of China, to share the gospel with the people there. 70 years later, in 1955

John Wheatley-Price,, a student at Cambridge had the vision of sending out 70 people to spread the gospel. Just after my own call to mission I heard about this and decided to go and talk it over with Richard. He agreed that I had been called and I was enrolled amongst the 70. Years went by. The number grew to over 80. The others all got to work, almost all in countries overseas, but I stayed at home. Then many of them returned after their years of service, some died, but still I stayed at home,

So now, in November 1993, could God possibly be asking me to fulfil that promise that I made so many years ago? I decided to visit my vicar, James Jones (later Bishop of Liverpool) to talk things over.

"I am wondering if God could be calling me to be a missionary," I said to him tentatively, wondering how this younger man would respond. Would he laugh it off?

At first he was politely interested. He wanted to hear all of the verses and together we gradually grew more excited. "I think you should meet with our Missionary Committee," he said, "so that they can assess your call."

The appointment was made for two weeks' time. I was to pray, but not to tell anyone about it, except my family, to see how they would feel about their not-so-young mother going off to some dry and sun-scorched land. I called my three grown-up children and explained. They were at first rather taken aback, but then they too became excited and each of them gave me their blessing. I was relieved, but also had to smile to myself. Usually it is the young person going to their parents and asking their blessing on a new undertaking. Now the situation was reversed.

Finally the days passed. On the evening before the committee meeting, I asked God if He could just give me one more verse, to assure me of my call. Next morning, I opened the reading set for that date and read the story in John 21 of Jesus testing Peter's love, after his resurrection. He had denied Jesus three times. Now, also three times, Jesus gave him the opportunity to put things right.

"Simon, son of John, do you love me more than these?"
The study notes told me that the word 'these' could have a variety
of meanings. But for me, it was a direct and challenging question.
"Jan King, do you love me more than these?"

I sat in my bed in my new and delightful small house, with
all my favourite things around me. After my recent divorce, my
husband had allowed me to take anything I really liked. I looked
at the photos of my three married children and Samantha, my one
small grand-daughter. My eyes strayed out of the window to the
small but beautifully laid out garden. In my mind, I travelled up
the road to my church with all its activities and of course to all
my friends. Again, the words penetrated my heart. "Jan King, do
you love me more than these?"

Here was my challenge to let go of all the known and move
out into the unknown. The internal debate went on for only a
matter of minutes. I have always responded to a challenge, and I
really truly wanted to accept this one, even if it meant letting go
of all these ties. It would mean putting my hand firmly into the
strong and secure hand of God and moving out of my comfort
zone.

I waited for the question to sink deep into my heart. Then I
made my response – "Yes, Lord, I do. I love you more than I love
all these." The next verse reads, "Feed my sheep."

The Missionary Committee had no doubt that it was a true
call of God. Have I ever regretted that initial letting go? No,
never! I sometimes try to imagine what my life would have been
like, if I had not answered God's call. It's hard to express just
what I would have missed. My fifteen years in and out of Sudan
were some of my very best years, certainly the most exciting
ones. I went expecting to give so much of myself. I was able to
give something, but what I received from being with these
wonderful Sudanese Christians is immensely more. I learned so
much from them, particularly their deep trust in the Lord and their
ever-ready smile in spite of problems. I was constantly challenged
by their faithfulness and joy in the Lord. I also learned a great
deal about myself, which is not always comfortable to know.

WAITING

The next year and a half was a time of testing. There were rejections, delays, set-backs. I applied to five different Missions that I had had contact with over the years. Two rejected me outright, saying I was too old. Feeling somewhat incensed, I wrote back to one, explaining that people in their 60s could actually be a great resource. Many were healthy, with a life-time of experience behind them. That particular mission did reply, actually inviting me to come for an interview, but by then I was in contact with Africa Inland Mission, (AIM) who had no problem with my age.

The first assignment that AIM suggested was for me to teach English in a girls' boarding school in Kenya. English was definitely not my strongest subject at school, but I felt I should do as AIM had asked. A few weeks later I received a phone call from Peter MacLure of AIM. "Jan," came his voice, "You had better sit down. They won't have you, because you are divorced." This was a great shock and extremely hurtful – another rejection at a time when I was still feeling the pain of the divorce.

Two or three years later, I was invited to spend Easter with an AIM friend, Edith Currie, who was actually working at that very school. I soon realised that I would not have been happy in the confines of a girls' boarding school. Again and again I have realised that God, in His infinite wisdom, will guide us in the best possible way, as long as we are open to His voice. I still sometimes wonder – What if I had not accepted His call to Africa? What if I had thought the whole idea was simply preposterous? Just think what I would have missed! I cannot thank God enough for His master plan and for teaching me so much. I realised that in the west when I prayed for something – and did not receive it, I could probably sort out an alternative by myself to get round the problem. But in Sudan in particular there were no other options, so the people put 100% into their trust in God. I certainly had a lot to learn!

Before I left, there were other delays and time seemed to be passing, with still no assignment in sight. I was getting older all the time – would I soon be too old? Meanwhile, I decided that it would be useful to get a qualification in teaching English as a Second Language, so in September 1994 I enrolled in a six-month evening course and gained my certificate.

The delays and the rejection were hard to accept but, with hindsight, I can now see that God was testing my call and my readiness. Also, although I was not aware of it, a good deal of healing had to go on within me after the divorce. Thankfully, it hadn't been acrimonious, but there was still a lot of hurt and the sense that I had failed in our relationship. Gradually, in his great love, God was bringing me to a position of forgiveness for myself, my husband and all that went wrong in the marriage, releasing me from the trauma of the past and healing my memories.

Then, at an AIM conference I met Doug and Gill Reitsma, who began to talk to me about southern Sudan and all its problems. They showed me pictures and as they talked a strong conviction came over me – a gut feeling that at last this was to be my assignment.

Slowly things became clearer. The 'sun-scorched land' was indeed to be southern Sudan. I have to confess that I knew very little about the country. Looking in my school atlas I saw that it was a huge country (I later learned that it was the largest country in Africa) due south of Egypt, with the Equator running through it. But Sudan itself was deemed to be too dangerous for missionaries. After they had all been evacuated in 1972 a number of groups came together to try to continue their work for the Sudanese, but working from outside the country. The group consisted of Africa Inland Mission, Sudan United Mission, Sudan Interior Mission and Missionary Aviation Fellowship. They called themselves ACROSS – Association of Christian Relief Organisations Serving Sudan. One of the departments of ACROSS was the Sudan Literature Centre (SLC). They were looking for someone who had taught in both Primary and Secondary Schools and had basic (very basic at that time) computer skills. I would be based in Nairobi, Kenya and would be working in SLC, editing church literature and school books (in

English). Although I had always disliked English in my school years, I felt I should be able to edit materials, so I was happy with the assignment.

However, in February 1995, before I left for Africa, I received a letter from Russ and Lyn Noble, who were already in SLC. It went like this: 'Dear Jan, We understand that you are going to join us at SLC. We are writing this from southern Sudan, where we are working, training Sudanese teachers. We are teaching them how to teach English. We hope that you will be able to join us.'

I have to confess that my heart failed me at the thought of actually going into the war zone, while the war was still raging. From the perspective of the relatively safe UK, it sounded pretty dangerous. Then she added, 'The temperature today is 106 F and we keep an axe in the tent to behead the snakes. Will you come?'

"Lord, I need another verse," was my urgent prayer. The next morning, it was the 8th February, I opened my Bible and the notes I was using at the time. I was back again in Isaiah, in chapter 18. My eyes nearly popped out of my head when I began to read. Verse 2 says, " Go, swift messengers, to a people tall and smooth skinned, to a people feared far and wide, an aggressive nation of strange speech, whose land is divided by rivers." The footnote read: That is the upper Nile region. I laid down my Bible and began to praise God for his amazing love in giving me such exact guidance. I wrote the date in the margin of my Bible beside what I call my miracle verse.

So it was with total confidence that this was what God had planned for me, that I wrote back to say that I would be very happy to travel with them. Although English was not my strong point, I had taught for some time in Junior Schools where of course English was taught every day.

GETTING READY

Now there was a lot to do. AIM (Africa Inland Mission) had said I must gather a good group of 'prayer partners', who promised to pray for me. I was also to raise my own financial support. AIM is a so-called 'faith mission' with the belief that if God has called someone to work, then the money can be 'prayed in'. Actually the finance was not difficult for me. Young people often find it extremely challenging, when trying to find support among their young friends. But I belonged to a missionary-minded church and my older friends were very generous. Again, in seeking prayer partners, I had a good start with my church and a wide spectrum of Christian friends. I also felt it would be good to have other churches to support me in prayer. Several of my friends went to churches which did not support a missionary of their own, so I made contact with them and was invited to come and speak about my exciting new calling.

By the time I left, six of these churches had pledged to support me in prayer. Of course, my own church, Emmanuel South Croydon was my chief supporter and donor. Some of the other churches also became very generous in gifts. This was to be a real godsend, as I never had to worry about my financial needs and was well supported in prayer.

Next I had to prepare a Prayer Card to distribute among my supporters. I didn't fancy a picture of myself but I found a black and white picture of school children sitting on stones under a tree, holding slates and listening to a teacher, who had a blackboard on an easel. It seemed to sum up what I was hoping to be involved in. Barbara Ashton and later Fiona White were my faithful prayer secretaries, who had agreed to send out my prayer letters four times a year. At that

Please pray for
JAN KING
working with Africa Inland Mission
on behalf of the children of Sudan

c/o ACROSS, P.O. Box 44838
Nairobi, KENYA

time, few of my friends and supporters were on email, so these mostly had to go out by post. However, as the years passed, the use of email made it very much easier – and less expensive.

Some of my prayer partners kept in touch really well. I received lots of letters and was overwhelmed with birthday cards each year. (I suspect that my daughter Alison had a hand in reminding people!). Each time I came home, I sat with Fiona, my prayer secretary and went through the list. Occasionally someone had died or had decided they could no longer pray for me. There was always a good number who never made any contact. I remember discussing with Fiona whether I should take them off the list. Happily we left them on. After I came home I finally met some of these 'hidden' people and was amazed when several said, "I prayed for you every day while you were in Africa." How I thank God for all these faithful 'prayer warriors'.

Next was the problem of what to do with my house. I did not want to leave it empty for a year. At that time, Peter Graystone, a member of our church, was looking for a temporary home. He had been working with Scripture Union, but when they were moving to Milton Keynes, he decided not to go with them. His hope was to become a free-lance writer. (He is in fact very successful and has published a good number of books). So I was able to offer him the house, on a very low rent, just to cover any expenses. He was very happy to accept the offer. We both expected that this would be for just the one year. So there was none so happy as he when I extended my contract for another – then another and yet another year. He was a wonderful tenant and cared for the house beautifully. I remember an email I received from him, which read, "One of the tiles has fallen off in the bathroom …. So I have taken the day off to get it fixed." It was only the garden that was a really great challenge for him! He stayed in the house until 2003 when he was asked to 'house-sit' by another friend for three years. Now he has his own flat.

There was also the matter of my contract with AIM. As Sudan was deemed dangerous, I had to sign an indemnity form and also get my family to read it and agree that I should sign. Part of it read,

I acknowledge that the mission field I have chosen is located in an area where there have been civil and political disturbances that may affect my personal freedom and safety. I

18

have carefully evaluated the potential risk of a personal injury or detention, and I believe that risks are worth undertaking in order that my missionary services can be accomplished. I hereby agree to personally assume all the risks associated with this mission service.

The mission also asked the family what they would like to be done with my body, in case I was killed in Africa! As you can imagine, this was not easy and it was the last question that brought tears. However they could see that my heart was set on it, so we agreed that I would be buried in Sudan. It was not without some qualms that I finally signed the document.

PACKING UP

I managed to make some mistakes – very common for enthusiastic new missionaries. It seemed to be a very good idea to take lots of children's clothes with me, to distribute, particularly

any school uniforms. One school had recently changed their school dress so they gave me a large number of purple and white gingham dresses. A group of willing helpers joined me in sorting the clothes. However it slowly dawned on me that I was only allowed 20 kg on the plane and the clothes would have to be sent separately. We found that that would cost far too much, so we found another 'good home' to send them to.

The other project was pencils. I was sure that this would be something really useful, so appeals went out for pencils. People responded generously, some people buying new ones and others raking through their desk drawers. Soon we had nearly 1000 – and these I was determined to take with me.

My local paper, The Croydon Advertiser got wind of this and came to interview me. They brought a camera with a large shiny disc which was used to direct the sun on to my face. The resultant picture showed up every wrinkle I possessed! When it was published, we noticed in one corner of the page an advert for Wrinkle Cream! I later inquired whether the advert was just a coincidence, but they confessed that it was their little joke! The article, in the issue for August 8th, 1995, was actually quite good.

PENSIONER HEADS FOR BATTLE ZONE CLASSROOM

Pensioner Jan King is defying Foreign Office advice and flying out to an African war zone at the end of this month. ...

She has raised £20,000 for living and travel expenses without asking anyone for money. The money accumulated thanks to people learning about the needs in Sudan and her strength of belief in God, she said, "God has spoken to me through the Bible and told me to act."

Daughter Alison Lawton said, "I hope she will be safe. We are really going to miss her. ... We were quite worried at first but it is a wonderful thing she is doing and we'll be supporting her wholeheartedly."

A spokesman from the Foreign Office said, "The security situation in southern Sudan is still unstable despite the ceasefire. Our advice is do not visit these areas unless on an essential visit."

After this interview, there was still a lot to do. I had a good number of injections to face – typhoid, rabies, meningitis and yellow fever, were all on the list. Then there were decisions about whether to take malaria tablets, or just try to build up my immunity while in Africa. Fortunately Nairobi, where I was to be based, is about one mile above sea level, so mosquitoes are not a problem, but I would need to consider the trips into the heart of southern Sudan. The advice was only to take tablets for my trips into Sudan. Happily they were totally effective, so I never succumbed to malaria. This, I'm sorry to say, was not true of the other diseases as, in spite of every precaution I contracted typhoid twice, as well as other tropical sicknesses.

I was only going on a one year contract (or so I thought at the time), but there were still so many decisions! What did I need to take in the way of food – if anything? It seemed that people already there would value Marmite, so that had to go into the luggage. What clothes? What shoes?

My flight was booked for Monday 28th August, 1995 and I knew I was only allowed 20 kg of luggage. But as I gathered all my goods, as well as all the pencils, it was well above the 20 kg. So I put as much as I could into my hand luggage (a backpack) and we all prayed that I would get through.

Before going on with the story, it might be helpful to write a little about my early life.

CHAPTER 2 EARLY LIFE 1933-44

I was born in April 1933 in Leeds, in the north of England and was baptised into the Church of England on 18th June, the same day as my grandparents' golden wedding. They had a big gold cake – with a little white one on top, for me. I still have a photo of the event, although I do not of course remember anything about it!

I was not exactly 'born with a silver spoon' – or perhaps I was, for I still have one given to me by my godmother, but I did grow up in comfortable circumstances. My father was a doctor, the old-fashioned sort, who was much beloved by his patients and cared for them day and night.

FAMILY HOLIDAYS

When we were young we mostly went for lovely seaside holidays at Scarborough and Filey, on the Yorkshire coast. But being a Scot, our father also took us to Scotland. He had a number of cousins in the borders, in Selkirk, Galashiels and the small village of Bowden. We sometimes stayed with his two maiden great-aunts, Aunt Isa and Aunt Cissy, a very eccentric pair! Aunt Cissy had a passion for foreign missions and when my father stayed in Bowden she sometimes had a missionary staying with her.

They really belonged to another world. In their younger days they travelled in a small 'dog cart' drawn by their pony. They were very conservative in their dress and rarely bought any new clothes, as long as the old ones were still serviceable. However Aunt Cissy had a particular penchant for black bonnets and often treated herself to one. After she had died, seventeen nearly identical bonnets were found in her cupboard.

My father told me a story about one holiday when I was four years old. We were staying in Bowden near the Eildon Hills, a group of three hills, the middle one (the Melrose Hill) being slightly over 1000 feet and so just qualifying to be called a mountain. My parents decided we were old enough to tackle the Melrose Hill. We set off in good heart, but after quite some time, my father could see that I was lagging a little. "Would you like a piggy-back?" he asked.

"No," came the determined reply. A little later, he asked again – and again and again. Finally when asked if I was tired, I replied, "Yes, but I like being tired!"

In many ways this has been true for the whole of my life. I still love to go to bed tired, feeling I have done a good day's work.

I was the second child, with a brother Ian, two years older. Ours was rather a Victorian upbringing, as we only really saw our parents on our family holidays and when our nurse, having prepared us for bed, took us down to say goodnight. We had a nurse when very young, followed by a nanny. Then in 1938 my parents provided us with a German woman, who today would be described as an au-pair. She was very strict, a great contrast to our previous nanny. Ian did not like her at all! I got on better and she began to teach me some German songs, one of which I still remember. I think this might have been responsible for the love of the German language that developed in my later years. However she did not stay long, as war with Germany was looming, so she departed hastily before being interned in England. Ian and I viewed her departure with some relief.

At five years old, I started at St. Agnes' School, a small private establishment. The fees were three pounds, thirteen shillings and sixpence a term, with French, music, dancing and eurhythmics as 'Extras'. However, my stay was to be short-lived as the Second World War was upon us. We were evacuated as a school to the safety of Nunnington Hall, near York. It is now a

National Trust property. I have few memories of that time. One was of sitting on a swing crying for my parents. However I soon got over my homesickness and began to enjoy it. My parents remember a letter I wrote home. I had clearly been learning spelling like bough, bow, rough etc. So I informed them that I was in bed with a cow!

My father had a number of second cousins in America. They began sending messages, saying "Send the children to the safety of America". At that time it was thought that the war would soon be over, so my parents decided to act upon their invitation. I was far too young to understand fully what was going on, but when my own children were of similar age, the thought of sending them away was extremely challenging. I am sure my parents must have gone through a variety of conflicting thoughts and emotions before taking such a major decision. But evacuation was all around us. Thousands of children from London and other cities like Leeds were being evacuated to the countryside, so my parents took the final decision and made arrangements for our trip to cousins in Buffalo, New York.

OUTBREAK OF THE SECOND WORLD WAR

In 1940 my father had volunteered to join the Royal Army Medical Corps with the rank of Captain and was drafted into the 1st Battalion of the 1st Regiment of the 1st Expeditionary Force and soon found himself in France.

My father leading his men

As they advanced into France, he was in charge of the 1st Field Ambulance. He worked out a plan for how the ambulance should be arranged, so all that was needed was easily available. This pattern was then copied by all the other ambulances in his group.

As he travelled through France, he found many men sitting around idly, so he asked them why they were not with their battalions. They told him that they all had minor orthopaedic problems, like in-growing toe nails, so they could not march.

"Why has no-one treated you?" he asked.

They explained that as soon as any orthopaedic surgeon arrived, he was immediately sent on to another location. Although my father was only a General Practitioner, in those days GPs often did minor surgery, including taking out tonsils. (My tonsils were removed by his GP partner, under anaesthetic, lying on the kitchen table!)

After a makeshift operating theatre had been erected, my father asked if any of the other RAMC people could do anaesthetics. One man volunteered, explaining that he had not done any since his student days, but was sure he would be able to do it.

The men were brought in one by one and my father performed their operations. After it was all over, he casually asked the 'anaesthetist' what had been his job as a civilian.

"Oh," he replied," much to my father's surprise. "I was an orthopaedic surgeon."

"Why didn't you say so?" demanded my father.

"I thought it would be good experience for you, "he replied. "If you had made a mess of it, I would have stepped in and taken over. However, you did a splendid job!"

DUNKIRK

The British Expeditionary Force advanced into France. On May 10th, the Germans began air raids, followed by land attacks on Belgium and Holland. On 14th May the Dutch surrendered, followed by the Belgians. It was also becoming clear that the BEF was in a perilous position. The German army was advancing and there was the danger of the British forces being trapped between them and the sea. So on 26th May, 1940 the difficult decision was made for the British to withdraw towards the French port of Dunkirk, holding back the German advance as much as they could. When they reached the coast, their position seemed hopeless, as more and more allied troops arrived on the beaches.

There then followed one of the most amazing yet unlikely evacuations that has ever taken place. Messages were sent out asking owners of boats to cross the English Channel to Dunkirk to rescue our men who were trapped between the approaching German Army and the sea. As well as our naval craft, over 850 boat owners responded and a flotilla of small boats, pleasure craft, fishing boats, lifeboats crossed the Channel time and again over the next nine days. Thousands of men lined up on the beaches and then waded out, often up to their necks in the water, to get on board the bigger ships that were not able to come nearer to the shore. The bigger boats were raked by machine gun fire

 from the German planes, but over 300,000 men, both British and French were brought to safety. One of the last boats to get through was a paddle boat called the 'Medway Queen' and that was the boat on which my father returned.

After ensuring that all his men were on board, he also climbed on board and began the very slow six hour trip back to England. After landing he was able to contact my mother, to her infinite relief. He was home! He was offered the Military Cross for Gallantry, but refused it, saying that his men deserved it just as much as he did.

The paddle steamer 'Medway Queen' is the last estuary pleasure steamer surviving in the United Kingdom. She was built in 1924 on the River Clyde in Scotland. The ship is 180 feet long and 50 feet wide over the paddle frames. She had been built for service between the Medway Towns and Southend-on-Sea. However this comparatively simple task was put aside when she was requisitioned by the War Office. She saw active wartime service between 1939 and 1945 with her finest moment in 1940 when the ship and her crew made seven crossings to the beaches of Dunkirk rescuing 7000 British and French troops. Her bravery and that of her gallant crew lead to the title "Heroine of Dunkirk" being bestowed. After the war the 'Medway Queen' returned to pleasure steaming on the rivers Medway and Thames, under her original owners, until withdrawal in 1963. Now there is a Preservation Society which is seeking to restore her to her past glory. Recently I had the opportunity of going to see her. I felt very emotional when I stood on the deck of the ship that had saved my father.

That was actually the end of my father's military career. So many doctors had been drafted into the army that our people back home were lacking medical care, so for the rest of the war, he ran two GP practices single handed. In 1948 he very surprisingly received a telegram from the war office, telling him that as he had never been officially demobilised, he was still in the army. It included an order to report to Catterick Camp within 48 hours! After a recent X-ray it had been discovered that he had a hairline fracture on one of his vertebrae (an old rugby injury). So he sent a telegram back, to the effect "I am 48 years old and have a broken neck." Needless to say, he heard nothing more.

After sending the message, he remembered an amusing story of army parlance. A friend was claiming his expenses and wrote – porter 1 shilling, cab – £1.00. The reply came back, "Do you mean porterage?" So he wrote 'porterage – 1 shilling, **cabbage** – £1.00." His expenses were duly paid to him, without further comment.

Another incident relating to Dunkirk happened many years later. In about the year 2000, a lady called Maria Randell belonged to the same Keep Fit class as I did. We got talking and discovered that both of us had been to Leeds Girls' High School, although I later went on to the Mount School. Unlike me, she was still receiving the Old Girls Newsletter. In one issue she noticed a small advert asking Janet Scott, who had been at Leeds Girls in the 40s and 50s and had gone on to boarding school, to ring a certain phone number. Although she did not know my maiden name, she guessed that it was probably me – and she was quite correct. I was very intrigued, so I rang the number, which belonged to the editor, who then put me in touch with Dr. Douglas Inch, my father's junior partner – now 90 years old. They had been doctors together until my father retired in 1965.

It turned out that after many years, the medical practice was finally moving to new premises. During the packing up stage, they found a silver inkstand, with the following inscription:

PRESENTED TO MAJOR R.A.M. SCOTT, R.A.M.C

By A Coy No 1 FIELD AMBULANCE, 1940.

This must have been given to him after he ensured that all his men returned safely from Dunkirk. What a lovely thing for us to have returned to us after so many years. Only one of my grandchildren has Scott as a middle name, so I shall pass it on to Peter one day.

EVACUATION

The decision for us to be evacuated was taken after the Dunkirk evacuation in 1940, when it appeared that Hitler might well invade England next. Our mother rushed us to London to get passports and visas. We shared a passport and I was included on Ian's passport as his wife!

Our evacuation was well timed, for the German bombing campaign began in earnest. Hitler's hopes of invading England had been foiled by the success of the Royal Air Force in the Battle of Britain, in July 1940. As he could not invade without control of the air, he turned to bombing instead. We left England in August and in September the Blitz began. (Blitz is short for Blitzkrieg – Lightning War). It lasted from September 1940 until May 1941.

In order to confuse the enemy, if they were to land by parachute, many signposts were either removed or turned round so they were facing in the wrong direction. This caused my mother a lot of headaches! For after my father's return to his medical practice, she joined the Mechanised Transport Corps and became a Captain. Her task was to meet important army or navy personnel at Leeds station and take them to secret locations in the countryside around Leeds. So you can imagine what problems she had with the signposts being of no help whatsoever!

During the war, nobody took normal family holidays. However there came a few days when my mother was on leave and my father could leave his practice, so they took their tent out into the Yorkshire Dales and planned a short period of resting and being together. During their first night, a German bomber happened to be returning from a raid and had not yet dropped all its bombs. As the crew were not allowed to return with any bombs on board they decided to get rid of the unwanted bombs – and dropped them in the next field to where my parents were camping! I never heard the end of the story – whether they stayed as planned, or made for home.

All the able-bodied men were conscripted into the armed forces and the others were all working for what was called 'the war effort'. They were in factories making armaments and other materials needed by the troops. Others were in what were called 'reserved occupations' like doctors, police, hospital workers etc. Others were conscripted into the mines, digging out the coal which was so desperately needed to keep the factories going and to provide warmth for our homes.

It is hard for us in the new millennium to imagine what life was like during the war. For those in London, who suffered the blitz, with bombs falling and destroying property night after night, it was a nightmare that never seemed to end. Many families slept every night in the Underground Stations. The Chislehurst Caves, on the outskirts of London were another favoured destination. This extensive system of tunnels was taken over by families. Each had their own patch. Committees were formed who drew up rules of behaviour. No noise was allowed after 10 pm for the workers urgently needed their sleep.

All around the country people lived in real austerity. Bath water was meant to be only five inches deep. Coal was rationed, so people had to put on their warmest clothes in order to save this precious commodity. As clothing was rationed, people made their garments last as long as humanly possible. Younger children never had new clothes, but wore 'hand-me-downs' from their older siblings. It was the era of 'Make Do and Mend'.

Air-raid shelters were dug by those who had gardens and families, who furnished them with bunk beds and a little furniture. Many a night was spent by British families, sleeping in these shelters. Other families, who had cellars, did the same, putting bunk beds there. Another idea was the Morrison shelter, for those who did not have gardens. This was a large steel table, 6 feet 6 inches long (2 metres). It was given free to families whose joint income was less than £350 a year. It came as a flat pack kit, in over 300 pieces for the family to construct. Clearly, beds could not be put beneath it, so during a raid the family would cower together under the table. An elderly friend still has hers, which she uses as a kitchen table!

It was the combination of all these factors and the urgency of my father's cousins who offered to have my brother and me to live with them, that caused the decision to be taken that we should go to America.

OFF TO AMERICA, May 1940

Once the decision was taken to send us to America, my mother went up into the attic to find a trunk in which to pack all our clothes and belongings. It was a rather old red trunk, with the name of a ship painted on it – the Duchess of Atholl, a Canadian Pacific liner nicknamed the 'drunken duchess'. This was left over from a cruise my mother took before she married.

The fateful day came, actually during the evacuation from Dunkirk. We were informed of the place and time when we had to report to Liverpool docks, It was very 'hush-hush' and we were to tell nobody. As we drove down the street early one morning, there was this huge ship. It all seemed very exciting to me, although I cannot think what it must have been like for my parents.

We stood in line with our luggage. When we reached the head of the queue, the official looked at the trunk in surprise – almost alarm. "How did you know the children were going on the Duchess of Atholl? You must be spies. We certainly won't take your children," he announced to my startled mother. Fortunately the paint on the trunk was old and chipped, as my mother was able to point out. It was merely a great co-incidence that it happened to be the same ship. We learned later that had we not gone on the Duchess of Atholl, but on a later ship, we might not

still be here! For the next ship to depart with child evacuees was the City of Benares. This ship sailed in a convoy on 13th September, 1940 with 404 people, including 101 adult passengers and 90 child evacuees. When they had been sailing for four days, disaster struck. At 10 pm the ship was torpedoed by a German U-boat, U-048. The order was given, 'Abandon ship'. A force 5 gale was blowing and it was difficult to lower the life boats. Several capsized. In the pandemonium, not all the children could find life jackets. Many fell into the sea. Although help was sent, it was far too late, for the sea was very cold and rough. In all, 145 people perished, the majority of them being children. In fact only 13 of the 90 survived. Six of them spent seven days in a life boat before being rescued by another ship. The Duchess of Atholl was herself torpedoed in 1942, but in that incident all the passengers and most of the crew were saved.

Many stories have been told by the survivors. Perhaps the most poignant was of two brothers. As their parents said 'goodbye' they charged the older boy to look after his younger brother. When the order came to abandon ship, they had only one life jacket between them. The older boy insisted that his younger brother should have it. He was among the survivors, but the older lad drowned.

We were supposed to be under the watchful eye of a friend of my parents, who was travelling with her children. However, we ran wild and had a good time, until I was overcome by seasickness. Our ship's menu was in French, which did not help us. I remember having fish followed by pistachio ice cream every day. The ship was commonly known as the "drunken duchess" because she rolled so much being designed with a shallow draft for navigating the St Lawrence River. We sailed alone without escort, which was a little worrying as a German pocket-battleship was reputed to be in the vicinity. Luckily, and no doubt in part due to the foul weather we had no problems. Our total armament was one 4" gun and a lot of depth charges, which were stored in the pool!

IN AMERICA

It was a great relief when we finally sailed up the St. Lawrence River and landed in Montreal, Canada. My father's cousins met us and drove us across the Peace Bridge into USA, to Buffalo in New York State. I was car sick all the way and slept for a good 24 hours on arrival. My Aunt Jean Wood and her husband Uncle Luther welcomed us into the family. They had two daughters, both older than us, Jean Scott and Sally. I was enrolled in Elmwood Franklin Elementary School while my brother stayed only a short time at a school in Buffalo, then was later sent off to boarding school in Canada. It was thought that, as a boy, he should have a more English type of education, to prepare him for his return to the UK, where our grandfather paid the school fees for all his grandsons to go to Charterhouse School. We girls were clearly of no great importance to him!

Winters in Buffalo were extremely cold but lots of fun with plenty of snow, skating and tobogganing. We spent the summer with my Aunt Gay (another of my father's cousins) and Uncle Jack in their lovely house on the shore of Lake Erie, which was not polluted in those days and so we could swim in it.

We were well settled when the next problem arose. Uncle Luther had a heart attack and was told to cut down on his work and spend more time at home. Four children seemed too much, so one of us had to go. Of course Ian needed to be near to Canada for his schooling, so I was the one to go. After a short stay with my Aunt Gay on Lake Erie, I was finally sent to stay with a cousin of Aunt Jean, in Washington DC. So at 8 years old, off I went on my travels again, being sick most of the way!

THE DONOVANS

This cousin was my Aunt Ruth, married to a General called Bill Donovan, so I called him Uncle Bill. But he was no ordinary man, as I found out later. He was a general, with the nickname of Wild Bill Donovan, which he had acquired from his earlier exploits.

The Donovans lived in a very large house in Georgetown, the smart area of Washington D.C. on the corner of 30th Street and R Street, with servants and a lovely black butler called George, who wore a white jacket and a bow tie. It never entered my head to question the fact that white people had black servants working for them.

Bill Donovan had been involved in espionage and between the two World Wars had worked closely with President Roosevelt. During the Second World War Bill's espionage work now became of first importance. He was given a new office and a bigger staff. It was also given a new name, the Office of Strategic Services, the OSS. He was given the title of Co-ordinator of Information. As far as possible its activities and even its existence were to be kept as secret as possible. He also became very friendly with Winston Churchill, who occasionally came to dinner.

As a child, I was not aware of any of this. The Donovan's granddaughter Patricia was also living there, but she was only four years old. She had a French governess, who spoke to us in English in the mornings and French in the afternoons, so I became quite fluent in French during those years.

I was sent to a very select school, in Bethesda, Maryland, travelling by school bus every day. I do not remember being sick on the bus, which was a great relief. I do remember sharpening my pencil with a penknife on the bus and cutting off the end of my middle finger, which bears the scar to this day. The classes were very small and we came from a variety of countries. My best friend Astrid turned out to be a Norwegian princess. I sometimes stayed for the weekend with her, her father Prince Olaf, who later became King and her brother Harald, who is currently King. I caused a bit of a stir at my local cinema in Leeds, after my return. On the Pathe News they showed Olaf – now King Olaf. I commented in perhaps an over-loud voice, "Oh, I've stayed the weekend with them!"

The Donovans were extremely well-off. As well as the Washington house, they had a farm in Virginia, a sea-side house on Cape Cod, Massachusetts and a permanent apartment in the Ritz Hotel, New York. I would often be sent

CHAPEL HILL FARM

down to the farm for the week-end or in the holidays, travelling on a Greyhound bus. It was a lovely place to be, on the edge of the Blue Mountains and I used to roam about on my own. One day I was chased by their prize Aberdeen Angus bull, weighing over a ton. Fortunately bulls can't turn corners very quickly, so I kept darting round the one and only tree in the field until it got bored and moved away. Finally I plucked up courage and fled towards the fence, jumping over it to safety.

I was a lonely child. Although I have very few memories of my time in Virginia, I had an interesting experience in the 1980s. I was on holiday with my friend Pat Kingston, who sometimes has very vivid dreams. One morning she told me of a very odd dream of a young girl with fair curly hair (yes, it was fair then, rather than the current muddled grey/white.) The girl was sitting on a blue mountain, crying. As she recounted this dream, I found myself in tears, for the young girl was surely myself, in one of my lonely times in the Blue Mountains.

One comfort on the farm was the dogs. They had an enormous Great Dane called Elaine and a very small white Sealyham terrier, who loved to run in and out between the Great Dane's legs until it was exhausted. Then they would both lie down and sleep, with the terrier between the Great Dane's paws. There were the cattle (Aberdeen Angus as mentioned above) and horses. My Aunt Ruth (Uncle Bill's wife) had a wonderful glossy brown stallion, but I was not allowed near. Sometimes my brother Ian joined us at the farm in the holidays. We decided one day we would like to learn to ride. As the horses were forbidden, we decided to try to ride the two mules, called Muffin and Puffin, with somewhat painful results!

Every August we spent some weeks in Nonquitt, on Cape Cod, where I have memories of golden sands and clam bakes on the beach. Here I had my first encounter with a poisonous spider, which has left me to this day with a great dread of spiders – not very helpful when you later go to live in the wilds of Sudan. I had been swimming and was in a small beach hut. Having removed my swim suit, on the wall of the hut I saw a large hairy and very poisonous spider, a black widow, a few inches from my face. I was terrified, but did not dare rush out in the nude, so I had to very gingerly pick up a towel to cover myself and burst out of the hut. People came quickly and dealt with it, while I looked the other way.

Another unusual experience was in a hurricane. It was on the night of 14th September, 1944 when it struck. Warnings were given on the 'wireless' and in the local papers. Our house was near the top of a cliff, but the decision was taken that we should

35

stay put. Our mattresses were brought down from the bedrooms as a precaution. I didn't find it very frightening; with the carelessness of youth I thought it was all very exciting! The wind increased between 9 and 10 pm until it was blowing at 100 miles an hour. Fortunately the tide was already going down, or the results might have been even more devastating. Thirty-one people were killed in the storm. When the wind had died down we were allowed to go out. We could not believe our eyes. Many houses were in ruins, our beach huts were nowhere to be seen. The road was littered with boats, and many cars were in the sea. Falling trees (it was estimated that over 2,500 mature trees were destroyed) had damaged electricity cables and telephone lines. The State Guards of Massachusetts, the Red Cross, the Coast Guards and the Civil Defense (American spelling) all arrived to help the victims and to gradually restore order in the many towns and villages that had suffered in the storm.

I've just come across a letter I sent my parents in October, after the hurricane. It contains some rather terrible riddles and a letter, all of which had been opened by the Censor. It explains that we couldn't return to our home in Washington because there was a big scare about infantile paralysis (Polio) so the doctor told us not to come. It was now too cold in Nonquitt, so we went to stay in the St. Regis Hotel in New York in the apartment belonging to the family. I, of course, was delighted as we were able to visit the Empire State Building (at that time it was the tallest building in the world), Central Park, the Chrysler Building and the Statue of Liberty. There we were able to go up, first by the lift, then by the stairs (I counted 168 steps) in the head of the statue. The further steps up into the arm of the statue had been closed for security reasons during the war.

At that time, the war was dragging on, but it was clear that victory would soon be won. My parents wrote and suggested that it was time Ian and I came back home. They were very keen that my brother, who was rising 13, should get back to England to start his schooling at Charterhouse. It was arranged that he should cross the Atlantic on an aircraft carrier in August 1944. It seemed my time in USA would soon be over and I might soon be going home.

Here is part of my brother's story –

I was pulled out of school and whisked to New York in March 1943. I was duly outfitted for a return to England and taken to an elegant hotel for a secret rendezvous with officers of the British navy. It turned to be far from secret as the entire hotel staff knew I would be a passenger on HMS Premier, an escort aircraft carrier given to the British Navy by the US. A family friend, who knew Winston Churchill, had arranged for me to return in time for schooling at Charterhouse. Our group of about 20 was driven to the Brooklyn Naval Yard where we embarked. We joined a convoy of about 60 ships of various sizes and speeds. The trip was not uneventful.

One day while we were being shown how the radar worked, the operator noted a blip heading towards the convoy. It was a German U-boat and it torpedoed and sank one of the Liberty ships. It was duly rammed and sunk by another of our escorts. The survivors from the submarine were brought on board our ship and the destroyer had to limp home for repairs to its damaged bow with another destroyer as escort. We encountered one of the worst storms in the Atlantic during the war at times when we were in the hollow of a wave we could not see another ship from the flight deck which was 60' above the water. The remains of the convoy struggled on at the speed of the slowest ship. The crossing took two weeks but at last when we were a day or so from Liverpool we left the convoy and sprinted into port. We were sworn to secrecy and I returned to Leeds.

My turn to return home was soon to come.

CHAPTER 3 THE HOMECOMING 1944-55

At last it was my turn to return to England. We had to go to New York to complete the paperwork. I finally had my Departing Alien form, which was actually

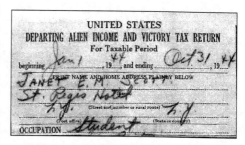

requiring departing people to pay their income tax! This was clearly not relevant, but I had to have the correct form. Finally in November, 1944 I was put on board the Rangitata, a banana boat, which the government had requisitioned to transport troops and evacuees. As usual, I was sick most of the way and also developed a very bad cough – as did many other of the children, in our crowded dormitory holding 40 of us. It turned out to be whooping cough but the ship's doctor did not give out the diagnosis. If he had, all 40 of us would have been kept on the boat in quarantine, for several weeks.

We arrived at Mersey Docks in Liverpool on a cold gloomy November day. It passed through my mind, that if this is what England was like, I was not impressed. I'd rather go back to America. After we landed we were greeted by the sight of a large number of adults, all looking for their sons or daughters, home from the States. Gradually parents and children paired up with great joy. After the crowd dispersed, there was left a tall man with a bristly moustache, who was wearing plus-fours (a type of knickerbockers)– and me. "Are you Janet?" he enquired. When I said I was, he told me he was my father. It was not an easy homecoming.

We drove back to Leeds, but of course I was sick all the way, as well as having a terrible cough. I was put to bed and within a day or two I was whooping loudly. It took some weeks to regain my strength.

Next I had to get used to rationing. I had come from the land of plenty to a very limited diet. Strangely enough, it suited me rather well and I began to flourish. I realised later that the American diet was far too rich for me. I had been compelled to drink a large glass of full cream milk twice a day, which I hated and was clearly not suitable. So rationing was actually an advantage. The ration at that time was still extremely severe. We all had to have a Ration Book (I still have mine). We were allowed so many 'coupons' a week, to buy other food items. At that time the weekly ration consisted of:-

4 oz (113 g) ham or bacon	1 lb 3 oz (540 g) meat
8 oz sugar	1 oz cheese
2 oz loose tea	2 oz butter
4 oz margarine	2 oz lard
2 oz sweets	8 oz jam or marmalade

1 egg per week or 1 packet of egg powder per month

3 pints milk, extra for children, invalids and expectant mothers.

24 poin ts per month for tinned or dried food.

36 coupons per year for clothing

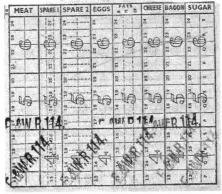

Here is a page from my Ration Book. Some items were not rationed, but were not always available. These included locally grown fruit and vegetables. Shoppers had to take their ration books with them and watch the shopkeeper carefully cut out all the relevant coupons. Later, they were given a rubber stamp to cancel the coupons that had been used. Then there was nothing more available until the following week, or until the following year for clothes. It was not until 1954 that all rationing ended, although some food stuffs were still in short supply and queuing was still the order of the day for some time after. I really missed the fresh fruit, as we only had apples, pears and berries in their seasons. Imported fruits such as bananas and oranges were never available. When the first bananas did arrive in the shops, we were only allowed one each. However, we never went hungry and there was certainly no problem of obesity!

AT SCHOOL IN ENGLAND

My parents wanted me to go to Leeds Girls' High School, an Independent School, in Headingley, on the other side of Leeds from our home. It was the sister school to Leeds Grammar School, where both my brother and my father had been pupils and years later my son-in-law David! There was one vacancy, with three of us competing for it and – quite amazingly I was the one to get the place. I remember that one of the questions on a general knowledge paper was, what does BBC stand for? Here was something I was sure of, so I wrote down

School was the next major hurdle I had to blunder my way over. I had returned on November 19th, 1944 and finally got over the whooping cough, so I was to start school in January, in the first form in the senior school, in a form called quaintly Upper III p2. As it was January, school friendships had already been made. Then my mother explained that I must wear school uniform, an unfamiliar concept. It was a shapeless, green garment, such as I could not remember having seen before, which she called a gym slip – and for which she had given up something precious called 'coupons'.

Christmas came and went and the fateful day arrived. I was delivered to the school gate, clutching my shoe bag. On arriving in the morning we had to remove our outdoor shoes and put on our indoor shoes. All the girls had plain green shoe-bags hanging from their pegs in the cloakroom. But there just were not enough

40

clothing coupons, so my mother had provided me with a bright, even gaudy bag for my shoes. It was a souvenir she had brought back from a trip to Egypt, with appliquéd pyramids on one side and a grumpy looking sphinx on the other. I still have the shoe bag and am now able to treasure it! But at that time, I felt terribly embarrassed by the bag and I could see the other girls making snide comments about it. So I tried to hide it under my coat. I felt so different, so apart.

The lessons were not difficult, but whenever I was forced to open my Yankee mouth, the girls quietly sniggered to one another. Then it was Break.

I trailed after the others out into the playground and stood rooted to the spot – a small girl, an island but not feeling 'entire of herself', watching a sea of green swirling around her, an ocean of girls in green. I glanced at my own unfamiliar green gym slip, but I still felt no part of it. I longed to be sucked into it, to swirl along with the others, but I felt myself to be a misfit, unwanted, unnoticed, unconsidered.

How long I stood there I do not know. Then I felt a tap on my shoulder. A girl of my own age held out her hand and said, "I am Milly. Will you come and play with me?"

I took her hand, entered gratefully into the swirl of green – no longer an island, perhaps only a small drop in this mighty ocean, but at last a part of it.' Farewell island of isolation' - wonder of wonders, I was beginning to feel that perhaps I could somehow fit in.

But it was difficult, for I was still a Yankee kid, with a marked Yankee accent and full of unspoken resentments. I quite quickly picked up a Yorkshire accent. But in the school, there seemed to be endless trivial and to me unnecessary rules that somehow challenged me to rebel. As time went by I tried my best to break most of them. My friends egged me on and dared me to do some outrageous things – and I usually got away with it. I soon had the reputation of being the naughtiest girl in the school and broke the school record by having more detentions than anyone else had ever had – and I hope has never had since. A

41

detention consisted of staying in after school and copying out a section of the dictionary, then being tested on the words. Who knows, perhaps that is why I have a pretty extensive vocabulary today!

Fortunately the rest of my form had only had one term of teaching before I arrived, so I was not too far behind academically. The one lesson I shone in was French, as I could speak it quite fluently, whereas the rest of the form had only just started. However when the January exams were marked I came bottom. The problem was that I did not know how to write it or spell it. So when required to write Qu'est ce que c'est, I produced something like kes-ke say. I was very incensed. Here I was able to speak the language, but then to be bottom in the exams seemed exceedingly unfair. However I did not give up, as I found that I actually enjoyed languages.

In the second year we started Latin, which I loved, and later had to choose between German and Greek. I desperately wanted to do both, but that could not be. So my father pointed out that both he and his father had studied Greek. It would be better to learn Greek at school, as I could pick up German later – which I did, but not until I was in my late forties, at evening school. Then many years later I was able to learn Italian. I had some time before started a little Italian at evening school, but the class had folded up. At that time I was teaching at a girls' grammar school in Croydon. It turned out that I had free periods at the same time as the Italian teacher was teaching a group of Sixth Form girls, and I was allowed to join and take the external exam – at my own expense.

To return to my school years, they were not always happy. I did not seem to have much of a relationship with my parents. My father was an exceedingly busy GP and I saw very little of him. My mother belonged to a lot of committees and was often out. We did not seem to be able to form a close relationship or communicate at a deeper level.

Looking back on those years, I now feel ashamed of my behaviour, particularly as I later became a Christian. My behaviour then was far from Christian! I think the root of my problem was the sense of rootlessness. I had been sent away from my home for nearly five years. Of course this was not all that unusual amongst my peers, as so many of us had experienced the trauma of being evacuated. Some children had a wonderful time with surrogate parents who took them to their hearts. Others did not – and I was in the latter group. It was not that I was abused in any way. I was cared for very well and given good homes and a good education. I think it was more the fact that I had been passed from family to family that had affected me deeply, although I was not aware of it at the time. Children are pretty tough and have a good way of accepting situations. But I found it difficult to make good relationships and became very independent.

My parents said that they were concerned about the hours of homework I was required to do at Leeds Girls, so they decided to send me to boarding school after I had completed my School Certificate. So at the age of 16, I was sent off- yet again - to The Mount School, York. As I saw it at that time, they had sent me away to America and now they were sending me away again. It seemed to be another rejection.

CHRISTMAS

One thing I really enjoyed was Christmas, as this was spent at my Grandfather's house in Barking, east London. My Grandmother died while I was very young, but my Grandfather lived on in the huge house, called Roden Lodge. He was an amazing man, a real Victorian. His children all called him 'the Governor' and we grandchildren called him Dandy. I gather this was because as a young man he had always dressed very stylishly. As a young man he had heart trouble and was told he might die before he was sixteen. In the event, he went on in good health until he was ninety-three.

43

Roden Lodge was named after the little Roden River which flowed into the River Thames. This location was very important, as he and several generations before him had been fishermen and in the early days they had been able to moor their boats near to the house. In later years the business expanded until they had the biggest fishing fleet in England. However as the years passed, he realised that fishing was becoming more precarious as a way of earning a living. He could see that steam was overtaking sail and that a good supply of fuel would be of the utmost importance. So he transferred the fishing fleet to Fleetwood, where gradually the boats became fewer and fewer until the business closed down. All that now remains is one stall in Billingsgate Market.

After some consideration, he decided to use his land as a depot for the import of oil. So Barking Oil Wharves became the family business, making a very good profit. The land became more and more valuable over the decades and now some has been sold to developers.

One of the highlights of the year was Christmas. My mother was youngest of nine children. The rest of the family lived in and around London, while we were up in the north. So we would make the annual trip by car. These were the days before motorways, so it was an exceedingly tedious journey along the Great North Road.

On my first visit to Roden Lodge I was quite overwhelmed. It was a very big house, with a huge hall, with a gallery above and a beautiful staircase, with stags' heads and heavy paintings of my ancestors hanging on the walls. The ancestors had a habit of

44

falling down in the night, giving everyone a fright! Upstairs there were creaky corridors and a series of bedrooms with iron bedsteads, each with a ewer of water and a big bowl, where we could get washed. The toilet, at the end of one of the corridors was a massive affair, with a heavy chain to pull and a splendid mahogany seat.

Downstairs was like a museum! The dining room was vast with a table which, with one small addition was able to seat all of us. The year before he died, we were thirty-four people, all related to one another. At one end was the billiard room, much frequented by the male members. The parlour was pure Victorian with a rug made of bear skin, with the head still on it, a table made from an elephant's leg, a big glass dome full of stuffed birds and so on. I can remember wandering around admiring all the amazing things, many in display cabinets. I really fell in love with an African table that Dandy had brought back from one of his journeys. It had been made from a section of a tree trunk. Two of the legs were two small pygmies, the other two being the head and tail of a spotted leopard, with the rest of its body underneath. After Dandy died, we were allowed to choose some things from his belongings, so I chose the table, which I still have in my house! The outside was equally amazing as there were a fernery, a conservatory and a fives court (a game rather like squash, played with a glove rather than a racket).

Christmas Eve was a very busy time, with great preparations going on all over the house. The turkeys were taken to the local baker's shop to be cooked in their huge oven. I used to get the job of shelling the chestnuts to make chestnut stuffing – a terrible job as they were very hot and removing the shells and skins was a real challenge. Then the stockings were hung. Anyone under eighteen and over ninety had a stocking. They were hung, in age order all around the gallery rail, overlooking the hall. The youngest child got the biggest stocking – a seaman's stocking and Dandy, being the oldest, had a baby's bootee.

Christmas lunch went on for hours! The turkeys were carved by some of my mother's brothers. Carving in those days was a special skill. One year my father, only an in-law, was invited to carve, which he took as a very great compliment.

A large amount of wine was drunk and people became very merry. After the main course the huge Christmas pudding was brought in with flames leaping from it. It was followed by a procession of all the grandchildren who either played an instrument, if able, or just had a drum, or failing that, a tin lid to bang. The pudding was held up high as we all processed round and round the table.

After the pudding had been consumed, it was time for the mince pies. There was a family tradition, no-one could say when it first began, that Dandy would throw a mince pie to each person. As I have said, the table was vast, so it was very much hit-or-miss, with crumbs flying everywhere.

Once the meal was over and cleared away, we all trooped into the parlour, where we played a medieval game called Dumb Crambo. Then all the grandchildren who were old enough were expected to perform – to sing or recite. I used to recite, carefully learning my piece beforehand. I can still remember two of them, after all these years. Here is the one I loved, which I think will be appreciated by any poetry lovers. I hope you will enjoy it too.

ROBERT REECE

Once there was a little boy whose name was Robert Reece.

Every Sunday afternoon he had to say a piece.

Now pieces he learned until he had a store

Of recitations in his head, but kept on learning more.

When called upon to recite one day,

He completely forgot what he had to say.

His brain he cudgelled – not a word remained within his
head

And so he spoke at random – and this is what he said –

46

My beautiful, my beautiful

That standeth proudly by

'Twas the schooner Hesperus –

The dashing waves break high

Why is the forum crowded –

What means this stir in Rome,

Under the spreading chestnut tree

There's no place like home.

And freedom from the mountain height

Cried 'Twinkle little star'

Kill if thou must this old grey head,

King Henry of Navarre.

Roll on thou deep and dark blue

Castle crag of Drakensfels

My name is Norval on the Grampian hills

Ring out wild bells

If you're waking call me early –

To be or not to be.

The curfew must not ring tonight

Oh, woodman, spare that tree.

Charge Chester, charge, on Stanley on

And let who will be clever,

The boy stood on the burning deck,

But I go on for ever!

AT SCHOOL IN YORK 1949-1952

In 1949 I arrived at The Mount School, York. Again I found it very hard to fit in as all the other girls had been at the school since they were eleven. Also, it was a Quaker school. I knew very little about the Quakers and I found it all rather strange. First there were all the periods of silence. Before a meal, no-one said grace. Instead we all had to sit in silence to say our own. Needless to say, I had no idea what to say to God, having never been introduced to him. Sundays were terrible as we had to walk across York, two by two in a crocodile to the Quaker meeting house. There we had to sit in silence for a full hour. Sometimes one of the adults would feel 'led' to preach to us. I was completely nonplussed by the whole procedure. The only thing we were allowed to do was to bring a Bible and read it.

The Bible was very important in the school. Every morning after the rising bell there would be the 'Fives' bell. This was to mark five minutes when we had to sit on our beds and learn a specified verse from the Bible. At breakfast one girl's name was called out and she had to stand up and say the verse. So there was no escape, we just had to learn the verses.

There was also a special challenge to all the pupils. If anyone learned the whole of the Sermon of Mount (Matthew chapters 5-7) off by heart, the prize was not a Bible, but a copy of the Oxford Book of English Poetry, on India paper. I was not too sure why India paper was so important, but it sounded very splendid, so I took up the challenge. I still have my copy of the Oxford Book of English Poetry – and yes, it is on India paper, signed by my headmistress on Nov. 11th, 1950.

At that time I had no Christian beliefs whatsoever. My parents had never sent us to Sunday School. We attended church only at Christmas and Easter. But I was learning a lot of verses, even chapters from the Bible, which would be a great blessing in years to come.

Having not really made much effort in my studies at Leeds Girls' High School, I did much better at The Mount. There were only three of us doing Latin and Greek. We also did Ancient History and Literature, as our third subject. We had a very delightful, but rather other-worldly and rather quaint elderly teacher for the first year, who brought us on well in our studies. Then she had to retire for ill health and there was no-one available to teach us. So, wonder of wonders, we were allowed to go on our bicycles, unaccompanied (!) to the boys' Quaker School, Bootham and were taught by the classics master there. We were the envy of the whole of The Mount. He was an excellent teacher and all three of us did very well under his tutelage.

The three of us were very interested in the Romans, particularly as the school was in York, an ancient Roman city, once called Eboracum. In our final year, something occurred which to us was extremely exciting. The Ministry of Works opened an archaeological dig in York, not far from our school. It came about when some children were playing. In those days, we often played games based on war time experiences. One favourite was digging tunnels, to escape from imaginary prisoner of war camps. While digging their tunnel, the children came upon some human bones. They were examined and declared to be Roman. So the dig began. The timing was perfect, as the three of us in the Classics department had finished our A-levels and had plenty of free time. To our great joy, the Headmistress allowed us to go, unaccompanied, to help at the dig. It was a magical time for me and there began my fascination for archaeology. This was so much so, that I ended up reading for a degree in Archaeology and Anthropology at University.

The dig turned out to be a large Roman cemetery for the British inhabitants of York, rather than for the army. Over 600 skeletons were found in their entirety or in part. Several were found with coins in their mouths to pay their fare to Charon, the boatman who would take them across the River Styx to their final destination. The people were clearly poor, as there were few items of value found. However we found five Roman vases – and I was the lucky one who found four of them. In the picture I am seated near the centre, holding one of the vases.

One of them found its way into one of the Museums in York. This, of course, did much to fuel my love for archaeology. I dreamed of myself in charge of an amazing excavation somewhere in the Middle East, making earth-shattering discoveries. Of course, such dreams rarely come true and this was certainly the case with me.In 1951, after the dig had closed, life seemed flat. However it was the summer holidays. Most of the Upper Sixth had now left school, but those of us who hoped to get into Oxford or Cambridge returned for a final term, followed by the various entrance exams. During our last term, the three of us still had a great interest in archaeology. We found maps of the Roman road going through York and realised that our school was situated quite near to the road. One of our dormitory buildings was across the road from the main school buildings and had a rough area of garden. We begged the Headmistress to be allowed to dig it up to look for more Roman remains. She granted us permission, so we planned out the site, with a grid of squares marked out with pegs and string and began to dig. Amazingly we did find something! We found the skeletons of a man and a baby and also some pieces of what was definitely Roman pottery, which proved that the whole find was indeed Roman.

The Yorkshire Post heard about our exploits and came to interview us and take some pictures. We bought a copy of the paper and opened it with trembling hands. There we were, busy in our trench with a small inset of the finds. The joke for me was that I had just had my appendix out so I was leaning very heavily on my spade and was in no way fit for any digging!

Picture from the
Yorkshire Post

THE FESTIVAL OF BRITAIN

By 1951 Britain was making slow progress in rebuilding a good deal of the infrastructure of the country that had been devastated during the war. Many foods were still rationed. Troops who had come home were settling back in this country with varying degrees of success. Many wives, who had taken major roles both in the family and in the workplace, were finding it difficult to return to the comparatively dull role of dutiful wife and mother. The British had all lived in austerity for a long time and needed something to cheer them up and give them a boost.

In 1851 in the time of Queen Victoria, Britain had hosted The Great Exhibition. Its full title was the Great Exhibition of Works and Industry of all Nations. While allowing many nations to display their work, the British works took the lead in nearly all fields. An amazing glass building was constructed. It got the nickname of Crystal Palace. It was a huge success, with over 6 million visitors. The profit was used to found the Victoria and Albert Museum, the Science Museum and the Natural History Museum, in London. After the Festival, it was removed to Sydenham an enjoyed several decades of popularity as a major venue, but sadly it was burnt down in 1936.

51

So 100 years later in 1951 the government came up with the idea of something similar. They called it the Festival of Britain. Its aim was to raise our spirits and also to promote British art, design and industry.

The Festival's centrepiece was the South Bank Exhibition, with displays of British advances in the fields of science, technology and industrial design. The Royal Festival Hall was built at that time, in a clearly Modernist style. It still stands as a centre for the arts, although it was altered and improved in 1964 and refurbished in 2005. After the Festival was over, most of the buildings were taken down, but the Royal Festival Hall still stands as a symbol of our recovery after all the years of war.

I can remember my parents talking about it, but it was to be in London, far away from our home in Leeds. So you can imagine my delight when they decided that we should all take the journey during the summer holidays and attend the exhibition.

I can recall going into the huge dome, not dissimilar in design to the Millennium Dome (now known as the O2) and also used as the Olympic Stadium for the 2012 Games in London. As we entered, I looked all around with wondering eyes. The whole area was divided into sections, representing different aspects of British life and endeavour. These sections included The Living World, the Earth, Sport, Homes and Gardens and one called Television! This seemed very wonderful to me. We did not have television in my home until 1970. One of the most fascinating sections was The Natural Scene, which was cleverly laid out as though we were climbing a tree as we moved through it.

The aim of the festival was to give us a feeling of recovery and progress, a feeling that in spite of our present austerity, we could still produce great products and hold our heads high in the world. I believe it gave the population a real sense of hope for the future, which had somehow dwindled since the end of the war.

FAMILY HOLIDAYS

After the war, my brother and I were deemed fit for rather more adventurous holidays. My parents had a boat on the Norfolk

52

Broads, so every Easter we would take the long and tedious journey to Norfolk. My first experience of sailing was at Easter when I was twelve and my initial reaction was pretty negative. Easter often falls around the Equinox, when the night and day are of the same length. But it is also the time of wild blustery winds and temperatures can still fall below freezing during the night. At first I was just cold and rather miserable – and my father kept shouting at me. My mother could see that I was getting upset and explained that the 'skipper' always had to shout his commands, because if we did not obey at once, the boat might capsize! Later in my first week, the wind dropped a little and the sun came out. I got to know the difference between a halyard and a sheet and soon sailing became one of the loves of my life. I still have a poem I wrote for the school magazine, in 1950, which tries to explain some of the joy and fascination of bowling along at great speed, only relying on the power of the wind.

The coolness of the leaping spray

Sparkling in the sun's bright ray,

The swishing water past our bow

As through the rolling waves we plough,

This is sailing

The flapping canvas shinng white,

The phosphorescent gleams at night.

Strong winds blowing in your hair,

Joy in weather, foul or fair,

This is sailing.

The sudden jerking of the sheet

Which nearly pulls you off your feet,

The heavy tiller's steady pull

When the sail is taut and full,

This is sailing

The noisy slapping on our side

Of the swift incoming tide,

The cheery wave, the hearty hail

As boat meets boat, sail passes sail,

This is sailing

UNIVERSITY YEARS

To get back to my schooling, the change to The Mount School had had the effect of at last getting me down to doing some academic work – and actually enjoying it. To my delight I was accepted by Girton College, Cambridge. This was very different from the current Girton College, which now has men! In those days, Girton and Newnham were the only ladies colleges, followed later by New Hall. Each of them was a sort of female ghetto. Oddly enough I accepted this as the norm. Having been educated in single-sex schools, here I was again in a similar situation. I cannot remember anyone being a feminist and demanding equal rights with the men. I was just very grateful to have been admitted to the university. In Girton, men were only allowed on the ground floor, until about 9.30 pm. We girls all had to be back in by 10.00 pm, then the gate was locked. It was possible to 'sign out' until rather later, but there needed to be a good reason. We then had to ring the bell to be admitted. I'm sorry to say that I have vivid memories of climbing over the gate when I was returning well after 10.00.

The other late night excitement was due to students having to wear academic gowns in the evenings. They were particularly inconvenient to wear and when riding a bicycle, they billowed out rather alarmingly and occasionally caught on various objects as we sailed by. All students had to wear their undergraduate gowns when out in the evening. The University sported some men called Proctors, whose duty was to roam the streets looking for students not wearing their gowns and report them to their colleges. Being caught was called being 'progged'. The men students had the worst of it, as there were so many of them and they seemed the most obvious offenders. We girls had a better time of it, as we were comparatively few in number. I remember one evening when I was out without my gown, I spotted a proctor coming my way. One alternative was for me to run, but I think the proctors were chosen for their fleetness of foot. The alternative was just to wander along, looking as though I was merely a local resident. I took the latter alternative and breathed a sigh of relief when the proctors looked at me … and passed along the street.

My great love in the summer was cricket. From playing on the beach as a child, to practising in the garden in my brother's cricket nets, I progressed to the College Club as a fast bowler and a reasonable batsmen. Next year, I developed a minor back problem, so I changed to being a spin bowler. Most of our games were 'friendlies' against men's Colleges, who did not take us very seriously, with the result that we very often beat them by a big margin. I still have a letter I sent home to my parents, telling them that I had just taken 3 wickets for 6 runs! I was invited to join the Cambridge University Women's Cricket team to play against Oxford. We won in our first encounter. By my third year I had risen to being Captain, which meant that I had earned a coveted Cambridge Blue. In my final year I was invited to play for Cambridge County, against Norfolk County.

1939   1954

CHAPTER 4 WHO AM I?

ATHEIST, AGNOSTIC OR WHAT?

As I have explained, I had no personal faith at all. If challenged I would probably have said that I was a Christian because I had been confirmed in the Church of England. While preparing for university, my older brother had warned me against the Christian Union. "They are all religious fanatics," he told me. "Don't have anything to do with them."

I followed his advice. In my first week a member of the Christian Union (Cambridge Inter-Collegiate Christian Union, known as CICCU) called at my door. She was clearly visiting all of us new students (freshers) to invite us to join the CICCU. I told her in no uncertain terms that I wanted nothing to do with religion.

The first weeks at University are not easy. We all had to find our feet and discover where we fitted in. Meal times were difficult. Most freshers sat together with others who were studying the same subject. So you would find all the geographers together, etc. I was studying Archaeology and Anthropology and there were only two others at Girton College. One was an Iranian girl and the other came from Greece. They sat with compatriots from their own countries, so I was rather at a loose end. As I looked nervously around the huge dining hall I tried to assess the various groups. Some looked fearfully sophisticated – not my cup of tea. Some looked rather intense. However, there was a group that seemed to be very relaxed and laughed a good deal, so I went and asked if I could sit at their table. They were very welcoming and I soon made friends. It was not until a couple of weeks later that I made the great discovery – they were all members of the dreaded CICCU. But as I was enjoying their company, I decided to stay with them, but have nothing to do with the CICCU.

Most weeks one or other of the group would politely invite me to a CICCU meeting. I equally politely declined. This went on for a full year. Little did I know that all this time they had been praying for me. At the beginning of the second year, I was

56

becoming rather tired of all the invitations and decided to go along just once, to satisfy them. I agreed to go to what was known as the Freshers' Sermon (although I was no longer a fresher).

To my surprise, the church was packed, very unlike the church I had occasionally attended back home. Instead of the 'holy silence' I had expected, there was a real buzz of chatter and a sense of expectancy. Two clergymen came in and I settled down to what I expected would be a boring service.

The first hymn was a rousing one and unlike any previous experience I had had of 'church' as everyone sang with real gusto. Then there was a reading from the Bible, read by a student, to which, I have to confess, I paid very little attention. But what I was aware of was that other students seemed to be listening with rapt attention.

Then without further ado, the preacher began his sermon. He started by telling a couple of jokes! This again was way out of my expectation for 'church'. Then he spoke simply and, to my horror he seemed to be talking straight at me. I wriggled rather uncomfortably, but I did begin to listen. The gist of the sermon was that I (and it seemed to be I and only I) was a sinner and needed to be saved.

After another hymn, we all surged out of the church. As soon as we were free of the crowds, my friends who had taken me, turned to me and asked rather diffidently what I had thought of it.

"How dare he tell me that I'm a sinner," was my immediate response. "I'm just as good as lots of people, and better than some." And with these words I stomped off and returned to my room. But that night I could not sleep. The preacher's words kept coming back to me, making me feel uneasy.

All next week, I felt ill at ease with myself – and everyone else. My friends told me afterwards that they had been gathering to pray for me. Had I known, I would have been very angry. So when they asked me if I would like to come again, something inside me said, "Yes."

57

This time, the preacher was Rev Keith de Berry, who had come over from Oxford. The service again began with a hymn and then a reading. This time I did listen to the reading, in which Jesus told three parables, about a lost coin, a lost sheep and a lost son, known as the prodigal son. At least I had heard that story. The coin was lost by a woman, probably a young bride, who knew her husband would be angry, so she swept the room and searched until she found it. The lost sheep was different, for the sheep was just one of 100, who had wandered off, probably looking for 'greener grass on the other side'. The shepherd had a terrible time trying to find it, but finally brought it home safely. The lost son went off on purpose, then messed up his life. Finally he came to his senses and returned very shamefaced, but was welcomed back by his father. However his older brother was angry and jealous and refused to welcome him back.

"Listen, friends," he began. "This reading talks about four types of people." As I had only made it three, I listened to see who I had left out.

"Let's begin with the lost coin," he continued. "The coin is lost, but doesn't realise it is lost. The sheep is lost and is perhaps enjoying itself – or perhaps wanting to get back to the sheepfold. So it knows it is lost. The son is lost because he chose to be lost. Then there is the older brother, who stayed at home and felt angry and self-righteous and jealous of his brother."

I was beginning to get the picture. Then came the crunch line. "I have given you four categories of people - those who don't know they are lost, those who are happy to be lost, those who were lost but came back and those who just feel superior. Where do you belong?" Then he paused, giving us time to think about our own position.

I guess I went into the church as a lost coin, because I really had had no idea that, in God's eyes I was lost. By the end of the sermon, I had 'graduated' to being a lost sheep. In my heart of hearts I knew that I was not feeling confident about my life or my future and a deep down voice in my heart was telling me that I was lost.

The preacher continued, "If you feel that you would like to ask more questions, or take a step of faith, please wait behind. Otherwise, you can come back tomorrow morning and there will be people to talk with you. Meanwhile, let me share a verse from Revelation chapter 3 verse 20 – Jesus said, "Behold I stand at the door and knock, if anyone hears my voice and opens the door, I will come in."

No way was I going to stay behind – or come back next morning, for that matter, as I was far too proud to admit my need. I told my friends I did not want to talk to them and went back to my room on my own. Again, sleep departed from me and I had a very restless night. The verse about Jesus knocking kept coming back to me. This continued until the Wednesday, By then I had had enough. I was on my bicycle, on my way to a lecture, pedalling furiously, but feeling a bit desperate. The preacher had said that Jesus had promised to 'come in' if I asked him. I did not really understand it fully, but as I continued to pedal, I said, "OK, Lord Jesus. If you really are there and you really are knocking, well …..please come in."

I reached the lecture hall, listened to the lecture then cycled back up the hill. When I sat down on my bed, I was aware of a feeling of peace. The restlessness had evaporated. Something had clearly happened to me. At last I felt I should go and talk to one of my friends. I knocked rather timidly and was invited in. "I think something has happened," I said.

She questioned me and then called some of her other Christian friends. They were so excited and happy – and I began to feel the same way. They confessed that they had all been praying for me earnestly for the last few days. This time I was happy to hear such news. That night I 'slept the sleep of the just'!

It was 23rd October, 1953 and I've kept it as my 'second birthday' ever since. So began my walk of faith with Jesus Christ as Lord. It did not always go smoothly. At the age of 20 I had a number of unhelpful habits to overcome!

One of the joys of being at Cambridge was that the Christian Union had some really great Bible teachers who came to preach and to teach. I began to learn quickly and at once got into the habit of daily Bible reading, which I've kept to ever since, barring times of desperation when I had three children under the age of four! But otherwise I've always slotted it in somehow.

In one of the Bible studies I had heard a talk about the fruit of the Spirit, from one of St. Paul's letters, the Letter to the Galatians. It begins, 'The fruit of the Spirit is love, joy, peace, patience, kindness, goodness, faithfulness, gentleness and self-control.'

"HELP!" I thought, "I can never be like that. But perhaps if I work on each of them, one by one, I might get somewhere." So I started working on love. I soon found that I was not getting very far and began to despair. A friend asked me what was my problem, so I explained to him what I was trying to do.

He laughed and then said, "Do you tie apples on to an apple tree?"

"Of course not," I replied. "They just grow."

"And how do they grow?" he persisted. Not being great in science, I replied, "I think it must be the sap – and that must come from the roots."

"Exactly!" he cried. "You must just put your roots down into the Bible and deepen your relationship with Jesus and then He will begin to grow the fruits in you. But it won't happen overnight."

What a helpful lesson that was in my early days as a Christian. How right he was, in saying that it wouldn't happen overnight. Christian maturity is a lifelong journey.

As I have said, it was wonderful to be able to get so much really helpful teaching. I began colouring my Bible in nine different colours, picking out themes such as sin, salvation, the Bible, the Holy Spirit, prophecies about Jesus etc. That was also a great blessing. So I became what I might describe as a 'head-knowledge Christian'. However, my relationship with Jesus did not deepen as much as it should have done. I was being fed with 'head-knowledge' but what I needed was 'heart-knowledge'. It

60

was not until the 1970s when there was much more teaching about the Holy Spirit that my 'heart-knowledge' began to catch up and I was able to enjoy a much deeper relationship with Jesus.

MY FIRST JOB

I graduated in 1955, with a degree in Archaeology and Anthropology.After becoming a Christian I had decided that I did not think that archaeology was what I wanted to do as a career so I began to pray about it. My prayer went something like this, "Father, I do not think you want me to be an archaeologist, so I'll do anything else but teach." That was rather a dangerous sort of prayer to pray, for, as you have already guessed, He had His own plan for me and it was quite definitely to teach. I tried various other possibilities, but

every door seemed closed except going to a Teacher Training College. My parents were very happy about this.

The next problem – I didn't have a subject to teach in secondary school, as neither archaeology nor anthropology was on any curriculum. My Latin and Greek were only to Advanced level, which was not considered adequate. So I decided to apply to Homerton College, Cambridge, to train as a Primary School teacher. My tutor in Cambridge was horrified. This was not something that Cambridge University graduates were expected to do! However, I stuck to my guns and put in my application for a one-year training and was accepted.

It was an interesting year, but not very profitable. We learned a good deal about child development and psychology, but very little about how actually to handle classes. We had only 6 weeks of actual time in a school on teaching practice, and I was ill for two of those weeks. I had only a vague idea of what went on in

English primary schools as I had had most of my primary years in America. So I was about to face one of my greatest challenges.

I passed all my exams with distinction and was allocated a school in Chapeltown, a poor area of Leeds, not far from my home. My first year was pretty much a disaster. I had Class 1C, consisting of 44 7-year olds who had already been graded as 'C' – and were aware of it. I had little idea of how to handle such a large group, who already knew that they were seen as failures. Several of them had fathers in prison and fourteen of them could not read at all. The class soon got out of hand. I did have some good times, when I was actually able to teach them, but there were trouble makers who could quickly turn the class into an unruly mob. It was a horrible situation. To add to it, I was lonely as there was no staff room, so at Break time a monitor brought me a cup of tea, which I drank in sole state in my classroom. Wet days were even worse, as the children were also in the classroom.

I began to have stomach pains and headaches. On Saturdays, when I went into Leeds on the tram for shopping, I passed the school, but always averted my eyes. I could not bear the sight of it. I might well have given up in despair, but mine was a generation that did not give up when things got bad. nly other redeeming feature was that all the other members of the staff were very much older than I was. One by one they came to me, asking me to take over their Physical Education lessons. This I gladly did and even more gladly swapped them for the subjects I really disliked such as Needlework and Handwriting. In those days, we had no free periods at all. However, if you joined up with a parallel class, you could have half an hour free on alternate Friday afternoons, but the following week you had to have both classes – about 90 children and read them a story.

My other dread was the swimming lessons. Once a week two classes, about 90 children, were shepherded on to a double-decker bus, three to a seat and we proceeded to the swimming baths. There were two pools and two instructors, who then took over. However on some occasions – far too many – one of the instructors was away, so I was expected to take over one group. Try to imagine 40 7-year olds, a number of whom were really frightened of the water, standing on the edge of the shallow end. I'm not sure who was more scared – them or me! The first task was to get them into the waterThe children had to sit on the edge, with their feet in the water – which mercifully was quite warm. The first command was, 'Put your left hand on the bar.' This could take time, as a good number could not tell right from left. Then 'Put your right arm across your body and put your hand down on to the bar, beside your left hand. Now slide into the water.' The biggest sense of relief every week was when I had returned to school, with every one of the 90 children accounted for!

There were also some joys in my early days, when pupils had been struggling with something and suddenly they 'got it' and gave me a big smile. This is one of the greatest pleasures of teaching.

Spelling was always a big problem to both the children and the teacher, who had to sort out their efforts. In Norwich, they often spelled words like smoke as smook. In Leeds a boy wrote a story about an *egog*. It took me some time to realise he was writing about a hedgehog!

There were of course some amusing moments. I was – probably rather misguidedly - trying to teach the difference between *may I* (asking permission) and *can I* (am I able). After quite a long session, Alfred put up his hand. The conversation went like this

Alfred, "Can I go to 't toilet?"

Jan, "Alfred, **may** I go to the toilet."

Alfred – after some thought, "You can if you like."

I disappeared behind the blackboard and had a little giggle to myself.

I only taught full-time for two years (so, on retirement my pension was 27p a week, which they suggested I should take as a lump sum!)

FAMILY YEARS 1958-1993

In 1958 I married John King. I had first seen him when I joined the Christian Union as a very new Christian, sitting at the back of the meetings. He was very handsome, sitting on the front row, as part of the Executive Committee and I admired him from a distance. However we became very good friends and later married. We moved to Norwich then to Maidstone, where our three children were born, Alison in 1961, Valerie in 1963 and Murray in 1965. Finally in 1966 we moved to South Croydon, to be nearer London, where he was working with IBM. I have had my home there ever since.

I did not always find motherhood easy. I had three young children under the age of four and I loved them dearly. But by 6 pm tre all crying – and sometimes I was too, not knowing which one to deal with first. All three had colic for their first few months and Valerie did not sleep through the night until she was 14 months old, by which I time I was again pregnant. As we had just moved, I did not have many friends. We went to a congregational church, as it was within pram-pushing distance. It was a church where people came in, sat in silence – except for the hymns – then got up quickly at the end of the service and left. There were no toddlers' groups or Young Wives meetings. We were still living in Maidstone, but John was by then commuting to London and not getting home until 8 pm. It was a tough time.

When in 1966 we moved to Croydon, things changed dramatically. We were warmly welcomed into Emmanuel Church and quickly felt at home. Our new house in Croydon cost £9,999, which today sounds ridiculously cheap. In those days, we could only just afford it, so all of us, except John, wore clothes from Jumble Sales. At Sunday School Alison proudly told one of the helpers, "My mummy bought this cardigan for only sixpence" Oh dear, what a reputation!

SECONDARY SCHOOL TEACHING

I took off several years from teaching while I had the children. Murray, our number three, suffered from asthma and eczema, but by the time he was six I was at last able to get back to teaching. I started with just two days at the local primary school where my children were pupils and could well have stayed in primary education. However, that was not to be. God had other plans for me.

Alison was now attending a local independent school, called Old Palace. One day I had to see the headmistress, then at the end of the time I suddenly said, "Do you happen to want a part-time teacher?" She asked me what subject I might be able to teach. This was a bit of a problem. My A-levels had been in Latin, Greek and Ancient History and Literature, but I didn't feel qualified to teach any of them. I thought quickly and said that I would like to teach 'Scripture' (the old name for what is now called Religious Education).

It so 'happened' (God is good!) that she was looking to fill that very post. Although I had no qualification for teaching the subject, the fact that I had a Cambridge degree (which would look good on the school prospectus), meant that she offered me the post. When I told her of my classics background, she was very interested. At that time many schools were starting to teach Classical Studies and she was looking for someone to develop a curriculum and teach the subject. It was agreed therefore that I would work only with the first three year groups, ages 11-14, teaching them Scripture and Classical Studies. This suited me very well indeed,

As Barbara Nunns, the Head of Department of Scripture happened to be free at that time, the headmistress took me to meet her. She had been teaching at Old Palace for many years. We immediately took to one another and found that we were both from very similar Christian backgrounds and were therefore very pleased indeed to be able to work together.

I came away from what I had thought would have been a short session with my head reeling! When reality finally set in, I realised that I had a lot of work to do. Barbara gave me a syllabus for Scripture, but Classical Studies was uncharted water – and there was no Internet to go to for help. A school year would be about 36 weeks and I was to teach twice a week. This meant developing 72 lessons, for each of the three year groups. HELP!

The 1st year girls were to study the myths and legends of the Greeks and Romans. This was a joy to teach. The girls, having come in from fairly easy going primary schools, were now faced with many subjects like Science, French, History and Geography, with all the demands of a more academic approach. This was pretty daunting for many of them. In Classical studies they could be more relaxed. I was able to tell them exciting stories and get them to write them up and decorate their books with pictures and Greek patterns. For many, this became their favourite subject.

The 2nd years were to study the Greeks and the 3rd years the Romans. This was a tremendous challenge, to get 72 lessons for each year prepared. I set to and finally finished at least the bare bones of it. I was able to add more 'flesh' as I went along. In my second week at the school I faced a terrible disaster. The folder containing all my notes went missing. I had dropped it somewhere. I was in the staff room, nearly in tears – all that work lost. Happily another teacher had just come from the school Car Park – and guess what she was holding? Yes, the precious folder.

Dear Mrs King,

I am very upset that you are leaving, but I realise that it's for a good cause. You are very brave and I admire you for going on your journey. One day I want to be just like you. I am worried about you and your mission but I am sure that God will protect you. Please look after yourself, so I won't have to worry about you. God will be with you.

To her surprise, I hugged her – and now the tears did flow, but they were tears of joy!

When I finally left, I received many heartfelt messages of goodwill from both pupils and staff. I find that I have kept one of them from a 10 year old in the Prep School. I taught at Old Palace for twenty years! After I had received my call to the mission field, the staff and the girls became very interested. I was invited to speak in Assembly to the Main School and also to the Sixth

For some years, I was invited back to speak at Assembly, telling the girls about my adventures in Africa.

EXCITING DISCOVERY

When I joined the staff of Old Palace, the school had been run by a delightful group of Anglican nuns. They did their very best for the girls, but were getting too old. So in 1972 they retired and handed the school over to a Trust. One of the sisters' gifts was not tidiness! Soon after I joined, I was turning out a cupboard in the Classics room and found a cardboard box tied up with hairy string. I opened it carefully and found it contained some old pots. On looking more closely, I realised that some of them looked very much as if they were Roman. I showed them to my Head of Department, who agreed. So I took them home and washed them very carefully. By then I was sure they were Roman. So we agreed that as I was only teaching part-time, I should take them to the British Museum. I made an appointment, wrapped them up carefully and off I went. It was very exciting to be ushered into the inner sanctum of the Classical Archaeology Department. I was given three trays lined with purple velvet to lay out our finds. First the expert on lamps came to have a look and dated them all as Roman and also Greek, going back to 600 BC. I was flabbergasted! As well as the pots, there was also a flat plaque, with the face of a woman on one side and snaky hair on the back. He looked closely at it and said he had no idea what it might be. The second expert looked at the pots and the third at the statuettes. Everything was genuine Roman or Greek ware. But, as with the first man, none of

67

them knew anything about the plaque. As they were finishing, a young man from the Western Asiatic Department took a short cut through the room. When he saw the plaque, he became very excited. It turned out to be from the Cyclades and was dated 1200 BC. "May we have it for the Museum?" he enquired.

I explained that it was not mine to give, but would ask our head. We later gave it to the Museum, on permanent loan and it is still there today. The next question was, what should we do with all the antiquities? Among the Greek and Roman items, there were two Egyptian scarabs. As my children were quite young, they were making things with a type of hard-setting clay. As the scarab was engraved on its base, I pushed it firmly into the clay. It gave a beautiful impression of an Egyptian cartouche, the symbol of an important person. At that time, pendants were very fashionable, so I was able to make pear shaped pendants, with the impression of the scarab picked out in gold paint, and painted the border in various colours. I sold these for a small sum to the girls and staff, who were very pleased to have them. With my first £100 I was able to have a cabinet made, to display our items.

It was almost two years later when I went up to the British Museum again, to have the scarabs dated. To my horror they told me that they were fakes! However, the expert assured me that they were very good fakes, but had a slight spelling mistake in the cartouche. So, rather shame-facedly I stood up in Assembly to tell the girls that I had sold them fakes. I offered to return their money, but they enjoyed the fact that they were fakes, as it added a bit of spice to the story.

YOUTH WORK

In 1971, our church agreed to open a youth group called Campaigners, for 6 to 18 year olds. This is a uniformed movement, similar in many ways to Scouts and Girl Guides, but with a strong Christian base. My friend Pat knew the movement well and invited me to join her in leading the the Girl Inters – the 10-14 year olds. Other members of the congregation were invited to help and when we opened the new leaders between us had 27 children of our own as founder members.

Our three children were of the right age. Here are Val and Murray, rather shyly showing off their new uniforms and Alison is in the garden, practising being the colour-bearer.

It was a great success and we soon had over 100 children. Among other activities, we had a marching band, including 16 fifes. At one time, Alison played a fife, Val played a snare drum and Murray managed the big bass drum! We had church parade once a month, when the band marched round a few streets near the church. This gave the members great joy, but I am not so sure about the neighbours!

Once a year, we went to camp and were blessed with very good talks about the Christian life and in later years, I had the privilege of being the Chaplain.

That is enough about the past. In 1995 I finally set off to Africa.

CHAPTER 5 EARLY DAYS IN KENYA 1995

I have in front of me my 2nd Prayer Letter that I sent out in June 1995 before I left, written on our first IBM computer, using DisplayWrite 2. (How different are our current prayer letters with their lovely coloured pictures.) I was encouraging people to pray for me. One paragraph said,

Think what I am like – always in a hurry, inclined to be impatient – how will that go down in an African culture? Think of the problems of adjusting to a new culture, a new job, a new language, new relationships, a new church, new food. HELP!

I'll need a lot of prayer. Then there will be times of loneliness, when I can't just pick up the phone for a chat. Think how I'll miss my children and two small grandchildren, Samantha and James.'

On Sunday 27th August, my church, Emmanuel South Croydon, hosted a Farewell Service for me, before I left following day. It was a very moving time, with family and friends gathered to wish me well and to pray for me. During the service, we sang the hymn 'Great is Thy Faithfulness', a family favourite, which we had sung at each of my parents' funerals and each of my children's weddings. Then the final hymn, which I sang with tears in my eyes:

> We trust in you, our shield and our defender,
>
> We do not fight alone against the foe;
>
> Strong in your strength,
>
> Safe in your keeping tender,
>
> We trust in you and in your name we go.

When we reached the lines 'We go in faith, our own great weakness feeling' a big lump arose in my throat, as I faced a very unknown future.

Next day, my son Murray took me to Gatwick Airport. My daughters offered, but I felt that we might well dissolve into tears. As Murray and I approached the desk to check in, my luggage was weighed, including the carton of pencils and it came to 32 kgs, well over the 20 kg limit. So I launched into an account of what I was doing and what the pencils were for and to my great joy, they accepted all of it. At that moment I put down my hand luggage, which landed with a loud thud. The clerk asked to see it and then weighed it. It was over 16 kg! Again my heart fell, but our prayers were answered. I was told to take out the few things I needed for the journey, then they attached a special orange label to the backpack and sent it also into the hold. How I praised God for this mini-miracle happened again. I had to keep to the allowance.

As we came to the Departure Gate, my heart was in my mouth and tears were very near. So with a bit of a gulp, I hugged Murray, said goodbye and passed through the gate, into a whole new life! Murray said that he watched me go, a small, lonely figure gradually disappearing up the ramp into the departure lounge.

The over-night flight was long and tedious. What with the excitement and the uncomfortable seat, sleep eluded me. With a sigh of relief, I heard the Captain announce that we were nearing Jomo Kenyatta airport, in Nairobi. As we taxied in, my eyes were glued to the window, taking in some of the sights. We finally came to a standstill and the doors were opened. It was 8.25 am on a dull grey day. I followed the crowd, passed through immigration and with some difficulty found a trolley. To my great joy, all my luggage appeared, including the pencils and the backpack. Pushing the rather unwieldy trolley, I finally emerged into the open air and looked around to see who was there to meet me. No-one came towards me. I saw a number of men holding up cards with people's names on them, but my own name was nowhere to be seen. Gradually people dispersed, but I still stood alone. Taxi drivers began to surround me, with ever more pressing offers of transport. There now followed one of the most alarming experiences in my whole life.

Here I was, in Africa, all alone. I had been given no address or phone number. All I had was the Post Office Box number. I finally spoke to one of the taxi drivers and asked if he knew

71

where the AIM headquarters were. He did not, so he spoke to his colleagues. Soon there was a circle of babbling drivers around me, all trying to be helpful and all touting for my custom. But I just did not know where I was to go and had no Kenyan money.

After what seemed an eternity, I spotted Rachel and Julian Jackson, an older missionary couple who had been sent out by my own church many years ago. I nearly fell into Rachel's arms with relief.

Then another English voice asked if I was Jan King. It was my colleagues-to-be, Russ and Lyn Noble. A few minutes later, Roger Gastineau, the head of Across appeared and then Christopher Kenyi, the head of the Sudan Literature Centre, where I was to be working. Then what a welcome ensued! They gathered up all my things and ushered me into the Noble's car and off we went to their house, where I was to stay at first.

On our arrival, Russ and Lyn gave me a very welcome cup of tea and asked if there was anything I would like. I innocently replied that I would love a bath. They looked at each other and then said they would see what they could do. It took nearly half an hour to fill and then was only lukewarm. Even so, it was a pleasure to relax in it. I was told not to pull out the plug, as the water could be re-used in the garden.

Next they broke the news to me that we would be setting off for southern Sudan on Friday, just three days after my arrival! The United Nations would fly us to Lokichoggio, (known as Loki) a UN base in the far north of Kenya and then the following Thursday they would take us into a remote area in the Upper Nile Region. Although that was a bit of a shock, I knew that that was what I really wanted to do, so I tried to prepare myself mentally.

The rest of the day passed quietly and I slept very well and woke up refreshed. Jet lag is not a problem as the flight is in a north/south direction, so there is only a difference of two or three hours. To my great surprise, it was quite chilly, so Lyn had to lend me a sweater – I had fondly imagined that it would always be hot, forgetting that Nairobi is one mile above sea level. In the evening Russ lit the fire.

As mentioned above, I had been seconded by Africa Inland Mission (AIM) to work with ACROSS (the Association of Christian Resource Organisations Serving Sudan). Lyn took me to the ACROSS offices of the Sudan Literature Centre (SLC) to have a look around and to meet some people.

My new boss was called Gordon Tikiba. He talked to me for some time, explaining what I would be doing and then took me on a tour of the building. We moved from office to office and finally into a small one with a dark-haired lady of indeterminate age, crouched over a computer. She was slightly unusual, with her hair awry, no shoes on and her glasses held on by a piece of hairy string.

"This is Rhondda Price," Gordon told me. "You will be sharing a house with her and Pat Champion, who is currently on furlough in Australia."

Rhondda looked up, startled. "Oh, hello," she said. "It's Rhondda, spelled R-H-O-N-D-D-A". Then she resumed her work. My jaw dropped open, my hopes, my emotions plummeted. What an odd person. At the thought of living with such a strange person, I felt tears pricking in my eyes and hastily squeezed them back. When I saw her later, I noticed that she was tall, probably in her late 30s, wearing a skirt with a tear on the hem. The glasses, as well as being held on by string were also broken.

Although I was really taken aback at first by Rhondda's appearance, we became very good friends and worked together happily both in Nairobi and occasionally in Sudan. It was just that Rhondda really wanted to be an African, so she preferred to dispense with shoes and to carry her shopping basket on her head!

The next day was filled up by paperwork. I had only an Entry Permit, but now I needed a Work Permit. Happily,

73

ACROSS employed Duncan, a Kenyan who had the right touch with people in offices. If ever they were crossed or annoyed in any way, they had the ability of losing documents and never being available for a meeting. Before I came I had read the classic book 'The Man with the Key has Gone Away'. It was written by Dr Ian Clarke, based on the endless frustrations of having to visit a series of offices in Uganda to get the correct rubber stamp on to each vital document. When some time later I went to the General Post Office to collect a parcel, I experienced this first hand. I had to visit six different desks (one of them twice) in the correct order and collect the correct rubber stamps on my paper work. It could take a very long and weary time! So I thanked God for Duncan who worked wonders and soon obtained my Work Permit. I also had to carry an Alien's Card. It felt very strange to be classified as an 'alien'. But the police had the habit of stopping people unexpectedly and asking to see their card.

I also needed a Kenyan Driving Licence. This did not entail an actual driving test, but it required a great deal of paper work. Having finally got it, I put it safely in the drawer in my desk. Almost a year later, I was being driven by a friend and we were stopped by the police, asking to see her driving licence. After we had driven on, I airily said, "Oh, I keep my Licence in my desk drawer." My friend was horrified, as it appears that it is a legal requirement to carry it at all times when driving. If you were found without it, you would be taken to the police station and charged. I really thanked God that I had not been challenged during all that time and made sure that in future I always had it with me when driving. I did have a couple of rather frightening incidents with the police, but more of that later.

As soon as the driving licence came through, Rhondda decided that I needed to be initiated into driving in Nairobi. We did not have a vehicle, but were able to borrow one of the ACROSS cars, for which we had to pay 13 US cents per kilometre. I was by then trying to get used to working in Kenya shillings, but ACROSS worked in dollars. So, trying to work out the cost in English pounds per mile, I was totally defeated. Anyway, there was no other choice but to use the car.

Driving in Nairobi was to be yet another challenge. Rhondda decided we should begin on Friday evening. It had not occurred to her that Friday evening rush hour would not be the easiest time for my first attempt. We set off and soon found ourselves in a huge traffic jam. No-one was willing to give way to anyone else. As soon as there was a gap, you had to move up quickly or you would find another car had zoomed round you and got ahead. To add to my trauma, Rhondda was not exactly helpful at giving directions! When we were part way round a roundabout and trapped in the left hand lane, she told me to turn right! This was not well received by the other aggressive drivers. We somehow survived and I soon became adept at coping with Nairobi traffic. Traffic in Croydon seemed pretty tame when I next came home.

TO WORK

Having arrived on Tuesday, on Thursday I went to see Dr..Kenyi, the head of Sudan Literature Centre to discuss my role and to know what was expected of me. The options were to work solely in SLC, editing and proof-reading, or to work in the ACROSS office, or to get more involved in Lyn's Teacher Training programme, or to do some English teaching. It was decided that I would work at SLC and help in the Teacher Training from time to time.

In those days, ACROSS had no programme of orientation. Africa Inland Mission did not have any orientation planned for me either, so I had to pick things up as they came along. This is very different from the way most missions work nowadays. Orientation has become an important part of the training of new mission partners. I had only had one week's orientation in the UK and that was all. Today, new recruits have a much longer period of orientation, preferably in the country where they are to serve. This involves one to three months of language learning, usually living in an African home and learning about the culture and generally finding one's feet. At the time I was very pleased that I could get straight to work – "After all," I said to myself. "That's what I'm here for." Afterwards I realised that I had missed a valuable experience, and in many ways lacked some important pieces of information (as with the Driving Licence).

By 7 am on the Friday we were ready to leave for the airport, finally on our way to southern Sudan, via Loki. Here is part of a letter home:

Here I am, safely settled in Lokichoggio, a small settlement on the northern border of Kenya, only a few miles from Sudan. It is the area of the Turkana tribe, a slim, very black tribe. We see the women and girls go by with row upon row of beads round their necks, stepping out so gracefully, balancing jerry cans of water on their heads.

It was a two hour flight, mostly passing over vast tracts of dry wasteland. As we disembarked from the cool interior, we stepped out into a very hot dry atmosphere – I could actually feel the skin around my face contracting and tightening.

We live in the Across compound, a fenced area with a number of small buildings called tukuls, which are round huts, painted white with green doors and with pointed thatched roofs. In my room I have a bed with an under sheet. There is a top sheet folded at the foot of the bed, but it's not needed, a small table, three shelves, a cracked mirror and a mosquito net hanging from the ceiling.

Loki changed dramatically in 1989 when the United Nations arrived with Operation Lifeline Sudan. Great numbers of people moved in, from all nationalities, working for over 40 Non-governmental

Organisation (NGOs) e.g. Save the Children, World Food Programme etc

It is extremely eventful here, with plans being made and changed at a bewildering rate. For myself, plan A was 1st Aug. to Loki, 6th Aug to Waat in Sudan to help in Teacher Training. Then there was a level 4 (the highest) security alert south of Waat, so plan B was to postpone the course until 17th September. However there is factional fighting in the area today and all personnel have been evacuated, so plan C is to postpone for yet another 2 weeks. The fighting is quite extraordinary – quite gentlemanly. The attackers warned the town that they were coming and offered options of joining them or leaving the town. Next day they arrived in force and entered the town with no fighting at all.

(written next day)

We're returning to Nairobi today, which will seem dull compared with Loki. We had torrential rain and went out to see the 'Irish bridge', so named because the rain flows over the road rather than under it! Cars and lorries were dashing through at tremendous speed, causing great waves of dirty brown water.

On the Sunday we had attended the local church, with openings for windows on both sides. It was a windy day, so the fine red dust was being blown in from one side, through the church, where it hung in the air until we could barely see the preacher! I later wrote a poem about it:

A DRY SEASON LAMENT

1. Dust, African dust
   Swirling, whirling everywhere
   Not our fluffy western dust,
   But scratchy, gritty dust,
   Pale brown to deep dark red,
         African dust.

2. Dust, African dust,
   Permeating, penetrating,
   Infiltrating my private world.
   When I arise, I see myself
   A white shape outlined by –
         African dust.

3. Dust, billowing dust,
   Raised by a passing car,
   Take a quick breath,
   Close your eyes tightly,
   Let it settle – until the next car,
   All pervading
         African dust

4. Dust, grimy, grubby dust,
   Under my nails, on my collar.
   I wipe my sweating face,
   I look with horror at the tissue –
   Am I in the army of unwashed?
   Stained, besmirched by
         African dust!

77

5. Dust, ever present African dust,

But who made the dust? God did!

And what are we made from? Dust?

"In all things give thanks" – even for dust?

O.K. Lord, Thank you for dust –

But must it be this very African dust?

AT HOME IN NAIROBI

Although I had enjoyed the experience of being in Loki, so near to the Sudan border, it was with a certain relief that I returned to Nairobi to settle down and begin to feel at home. I had coped with the extreme heat and the dust but it was good to escape from it.

In my first days, Rhondda had taken me to see the house where we would be staying. We had walked along an unmade road, with some huge potholes. Fortunately it was the dry season, but they told me that in the rainy season they would be full of water. I later found out by bitter experience, that this 'water' is actually thick, dark red liquid, which it is well-nigh impossible to remove from any clothing that gets splashed.

On our way, Rhondda strode on ahead, in bare feet and I was almost running to keep up. As I looked around at the unfamiliar sights, which soon would become part of my life, I felt a sense of bewilderment and my feeling of 'otherness' grew with every step. After ten minutes, we reached the house, which to my relief turned out to be quite 'western' in appearance. It was in a walled compound, like all the other houses in that area, with a large metal gate. A gate keeper was on duty in a sort of sentry box by day and three other guards took over at night. There were about twenty houses in the compound. As soon as I entered ours, I felt at home.

I'm not sure what I was expecting, (having seen pictures of people in mud huts) but it was a pleasant three bed-roomed house, with a kitchen and a large L-shaped living room downstairs and upstairs a bathroom with both bath and shower and three bedrooms. I was to be in the biggest one with my own en suite bathroom and plenty of cupboards. What luxury!

The house belonged to ACROSS, who also provided the furniture. There was a rather motley selection already in place and over the weeks we were able to acquire other items until we were very well provided for. When we did finally move in and began arranging things, we were very amused by the over-abundance of waste paper baskets – about two for each room!. For some reason this became a bit of a joke and if a waste paper basket was ever mentioned, we would go into fits of giggles.

I was particularly interested in the garden, which was so unlike mine at home. There was a banana plant (it is not a tree), with tiny little baby bananas beginning to appear behind a huge flower bud. Throughout the year, we were delighted by hibiscus, bougainvillea, canna lilies and other beautiful plants. What a joy!

Now I was back from Loki, I was at last able to move into the new home and unpack my things. My letter home began: *Three homes in 13 days!*

Unpacking has a certain finality about it – I'm here and here I will stay, in my own home with my own things around me. Although Rhondda was unconventional in many ways, including eating maize porridge from a calabash (gourd) for breakfast, we got on very well. In my letter home I said, It's far too comfortable – I really don't feel like a missionary at all.

On Sunday we attended Nairobi Baptist Church, a huge church with three services in the morning and one in the evening. The service was in English and we sang from Mission Praise. Afterwards we had a lovely Sunday lunch with Julian and Rachel Jackson. It was so delightful to spend time with them, but quite soon after my arrival they retired after nearly 40 years in Kenya.

I must just recount another experience I had with Julian and Rachel. It was in my first few days that they took me shopping in the local shopping complex called the Ya Ya Centre. We parked in the car park and as it was warm, I left my cardigan on the seat.

When we finally returned to the car – no cardigan! I was bemoaning the fact when Julian, with a big smile, produced the cardigan from his bag. "NEVER leave anything on show in your car," he warned me. "It won't be there when you come back." It was a good lesson to learn in my early days.

However I soon needed that cardigan. I had blithely set off imagining that Africa is always hot. How wrong I was! The temperature settled at around 60 F, with grey skies and rain. I was glad of the sweater Lyn had lent me and realised that I would need more warm clothes.

When I mentioned this to Rhondda, her eyes lit up. "Good," she said. "I'll take you to the Kibera Market. It's the place where the locals buy their things. There aren't many mzungus (white people) who go there."

So off we went, into a very poor area of Nairobi. We parked the car, paying a boy a few shillings to look after it, with the promise of more when we came back, and plunged into the most extraordinary market I had ever come across. We were the only whites, so we got quite a few catcalls and other comment. When Rhondda answered them – in Swahili, we were immediately welcomed in by the various stall holders, each of whom was determined that we should become their customer.

We bought a few food items first. Most of the fresh items were laid out on the ground in bundles or piles. For example, if you wanted tomatoes, you could choose a pile from the ground and they would pack them up in newspaper, or in our case put them in Rhondda's capacious shopping bag. She also bought some baby bananas. I had never seen such little ones before. She gave me one to try and they immediately became one of my all-time favourites, they were so very sweet and tasted delicious.

Other goods were displayed on often rickety wooden stalls, with vast amounts of cheap plastic bowls, cutlery, crockery, cooking utensils, stationery and all sorts of hardware. Finally we went into the area selling second-hand clothes. There were endless lines of stalls, with clothes hanging on racks, the cheapest

80

items in heaps on the ground, often with the seller standing on top of the pile, shouting out the price.

Rhondda, who had been there before, knew the best stalls. There were piles of sweaters, of good quality, going for only the equivalent of 20p. Then I spotted a Marks & Spencer's anorak, fully lined, for the princely sum of 25p. After I had bought it, I found a label inside from British Heart Foundation, £3.50! I wore that anorak for many years. Back home there is controversy about sending our unwanted clothes to 3rd world countries. Although Kenya produces various types of clothing, the prices are beyond a good proportion of the people, so it is a blessing to those living in this slum area, with huge unemployment. Be that as it may, I was delighted with my purchases.

After seeing the advantages of knowing the language, I redoubled my efforts at learning Swahili. Rhondda was a very willing teacher. I had bought a good textbook in England and had got started, but there was still so far to go! One thing that amused us was the verb to *fall down*. Every time it was mentioned, it was about a tree. So over the weeks, I learned to say a tree is falling down, a tree fell down, a tree has fallen down, and so on. This became a bit of a joke with us, but it cheered up the language learning!

I gradually acquired more language over the next months until I could use it for shopping. This was a huge asset, as when stall holders or shop keepers saw a white face, they immediately put up the price. However, as soon as I spoke in Swahili, the price came down by a considerable amount. However this was not the end of it, for this was the base for the bargaining that had to take place. Whatever sum was mentioned, I was told to offer about two-thirds or a half, then the bargaining began, until finally we came to an agreement. I would sometimes see white people being asked exorbitant prices and just calmly handing over the money. This sense of the power of language gave me an even greater incentive to teach English to the Sudanese. On the other hand, I have seen people haggling far too much and going away triumphantly with an item with little or no profit at all for the seller. This I could not do, considering the poverty of the people and the amount of work that had gone into producing it.

Another market experience happened later. In 1998 the arthritis in my knee suddenly became very much worse, so I needed a walking stick. On Tuesday there is a Masai market in Nairobi, so I set off to find one. I found a very nice stick, in a dark red wood with some decoration around it and bought it for the equivalent of £3.00. When I took it home, Rhondda and Pat Champion looked at it and looked at each other. "Is it?" said Rhondda. "I think so," said Pat. I asked what they were talking about. Pat took hold of it and pulled – and out came a sword! I was flabbergasted. Later I was able to bring it home at the bottom of my suitcase and is now one of my prized possessions.

NAIROBBERY AND THE POLICE

As Sudan was too dangerous for missionaries to live in permanently, we were based in Nairobi. But Nairobi itself is not a very safe place to live. Some people call it Nai-robbery. All the compounds need gatekeepers and guards. It has been said that one third of Nairobi are guards who are protecting one third of the citizens from the final third who are crooks of one sort or another. Some time later there was a very clever robbery in our compound.

A group of German musicians was staying in the compound. They had come from the airport in a taxi, together with several valuable brass instruments. They then asked the taxi driver to collect them next day, take them to a specific location and pick them up later and take them home, All went well at first. The driver duly arrived, delivered them safely, together with their instruments, and agreed to return at a specified time. So far, no problem (or as the Kenyans would say, Hakuna matata). He then turned up to take them back to the compound. The driver did not appear to be in a great hurry and seemed to take them on a slightly circular tour. As they neared the compound, the guard recognised them and opened the gate. The moment the gate was opened, four men erupted out of another car, threatened the guard with their guns and tied him up. They then forced the Germans out of the car and both cars made off, with all the instruments. Very neatly done! Happily they did not kill the guard, as happens all too often during robberies.

Unlike in the UK, the Kenyan police are heavily armed, but so are the robbers. As fast as the police get more powerful weapons, the robbers too get the same, if not better ones. Consequently the police are very unwilling to cope with emergency calls. They usually manage to time their arrival at the scene of the crime well after it is all over.

Many houses, including our own, had a heavy iron gate at the top of the stairs, which many people locked before they went to bed. We did have a gate, but very rarely got round to locking it. Some other friends had a horrid experience. They lived in a very fine house, well outside Nairobi, in their own compound, surrounded by a high wall and with secure metal gates. One evening a car drew up and several masked men jumped out. They were very heavily armed and demanded the key from the guard. He fumbled while looking for it so they shot him dead, opened the gate and drove their vehicle into the compound, spraying the house with bullets. The family inside fled upstairs and locked the heavy gate. Then all they could do was to hide well out of range, listening to the men rampaging through the house, smashing things as they went. There was a phone upstairs, so they phoned the police, who said they would come directly, but of course they did not turn up until the vehicle had disappeared with all the loot.

Within four weeks of my arrival I had a terrible fright in my own garden. I had gone out in the evening, when it was already dark. Suddenly I realised there was a man sitting on the patio! All I could see was the whites of his eyes, in his very black face. Fortunately Rhondda was just behind me and challenged him in Swahili. It turned out that he was one of the three night guards who worked on our compound. There had been several break-ins recently, so he was posted under my window at night. How was that for security!

A year or two later, when I had forgotten about this incident, I happened to look out of my window one night. There seemed to

83

be a large object on the patio, wrapped in waterproof sheeting. I crept downstairs and looked out of the French doors – and heard a strange sound coming from the big object – It was one of the night guards, fast asleep and snoring! As this is not acceptable behaviour for a guard, I woke him up and told him to do his job properly. He was there to protect us, not to go to sleep. It seems that the problem was that unskilled workers are very poorly paid, so many take on two jobs, one during the day and then acting as guard at night.

While on the subject of crime and the Police, let me add a couple of other incidents. Many of my colleagues refused to go out after dark, but I was determined to live as normal a life as possible. So one night when I was driving home in the dark, I was flagged down by the Police. I drew into a lay-by, with my doors locked and surveyed the scene. I knew that some crooks would pose as police and then rob the victim of all their belongings. They seemed to be bona fide police, standing by a police car, so I opened the window a little crack.

"Please get out of your car," one of them said. Rather gingerly I got out and stood between two very tall, very black men. "Please walk around your car with me," said one. I complied, but could see nothing amiss with the car. They then took me to the back of the car again, to show me that the tiny light above my number plate was not working.

"You must come to the station with us," they declared. My heart sank, but I had been told that such threats usually ended up as a demand for a bribe.

At first I acted the old and helpless role, hoping they might relent, but they persevered. Then they added that, instead of coming to the station, I might be able to give them something for their 'chai' (tea). Once it became clear that they were asking for a bribe, I exclaimed, with great conviction. "I am a missionary. Now please let me return to my home." With this, they realised that they were out of luck, as it was known that missionary societies instruct their members never to give bribes.

84

They knew they were beaten, so they told me I could go. With outward calm and composure, I got back into the car, with my head held high. Once home the composure departed and I began to shake and was dosed with hot sweet tea by my housemate. I could actually have done with something stronger, but as Christians in many countries of Africa never drink alcohol, we were encouraged to go without. This was a good principle as many new converts have previously been drunkards, so one sign of their conversion is that God gives them the strength to forgo alcohol. I kept this rule strictly while in Africa. The only quandary came on the flight home, when I was offered a bottle of wine with my meal on the plane. I used to have a good look around to see who were within sight of my seat – and if the coast was clear I would take great pleasure in the wine!

ARRESTED

There was one other memorable incident with the Police. I was attending a weekend conference, so I offered my flatmate, an American friend called Shirley, the use of my car for the weekend. After the conference, I returned, full of all that we had been doing. She was unusually quiet.

"What is the matter?" I enquired.

"I've been arrested," she announced, then added, "And it's all your fault!" I was appalled.

She told me what had happened. It was the first of March. She had been to the bank and was on her way home, when she was stopped by the Police. They pointed out that the Vehicle Licence was out of date, as it was only valid until the end of February. "You must come to the station with us," they declared. This time there was no argument. She had to go.

She explained that it was not her car, so they decided to let her go, on bail. Fortunately, having been to the bank, she had sufficient money, 2,000 Kenya shillings (about £20) to pay for her release. She was worried lest she might be stopped again on her way home, so they gave here a letter to carry.

"You must appear at the Court on Monday," they told her and released her.

She was in a great state of nerves, as the thought of standing in a Kenyan court terrified her. So when she poured out her story, I was horrified that this was all because of my negligence.

At the Police Station she had been told to come to the station at 7.30 am, where she would be given transport to the court. We had often seen these vehicles, like a Black Maria, with small windows near the roof, where we could see the prisoners' fingers holding on, during the trip. We tried to visualise two little white hands, also holding on, on her trip to the court. We discussed the situation, being determined that Shirley would not travel in the police vehicle. We

decided to ask our neighbour Harry Cotter, a Church Mission Society (CMS) missionary, if he would take us there and stay with us, for moral support. He readily agreed and we informed the police that we would be there.

As we shared the situation with other friends, they were full of compassion and also of good advice. "You will probably be there all day," was the general consensus, "So take some sandwiches and a paper to read."

On Monday morning, off we went, fully supplied with food, water, a crossword and a newspaper. The court was a square wooden room, with a bench for the judge and other seats for various officials. At the side was the dock, which poor Shirley regarded with some dismay. We were early, so we sat at the front. Slowly the room filled up. Then at 8.30 a door was flung open and in came the large and imposing figure of a lady judge, complete with wig and gown. Silence fell.

Opposite the judge sat a member of the police, a very large and imposing man, who had all the paperwork before him. Several prisoners were called, one by one. The first two were just remanded again. Then there was a disaster for the policeman, as he had mislaid some of the papers. He began to whisper to his colleague. "YOU DO NOT SPEAK IN MY COURT!" bellowed the judge. The large police man seemed to shrink visibly in his seat.

This did nothing to add to Shirley's comfort. Then the judge called Shirley's name. She got up and stood nervously in the dock. The Charge was read out. "Do you plead guilty or not guilty?"

Shirley answered saying she was guilty. "I see you have brought your supporters with you," the judge said with a smile and a pleasantly gentle voice. Encouraged by this change of demeanour, Shirley added, that it was not her car. I stood up and confessed that it was my car.

She gave her verdict, "A fine of 2000 Kenya shillings."

We all three walked out – on cloud nine! It was all over. The fine was the same as the bail she had already paid, so we were free to go – still clutching our sandwiches and other supplies. It was only 9.15. Harry then took us into the city, depositing me outside the office where I could update my vehicle licence. "Don't you come back until it is all legal," he cautioned me.

DAILY LIFE IN KENYA

Apart from encounters with the Police, life was fairly easy. I had a lot to get used to. I gradually became accustomed to all the unfamiliar sights, sounds and smells. My original sense of bewilderment and 'otherness' began to fade and I soon felt thoroughly at home.

Although there was the Ya Ya Centre within walking distance, with its array of western-type shops, I preferred to use the small local kiosks, which were ramshackle buildings, but with a surprisingly good stock of basic commodities, at a rather cheaper price than those in Ya Ya Centre.

After several visits and hesitant chats in Swahili, I was accepted as one of their customers and was greeted by name and offered the best of the stock. This picture shows a few of local kiosks. It was certainly very different from home. For instance when buying eggs, you would tell them how many you needed

87

and they would wrap each one up separately in newspaper. I soon learned to take an egg box!

Opposite the kiosks was a lady selling roasted maize. This was often the main ingredient of some people's lunch. The cobs were roasted to a lovely crunchy consistency and wrapped in a large leaf so you could carry them home. The smell was delicious and I was often tempted – until in my latter years, when my teeth were not quite equal to the task!

When walking home from the office, I passed a lady called Ruth who sold fruit. She usually had pawpaws, avocadoes and mangoes, depending a little on the season. With each of them selling for the equivalent of 5p, I generally chose two for my lunch. Just writing about them makes my saliva flow with longing! When I see pawpaws for sale here, for what seems to me an exorbitant price, I suffer from withdrawal symptoms and an intense desire for the real thing!

Transport was very varied. Some of the rich had four-wheel drive vehicles or flashy cars. The middle strata usually had Toyota Corollas, Nissans or Peugeots (pronounced by the people Pew-gee-ots). Drivers held on to their cars until they were literally falling apart, so it was not uncommon to see really old VW beetles around. The poor still used carts pulled by bullocks or hand carts which they pulled themselves. Many of the workers

were picked up by lorries provided by their employers, where they stood squeezed together like cattle. To save petrol, traders would pile up their goods on their vehicles in such a haphazard way that the load was often spilled.

The traffic in the centre of Nairobi could be a nightmare! Fortunately for the British, Kenyans drive on the left – or at least that was the theory of it! Some of the fairly crazy drivers, who have private buses called matatus, will drive on the wrong side, or on the pavement, to race their rivals and so get more passengers.

Our American friends, who were used to driving on the right, found it even more challenging and some lady friends of mine would drive for miles to avoid having to take a right-hand turn on to a main road. For many Kenyans, it was only a generation since they had been living in villages and often carrying out vendettas against their neighbours or struggling for survival. My colleague Agnes told me that as a child, she was usually dressed in animal skins. If ever a motor vehicle came into their village, she would flee into the bush and hide. Now she and her family are living in a very different environment. However, the old, deep-seated feelings were still there, leading to some pretty outrageous behaviour on the roads.

As I gradually learned more and more about Kenya and began to feel a bit more settled, I was able to concentrate more fully on the work I had come to do.

I wrote a poem trying to encapsulate its huge diversity.

Nairobi city of contrasts, Nairobi city so fair,

Bougainvillea, gardenia, hibiscus all scenting the air.

Nairobi city of contrasts, Nairobi city of fumes

Lorries and angry matatus pouring black smoke in plumes.

Nairobi city of contrasts, Nairobi city of stalls,

From ramshackle wooden kiosks to busy shopping malls.

Nairobi city of contrasts, sad city of despair,

The poor becoming poorer, hopelessness everywhere.

Nairobi city of contrasts, Nairobi city of crime,
  We have bars and bolts and padlocks, security all the time.

Nairobi city of contrasts, the city I've come to love,
With work and friends and fellowship, and blessings from
                                        above.

CHAPTER 6   SETTLING INTO THE WORK

My job description was 'Editor' at the Sudan Literature Centre (SLC). This entailed checking various documents or small books in English. I fondly imagined that it would be quite easy – I was wrong! All the books we were working with were written in a computer programme called Ventura Publisher, which was a very detailed and technical programme. So if I was to be able to edit, I first had to learn the programme. We were taught by our extremely patient colleague, Rhys Hall, who is a technical 'Whizz Kid' – though not exactly a kid, as he was then in his 50s. We spent long periods in his office, being shown just what to do, but on returning to our own offices, to put it into practice, that was a different story. Did we get it right? Certainly this was not the case in the early days. I remember writing lines and lines of instructions, following them carefully (or so I thought), only to find that at the end I had not achieved my objective.

To add to our problems, we were suffering from power cuts, so the electricity might suddenly disappear, with the result that we lost all our work. Of course, we were told to save it frequently, but as I got engrossed in what I was doing, I would often forget – then, in a flash, it had gone. Happily, in later years, we had a wonderful machine, which gave a signal that allowed us so many minutes grace after the power had stopped.

SLC was producing school books in English for Sudanese children. This was my primary focus. It also printed books and song books for the Sudanese churches, in a number of different languages, some with alphabets that contained extra letters such as Ŋ = nga. There were teams of writers, translators, editors, printers, collators and book binders, all within the centre.

To me, the most fascinating group was the collators. They sat round a huge circular table, made by Rhys Hall, which spun round on its axis. Piles of each page were placed all around the edge and the table was rotated, by hand. The workers then had to pick up one page from each pile, as the table turned. They became extremely skilled. I did try my hand at it, but could not keep up, so I missed several pages and was politely asked to leave it to them! The workers were lovely people and were so grateful to have a job. Although they were low-paid, they were always counting their blessings. Some were very poor indeed. I used to go home for lunch. On my return one day, I asked one of them what they had had for their lunch. "Air-burgers," came the reply. It took me some time before I realised that they had not had any lunch at all. Many of them managed only on their cup of tea which was made for them twice a day. They called it chai, and it is as far from an English cup of tea as you can imagine. To make chai, you put the tea leaves, the sugar, the milk and water all together into a large pot and boil it all up for a while, to get all the goodness from the leaves. When I first tasted it, I was rather appalled, but I soon came to look forward to it, not as a cup of tea, but as a nourishing drink. When I asked if I could have it without sugar, they were equally appalled.

Many of these workers came from Kibera, which is one of the biggest slums in Africa, housing about one million people. They live in shanties of one sort or another, with no plumbing. All the refuse is thrown out into channels running down the lanes. In the rainy season, it becomes a mass of mud and filth. No vehicles can get into the heart of the slum. Ambulances cannot get in either. If someone is very ill they will either be carried out on someone's back, or even wheeled out in a wheelbarrow.

As I got to know some of the staff and was trusted by them, I would be invited to visit them. There was no possibility of finding my way to their home, so they would meet me at one of the entrances and guide me. This sometimes involved jumping over open channels of refuse. They never invited me in the rainy season, as they were afraid I would not make it.

Francis was the first one to invite me. He met me at the perimeter and led me along narrow paths, jumping over open drains, weaving in and out of the various shanties. I was struck by the dirt, the ramshackle buildings, the piles of rubbish and the smell. Oh, the smell was nauseating.

As I entered his home, I found myself in one biggish room with a curtain which divided the bedroom from the living area. It was spotlessly clean. In one corner was a paraffin lamp and in the other a 'jiko', a small stove, heated by charcoal. This was meant to be used outside, but when the  weather was bad people used to light them indoors, which sometimes led to the whole house being burnt down.

In the dry season, if fire breaks out, it can be disastrous, as the houses are all crowded so close to one another. If this did happen, the culprit would run for his life, as the mob could easily turn on him and perhaps beat him to death.

Here in Kibera, for the first time in my life, I saw what real poverty looked like. People in the West may say they are poor, but are never found living in such conditions. However, what amazed me was that those who were lucky enough to have jobs, like our workers at SLC, always turned up at work clean and tidy. Their clothes, although of poor quality, were always clean and well ironed. Their shoes were always polished, although they often had to carry them in order to avoid having them dirtied in the mud.

Francis' family was there to meet me. For them it was an almost unheard of event, to have a muzungu (white person) in their home. They had been out specially to buy me a bottle of Fanta. Although I knew this was a great sacrifice on their part, I also knew that it would be an insult to them if I refused it. I drank some and then said I was satisfied, which meant that as soon as I had gone, one of the children would be given it. We chatted for a while, then they said, "You are free to go," which was their way of telling me that I could leave without causing offence.

I returned home in a very pensive mood. I had seen real poverty and yet I had seen people overcoming it in a quite amazing way. Since that time, I have never been the same; it has had a deep and lasting impact upon my life.

Funerals were far too common place, particularly among children and babies. One day I was approached by one of the staff. He told me his wife had given birth to a baby, but it had died the next day. He invited me to the funeral and also asked if I could transport him, his wife and the coffin to the cemetery. In no

way could he possibly afford to hire a hearse. So I took it as a great honour to be able to do this service for the grieving family. In this picture you can see it in the boot of my car.

At the cemetery I was appalled to see row upon row of little graves. It again made me recognise the huge divide between people in England, with our free National Health Service, offering free medicines to children and expectant mothers and those in Kenya. Although it is (or was) one of the best governed countries in Africa, infant mortality remains high. In Sudan the situation is even worse, with the sick often having to travel many miles to get any treatment and then at a cost most people cannot afford. The infant mortality in southern Sudan was one in six children under the age of four.

My car was again pressed into service by two members of staff, but this time for a much happier occasion. Our Stores' Manager, Wilbert, was planning to marry Dorcas, one of our collators. Sadly, western ways were infiltrating the country, which were raising people's expectations, especially about weddings. Whereas in earlier times it could have been a fairly simple affair with the couple in traditional clothes, now the demands had become greater. White dresses, page boys, flower girls and so on were now expected. This put a huge financial strain on the families who often fell into debt. These debts could take years and years to pay back.

So I was delighted to have been invited to the wedding and asked if my car could be used to transport the bride to the church.

It was a great day! Some of Dorcas' friends arrived at our house and decorated the car with streamers, most made of coloured toilet paper! Off we went to collect her. She, of course, was not ready! After a very long wait, she appeared, looking very lovely and was carefully tucked into my small car. The wedding invitation had stated that the service would begin at 12 noon. It was 2.45 before it actually began! Wilbert was waiting at the front of the church, when Dorcas came in, followed by six page boys, six flower girls and four bridesmaids. They came exceedingly slowly down the aisle, two steps forward and one step back.

IN THE OFFICE

At SLC the day started with Devotions at 8.30 am when we all squeezed in around the round table. It began with two people being asked to choose hymns from Golden Bells, a hymn book first published in 1925 in the UK and still much beloved by many African churches. Then there was what was intended to be a 'short' devotional talk, but which often turned into a mini-sermon. Then one person would be asked (without previous warning) to pray. Most of the staff took it in turns to give the talk. I was soon put on the rota. The fact that you might at any time be the one asked to pray, meant that I was always very attentive to the talk and any notices!

After Devotions, we all returned to our offices to begin work. SLC, a well-built single storey building, was originally used as a guest house for visitors to ACROSS. When SLC was developing, they moved in and tried to adapt it to their needs. At that time it was only a small concern, but when I arrived it had grown considerably and I was yet one more person to accommodate. The computer I was using was in a tiny room containing four computers, arranged around three of the walls. When we sat down, our chairs were touching at the back, so if one of us wanted to get up, we all had to move out of the way!

The staff was a mixture of Sudanese and expats. Over the years, there were more and more Sudanese and considerably fewer expats. Now it is almost entirely staffed and run by the Sudanese. This demonstrates the way 'missionaries' work. In earlier years, the whites came in and took control, sometimes seeing themselves as a cut above the 'natives'. Now, the term 'missionaries' is rarely used. Instead we are mission partners, underlining the fact that we come only at the invitation of the local people and churches. The great aim of the mission partners is to work themselves out of a job, so they can hand over the work to the local people and then move on to another location.

LITERACY

Before I left UK I spent 6 months doing a course for Teaching English as a Foreign Language (TEFL). It was a twice weekly class at the local Adult Education Centre, leading to a certificate from Trinity College London.

Soon after my arrival, I met an American lady who was working with a programme called Literacy and Evangelism. She encouraged me to join in the next training course, so off I went to enrol and take part. It is very different from TEFL as it is designed for totally illiterate people. I found it very interesting and challenging. It begins with different ways of teaching the alphabet, then moves on to different sounds like ea, ee, ai, etc.

As soon as the learner is able to read simple text, the examples, pictures and stories are based on Bible stories and Christian teaching. So it achieves its aim of Literacy and Evangelism. I took to it at once and really enjoyed the course.

The next thing was to find some students to experiment on. So I began praying about it. Quite soon after that, a Sudanese lady called Joyce Geri came into the office. She shared with me her great desire to help some of the other Sudanese women in Nairobi. Most of them had come with their husbands, who had jobs in Kenya. Many were illiterate and knew next to no English. Consequently many of them were trapped in their homes, not daring to go out. They just ventured as far as the nearest local kiosk-shops then went straight home again.

Joyce and I began praying about their situation and felt we should begin a programme to help them. I therefore had to get the consent of ACROSS to do such a task. At first they were not very happy about it. They pointed out that ACROSS was formed to serve the Sudanese **in Sudan**. However, when we were able to explain about the predicament of these ladies, they gave their consent. Next I had to clear it with my bosses at SLC, as it would mean being out of the office three afternoons a week. They also agreed, particularly as the wife of one of them would be in the group of learners.

After lengthy negotiations, we were allowed to have the use of an outbuilding belonging to the Africa Inland Church on Ngong Road, not very far from the office. They provided us with benches and a blackboard. Joyce then contacted some of the Sudanese ladies in our area. Meanwhile we spent all our time collecting pictures and making flash cards.

The great day came for us to begin. The Literacy and Evangelism teacher had suggested that we begin with four students. Joyce had clearly ignored this and had sent out a general invitation. 2 o'clock came – nobody had arrived. However, during

 the next half hour more and more appeared, rather hesitantly, until we had fifteen ladies! For some of them, this was an achievement in its own right. They had dared to come out, follow instructions from Joyce or their husbands and had actually made it!

It was also a first lesson for me about 'Africa time'. Two o'clock may mean anything up to four o'clock, or even later. I was to have many more examples of 'Africa time' during my years in Africa. Weddings were the prime example and could start literally hours after the specified time. In desperation, some of the Nairobi pastors started imposing heavy fines on couples who turned up more than half an hour late.

What an asset it was to have Joyce there at the classes! (After I left, she took over the whole programme.) She could speak the common language called Juba Arabic. This is a 'pidgin' language used across much of the south of Sudan. All of our ladies  could understand it, to varying degrees.

Most of the first lesson was taken up with finding out their names and greeting them. The only English many of them knew was, "How are you?" with the response "I am fine." I was soon to become really sick of this, as wherever I went the Kenyan or Sudanese children, seeing my white face, would call out endlessly, "How are you? How are you?"

It was a very mixed group. Some came and sat right in the front, whereas others slipped in quietly at the back. One of them called Neema sat right at the back, with her headscarf covering her face. Joyce told me that her husband had ordered her to attend, but she felt very nervous and very nervous and overwhelmed and suffered from a very low self-esteem.

Gradually the class settled down over the next weeks. We taught English vocabulary with the use of pictures, then moved on to the alphabet. We would hold up a picture of a cow and say "C for cow," etc. We taught simple English songs like 'God is so good' and 'One little, two little, three little fingers'. Although a class in UK might find that very childish, they had no problem and loved the songs and taught them to their children. Both TEFL and Literacy and Evangelism had taught us that we must teach four skills – Speaking, Listening, Reading and Writing. We began with speaking and listening and realised that most of them actually knew quite a lot of English words, but did not quite have the confidence to speak them out aloud. We encouraged them all to do so, often with a lot of laughter.

One of the first things they wanted to do was to be able to write their names. For some, this was an enormous challenge. I remember a bishop's wife, who had never held a pencil. We provided them with an exercise book and wrote their names clearly on the cover. They copied it. Once they thought they knew it, we invited them to come out and write it on the board. When one of them got their name right for the first time, we all clapped and they waved their arms in the air and did a little dance, sometimes punctuating it with a loud warbling sound called ululating.

I mentioned Neema, who at first was so lacking in confidence. She quite quickly learned to write her name and we saw a complete transformation in her. The headscarf came off her face, and she marched back to her place with her head held high. It was as though she were saying, "I'm no longer a failure. I can write my name. I am a big woman!" After that, she never looked back and became a really good student.

As we got to know them better, we began to hear about all their problems. Some had been brought to Nairobi, but their husbands had got jobs elsewhere and had pretty well abandoned them. Many of them had been cheated at the shops or market, but were unable to argue because of their lack of English. This became a big incentive for them to learn as quickly as possible. So we did a lot of role play on the subject of shopping and learning to demand their change after buying something.

One day Regina (in the red blouse in the picture) did not come to class. We were concerned about her. It transpired that she had been kidnapped by a man who was determined to marry her forcibly. We were all shocked and began to pray earnestly for her. Two weeks later she managed to escape and came back to us. She had not been married – or raped – but was still very frightened. What amazed me about all these women was their resilience. They had been through all sorts of traumas, but yet were able to smile and not be defeated by their experiences.

PREPARING FOR SUDAN

I had been extremely disappointed that my first trip to Sudan had only reached as far as Lokichoggio (Loki), in north Kenya. With hindsight I could see that it was actually too soon after my arrival in Africa and that I needed more time to get orientated. How often did I find out that God's plan was so much wiser than my own plans!

I was told by ACROSS that I was to return to Loki to attend an 'Orientation to Sudan Course', run by the United Nations. So off I went again to Loki. We took off later than planned and arrived in the middle of the day, which could have disastrous effects on the travellers. For as the heat rises, so the hot air thermals also rise, making the journey exceedingly bumpy. As we flew along, every time we hit one of the thermals it forced us up and then let us down again suddenly. As I have always suffered from travel sickness, this could have been a disaster. BUT.... a friend in UK had recommended 'Travel Bands', which uses acupressure. These are like elastic bracelets with a small button or bead on one side. You have to place the bead in the exactly right position – between the two tendons in your wrist - and they will control nausea. They worked every time. This really was a godsend. Had I been sick every time I travelled into Sudan, I'm not sure how long I would have persevered – those of you who suffer this way know just how terrible you feel and how long it takes to get over it. I must have travelled in a small plane over 50 times in East Africa, but thanks to Travel Bands, I was never sick.

The flight to Loki is always very interesting. Often the pilots fly quite low, so we can look down on the countryside. Leaving Nairobi, we usually circle over the slums in Kibera and look down on the hundreds of shanties, arranged with very little idea of order. As we gain height we can see the lovely Ngong Hills. These are a very long chain of hills – like a series of bumps. The word ngong means knuckles in the local language. We fly over the green heart of Kenya, dotted with villages and small farms. Soon we reach the Great Rift Valley and follow it for some time.

This is an extraordinary valley, more like a chasm, which was formed thousands of years ago. Later I was able to visit it myself.

As we fly further north, there is a subtle change, from green to brown, from sizeable villages to scattered compounds, from soft hills to rocky outcrops. It gradually becomes drier and drier until we reach Loki, which seems to be in the middle of a desert. As it is a small plane, flying low, we can soon spot the little airport and watch as we lose height and finally bump along the runway. As you alight from the plane, the heat hits you like a hot dry blanket, which nearly takes your breath away, until you get used to it. We hurriedly take off the sweaters we had been wearing in Nairobi and in the plane and make our way to the immigration desk. As I was alone, I was a little nervous about what to do next, but there was the beaming face of one of the Sudanese staff from the ACROSS compound to meet me. He grabbed my bag and off we rattled in the little pick-up truck.

Loki is in the area that is inhabited by the Turkana tribe. These people are a complete contrast to the tribes around Nairobi. They are proud cattle-keepers, somehow keeping their cattle alive in these near-desert conditions. I found them intriguing and wanted to take photos.

"Please don't," said the driver. "They might be very angry and throw stones or come and take your camera." I put it away hurriedly and asked the reason why. He explained that although they are very fierce warriors, they are also in the grip of witchcraft. They believe that if someone takes a picture of them, it will take away part of their soul. On another occasion, I did pick up my camera when I was with a group of women. They immediately got to their feet and fled.

The women are remarkable as they have very long necks which are encircled by row upon row of beads. These are a sign of their wealth, so their husbands will give them more and more until they become a really heavy burden to carry around. But it is also a matter of pride, so they hold their heads high to show them off. I'm sorry to say that they never take them off, so you may notice a not too pleasant odour!

101

Although Loki is in a remote area in the far north, it has become a very busy airport in Kenya, second only to Nairobi Airport. This is because it has the nearest access to Sudan. In the 1990s the United Nations ran Operation Lifeline Sudan, offering free flights to the numerous non-governmental organisations (NGOs) working in and out of Sudan. There were more than 50 different NGOs at that time, taking supplies to many parts of the south of the country. All the big names were there – Oxfam, Médecins sans Frontières, Christian Aid, etc. There were also various Christian groups, like Open Doors, ACROSS and various Catholic and Protestant church groups, all trying to help these dear people who were suffering so much in the civil war.

The orientation was very helpful and practical. It was not, as I had feared, just a series of lectures. Instead there was plenty of discussion and participation. The instructors were ten Sudanese people, including doctors, social workers, engineers and others who had taken refuge in Kenya. As they were aliens, they could not get a Work Permit, so therefore they could not get jobs. They were only too happy to have short-term jobs with the UN.

The procedure was to announce the topic for the session, then divide us into groups of three. The topics included the role of the father/mother, polygamy, rites of passage, the dowry system, etc. Each group then wrote down questions they would like answered, then the Sudanese team came up with the answers. At the end, all the groups reported back what they had learned. It was a very good teaching method, so much better than listening to lectures.

They also taught us various survival tactics, suggesting what we should pack – and what we should leave behind. We were introduced to pictures of the latrines – more of that later! We were shown different types of landmines we might encounter with advice as to what to do –which was to move away quickly, then report it!

What I found more alarming was a glass bottle they passed round containing a dead guinea worm, which was several feet long. When someone drinks dirty water, they may imbibe the larva of a guinea worm. This now makes its home in the gut, growing longer and longer. After about a year, it starts to come out. It can choose any part of the body to make its appearance, but more often than not it comes out of the calf. It may take several days to finish its exit. The important thing is not to break it before it is fully out, or infection will set in. Therefore, in spite of the pain, the sufferer must wind it up gradually, usually over a little stick until it has actually finished coming out. This was an extremely salutary lesson and I went to any lengths while in Africa to drink only water that had been filtered, boiled or treated chemically.

The UN had also developed a list of things one must carry, ready for a hasty retreat. This had some good suggestions, like spare socks, toilet paper, pencil and paper. But what horrified most of us was that we should also carry an amputation saw!

Much was also illustrated by role play. I was cast as the gullible English lady. People came one by one, begging for help of one sort or another. I happily gave them what I could – then realised that I had given away so much, that I had no alternative but to return to the UK to seek for more funds. It was another salutary lesson, as a white face immediately suggests that the owner is a useful source of income. We were warned that people would come with their heart-rending stories. We were told that we should resist such pleas unless we understood the whole situation.

I was once nearly taken in, back in Nairobi. I had been chatting with a friend on the pavement, near to my bank in Nairobi, telling her about my recent holiday. I walked away and set off for home. A young man accosted me, asking if I had had a good holiday. I was somewhat surprised, as I did not recognise him. He told me that he had seen me at church, when I was talking to a small group. He then went on to ask me for a loan, which he promised to return next Sunday. I hesitated – then realised that he had been on the pavement when I was talking to my friend. He had overheard our conversation and quickly made up his story. I told him in no uncertain terms to go away and not to try it on again.

Beggars are everywhere in the towns and cities in Africa. We see young mothers with two or three children, one of whom appears to be disabled or is crying, begging for *shillingi*. It is extremely hard to 'walk by on the other side', but that was often what I had to do. Some of the mothers had accumulated large sums by the end of the day, having borrowed a disabled child from a friend.

It was also a fairly common practice amongst educated friends or acquaintances. Elizabeth, who was highly educated, with a good job, asked me for a sizeable loan so she could finish the payment for a plot of land to build her house. She said that if she did not buy it now, the deal would fall through. I gave her the money – but in spite of constant promises of 'tomorrow' I never saw my money again. It was another useful, if costly lesson

BACK TO NAIROBI

When the orientation in Loki ended, I returned to Nairobi, somewhat sobered by what I had learned, but still longing to 'adventure' into the war-torn country of Sudan. Coming from the extreme heat and dust in Loki, I was greeted by the exact opposite. I was faced with mud! Both our unmade road and the footpaths were a sea of mud. I had to try to put my feet down on any possible dry patches. As I slithered about, my shoes got heavier and heavier, caked with thick red mud. It did not help that my knee had been a little troublesome, so this certainly made it more difficult. We all carried a spare pair of shoes to change into.

As I continued in the office, one thing began to trouble me. When I was at home in the UK, I was much involved in Bible teaching. As well as the R.E. lessons in school, I was teaching in a Home Group and was running three Christian Unions in school. I wrote home, saying, I would so much like to be involved in some Bible teaching ministry and am praying that God will guide me into the place of his choice.

However, it was not to be. I was firmly settled into what could be called a secular job, with no so-called 'spiritual' work. This began to open my eyes to the modern vision of 'Mission'. We were there on the whole, not to preach the gospel, but to work in the background, helping, encouraging and training the local pastors, teachers and ordinary Christians so that they could do the work of evangelism and discipleship themselves, in their native languages. Once I realised that by teaching English to Sudanese leaders I was enabling them to become more useful in their ministries, I began to understand my role better and be content with the work I believed God had given me to do. I also had the privilege of getting to know them, sharing with them and then praying for them.

In those early weeks, I was really enjoying living with Rhondda, but she herself was not too happy. She so much wanted to live like an African and felt uncomfortable in our relatively prosperous area. When she decided to move out, I was very sorry to see her go. (She did come back at a later date.) Instead a lady called Martha moved in. She was a semi-retired American missionary of 74, who had served in Sudan for many years and was involved in translating the Old Testament into one of the tribal languages. She had returned to Africa to check and hopefully to finalise the text. She was very different from Rhondda, a quiet lady, who liked her own space. However, we too became good friends.

Another 'goodbye' was to Julian and Rachel Jackson, who had been so supportive to me in the early weeks. They were such faithful prayer-warriors and great encouragers, so I knew I would miss them. They were finally retiring to England, in November, 1995. It must have been particularly hard for them to begin their retirement in the dark and gloomy days of November and December. I was sorry to see them go.

Our own weather was actually rather damp and dreary just then. I wrote home bemoaning the fact that I was losing some of my English suntan! The problem was that when the sun was out, it was far too intense for us to sit outside.

CAR PROBLEMS

It was at this time that I came to realise that I would need a car in order to move around in Nairobi. Pat, who was to be my house-mate, was still in Australia. She and Rhys from Sudan Literature Centre (SLC) had bought a car between them. It had been sitting idle for some months. Rhys decided he no longer needed it, so it was agreed that I should buy his half for £1000. The car needed a great deal doing to it. There was a hole in the floor, which let in water - and mud. It needed new shock absorbers (these very soon become worn out in much of East Africa, due to the terrible roads) and a new battery. A friend promised to give it the once over, to see if it was worth buying. I had to deliver the car to him. It was, inevitably, pouring with rain.

Four of the SLC staff bravely came out and gave me a push and it finally spluttered into life. Whenever I took my foot off the accelerator, it stalled and I needed another push. The only solution was to keep one foot on the accelerator all the time – but that meant I could not use the foot brake in case I stalled! So it was a hair-raising ride, in the rain, with some mud coming up through the hole in the floor, with very inefficient windscreen wipers and only being able to use the hand brake to slow down! As I did not know the way, I took a wrong turning and ended up in the wrong compound. The two guards nobly pushed me out again – backwards on to a busy road. When I finally arrived at my destination, I gave a prayer of thanksgiving as I scrambled out of the car and was offered a more than welcome cup of tea.

The car was eventually put right, so I bought Rhys' share and then had it to myself until Pat arrived. After that, we had to share it – which was not always easy!

I was learning more and more about myself and about life in Kenya. I was acquiring more information about Sudan, but I still had not set foot into the country. That was finally going to change.

CHAPTER 7 A SHORT HISTORY OF THE WAR

NOTE ON THE NAME OF THE COUNTRY

When I went to Sudan in 1995, the whole country was known as Sudan. However, there was a clear distinction between the Islamic north and the so-called Christian South. The area in the west of the centre of the country is the Nuba Mountain region. I worked only in the south and would not have been welcome in the north. I had hoped to go north and had been allowed another passport, but this never came to pass.

Most of my story is set in the time when Sudan was still one country. It only became two countries in 2011, when it was split into Sudan and South Sudan. It is surrounded by nine countries (Ethiopia on the east is not marked on this map). The south is land-locked, but the north has access to the Red Sea at Port Sudan.

THE HISTORY

The problems really began when the mapmakers, under pressure from colonialists of the 1800s sat down and drew lines on the map of Africa, dividing it into countries. It seems they took little notice of where tribal or national boundaries lay. The consequence was that Sudan became a huge country (the biggest in Africa) with not only tribal differences, but very grave religious differences, as the north was dominated by Arabs and black Africans who followed Islam, while the south was peopled by black Africans from a variety of tribes, the majority worshipping the spirits and the spirits of their ancestors. Historically, many of these tribes had been at enmity with one another for centuries, a good example being the two largest tribes, the Dinka and the Nuer. (As I write in 2015 these tribes are once again in conflict, with great loss of lives.) The north had been fairly well developed by the colonists, but the south, with its huge tracts of uninhabited land and the many warring tribes, had been largely ignored.

From 1899, Sudan had been governed jointly by a condominium of Britain and Egypt. In 1956, it achieved its independence. Almost immediately the Government in Khartoum announced that Sudan would now become a fully Islamic republic. At that time only about 10-15% of the people in the South were Christians, the rest following their various forms of spirit worship, ancestor worship, or some form of witchcraft. However, the one thing they were agreed about was that they did not want to be forced to become Muslims.

So the North declared Holy War – Jihad on the South. This war, known as Anya-Anya 1, went on until there was a short period of peace from 1972-1983. Fighting flared up again in 1983 and continued until the Comprehensive Peace Agreement (CPA) of 2003. During this second period of warfare, missionaries were not allowed to live in Sudan. However the needs of the people

108

were very great, so Operation Lifeline Sudan was born, as part of the work of the United Nations.

It was in the late 80s that oil was first discovered in the South. The map above shows the oilfields, all situated around the border between the two countries .Now the war took on a different aspect. Oil - lots of it - meant vast amounts of money. The fighting became more intense, with the north trying to appropriate more and more of the oil. The south of course retaliated, hence the war, which dragged on for the next 20 years. It is estimated that about one million lives were lost, very many of them being civilians. Nearly four million fled for refuge first to neighbouring countries, then all over the world. Thousands from the south fled to the north. Although they were not made welcome by the Muslim population, at least they could live without the fear of being bombed. Some managed to get jobs, but many were forced out into camps in some of the desert areas of the north. There was untold suffering amongst those who chose to live in the north, but it was much worse in the south with the innocent women and children often having the hardest time. Many fled to refugee camps in Kenya and Uganda. I will tell some of their stories later.

Finally in 2003 the Comprehensive Peace Agreement was signed. It was agreed that the fighting should end, the oil revenues should be shared and the south should have its own government. Elections were to take place and in 2011 there should be a referendum for the south to decide whether they would remain united with the north, as one country or whether they should become independent.

The elections were carried out, although there is great doubt as to whether they were free and fair. However, the South managed to set up a reasonably good system of government and the referendum was duly held, with a huge majority (97%) demanding that they become an independent country. So on 9th July, 2011 South Sudan was born – but many observers commented that it was a new country doomed to fail.

The clause concerning the end of fighting was never fully adhered to, and over the months and years the bombing from the North and fighting in various areas by both sides continued. The greatest hurdles were the oil and borders. It seems almost unbelievable that the decision to split into two countries was made before the actual border between them had been agreed. The border lies somewhere within the oil-rich areas towards the south of the country. The economy of both countries relies heavily on its oil revenues, so both countries demanded more and more for themselves. The ordinary people in the disputed areas continued to be under fairly constant bombardment and thousands fled to overcrowded refugee camps.

Those southerners still living in the north now found themselves to be aliens, being told they must have a passport, which most of them could not afford. President al Bashir promised to bring in full Shari'a Law, with all its harsh regulations, including forcing women to be fully covered from head to foot. Life became untenable for all Christians and also for all other southerners who were not Christians. There was therefore a huge exodus to the south. Sadly at that time many areas in South Sudan were suffering from shortage of food, as the crops had failed. There was malnourishment and even starvation in various areas. This made the return of the so-called aliens from the north even more difficult.

EYE WITNESS REPORTS

Later on, when I was teaching in Sudan, I asked the students to write on the topic, "How the war has changed my life. Below are two of their stories, the first by James Loki.

The war has brought great loss to me. In 1990 I was in secondary school, in the science department, with only two months remaining for me to sit for Sudan School Certificate to go to University. Unfortunately the war has blocked everything.

So I joined the Sudanese People's Liberation Army for five years, fighting on the front line with our opponents the so-called Arabs. I was injured in the leg, but not too badly and I recovered.

In 1997 I was invited to join the Timothy Training Institute in Imatong Bible College of Africa Inland Church and I received a Diploma in 1999. At that time the LRA attacked our compound and put everything to ashes. They killed many people with their pangas, cutting people to pieces and piling them in heaps. They killed children by beating their heads against trees. They took away all my cows and crops. We were in a bad crisis, with nothing to eat or to cover ourselves. We hid in the forest, beaten by the rain and many were affected with the disease known as measles, which killed many children from seven years downwards.

Being a leader in the church, I quote Job's words, "Naked I came into this world and naked I shall depart. The Lord gave and the Lord has taken away; may the name of the Lord be praised."

The war also separated me from my parents. It has now been fourteen years without seeing them. I have heard that they are alive, but far away.

NOTE James graduated from ECTC and is now serving as a pastor, with a part-time job in the local town. He is doing well, after such a sad time.

TABAN'S STORY –

Some years ago, I started to experience some changes in my life. It was when the Sudanese Civil War broke out in 1987 when I was eleven years old.

One night, I heard gun shots and called out, "Mother, mother, what is that? Are the army celebrating a big thing?"

"No, no, no," she said, "Be quiet." The rebels were burning grass and we saw some houses burning, including our kitchen. We stayed indoors from morning to night. Then we sneaked out to the National Army barracks for protection. There was no food there and we were surrounded by the rebels. One night we decided to escape to Moyo in Northern Uganda. When we were near the border, some rebels caught us and arrested us. They shot my father on the spot and put us in prison. After two weeks, we escaped to Uganda.

We were in the refugee camp for fours years, then the UNHCR moved us to another camp. In 1995 that camp was attacked and my mother was shot. I was left alone with one younger sister who needed my personal help.

I was born in a rich family of lovely parents. Now I was alone with no materials or financial support. I did some casual labour to continue with my education and reached Senior three. Now I need to work again to support my sister who is going to enter Senior 1.

I am now 23 years old. The war has changed my life, as I am an orphan, but God loves me so much in giving me Christ as my Saviour to comfort me in my terrible life.

TRIBAL TENSION

After South Sudan became independent, there were high hopes that the country would develop and people's lives would improve. There continued to be sporadic fighting around the oil-rich areas, but elsewhere life became less precarious. The Government was led by Salva Kiir, a Dinka as President with Riak Machar, a Nuer, as Vice-President, in the hope that these two major tribes would be able to work together. But problems abounded.

The country had been devastated by decades of civil war and the infrastructure had been totally destroyed. There was a dearth of schools, hospitals and clinics. The roads were well-nigh impassable or non-existent. Although efforts were made to rebuild, the people's expectations were not fulfilled. Many foreign groups and Non Government Organisations (NGOs) began to rebuild some hospitals, schools and roads, but the results were slow to appear and people began to get angry at the slow progress. Corruption crept into the government in all departments.

In 2013 the President sacked his Vice, who went off enraged. Observers held their breath, waiting to see what would be the repercussions, particularly in light of the enmity between the Dinka and Nuer and the ingrained desire for revenge. In early 2014 Riak Machar, who had gather great forces of Nuer soldiers, attacked various Dinka areas, with hundreds of people killed. What followed, was yet another devastating period of fighting and killing. Some of the other tribes joined in the fray. Thousands fled into the bush and more than a million looked for safety in refugee camps set up by some charities. As I write in 2015, the situation is still the same. The prophecy of South Sudan being a new country born to fail has at present been fulfilled.

I was based in Nairobi. The United Nations High Commission for Refugees was based in Lokichoggio, north of Lodwar, near the Sudanese border

.

CHAPTER 8 SUDAN AT LAST

I was told that on Wednesday, 8th November I would finally be going to Sudan. I was extremely excited. It meant an early start, as we had to be at the airport at 5.30 am. I arrived and waited eagerly. After two hours, I was told that my name was only on stand-by and there was no seat for me. Choking back my tears, a very dejected Jan King returned and went back to work in the office. However, the next day there was a seat – not on stand-by, but an actual booked seat. Again I was up early and this time I was able to board the plane and later arrived in Loki. Once there, I had to wait until there was a flight into our location. It was on Sunday 12 November 1995 when I first set foot in the country I had been preparing for and looking forward to, for the past two years.

I was helping to teach on a course run by ACROSS, for the UN. As it was under the UN programme called Operation Llifeline Sudan (OLS), they flew us in, free of charge on one of their small planes. (While we were teaching teachers, the UN was happy to transport us to and from the locations. However, once we began working with the churches, they could no longer take us.) On this occasion, our plane was just a 6-seater. It took two hours and was a pretty bumpy ride. The back of the plane was crammed with an assorted heap of items, including a bicycle.

On my return to Nairobi, I wrote down my first sensations –

- not finding weevils in my Weetabix - until the last mouthful
- finding a spider in my box of teaching aids. It was 3 inches across, light brown with spots
- crossing the compound in the dark, sweeping the ground ahead with my torch, looking for snakes or scorpions
- being regaled with stories about guinea worm

- lining up as we came out of church, shaking hands with about 400 people as they passed

- .standing under the black velvety night sky, looking up at the myriads of stars and praising God for the wonder of his creation.

The UN also provided food and all the materials the teachers needed when they returned to their schools. At the end of the course, they were each presented with a big metal box, containing 172 Primary School text books and teachers' guides, all produced by SLC. It also contained useful items like a blackboard, a football and two pairs of underpants! When the boxes were given to them, it was a real joy to watch their faces as they saw what was inside. In most cases, these teachers had no books whatsoever, so they were genuinely overwhelmed by such riches. Most teachers had to manage by passing on what they knew, with a blackboard and some chalk.

Our course was for 40 Primary School teachers. The first week was devoted to teaching intensive English to the teachers themselves. This was extremely important, as most of the students had received only a very sketchy education themselves, because of the war. After I had settled in, I wrote home. Of course I could not post it while I was still in Sudan, as there was no postal service. So I sent it after I got back to Kenya. Here is an extract from my letter, with a sketch of the tukul.:

Let me try to describe my surroundings. We are staying on the compound of a German Agricultural Mission. The compound is about half the size of a football pitch, surrounded by a 7 foot fence made of bundles of grass. There are two large huts, called tukuls. They consist of a large circle of upright poles, with the lower half filled in with thick

115

brown mud, which hardens like concrete. The top half is left open, as windows. There is a central post which supports a beautifully thatched roof, which is laid in steps. (Here the drawing I sent home.)

In one corner of the compound there is a small round hut which contains a very deep hole, aptly called the long-drop. There's no door, so you clap as you approach and sing while you're inside. Near it is another small screened area with a 'shower', which consists of a large bowl to stand in, a jerry can of water and a metal cup!

The ACROSS group has brought six tents, which is where we are sleeping. I'm sharing one with a very nice Australian lady. In one corner of the compound there is a large shady tree, under which we have 2 small tables and some camp stools. The biggest problem is the insects, coming in all sizes and shapes, all seeming to have the ability to bite or sting. It's not too bad by day, but when it gets dark (at 6 pm) we have to escape into one of tents and zip ourselves in to avoid being eaten alive.

Try to imagine a dome-shaped tent, about 8 feet across at floor level, but tapering steeply into the dome. Last night seven of us were packed in for the evening meal, by the light of a candle. Even then some insects managed to get in. The temperature was rising and rising until it was like sitting in a sauna

Once I had settled in, I joined in with the teaching. It was extremely challenging work. The students were really keen to learn English but, as explained above, some of them were well behind in their performance. We taught spoken English, often through songs. These were songs for them to teach to their pupils, so we included ones such as Old MacDonald Had a Farm.

I also enjoyed some of their efforts at English. Here are a few examples:

I became a teach in 1997. I am no get marry. This is my end.

I was born 1997 years ago.

In 1994 my wife was born a boy.

116

This was concerning the dowry system: *I have not marriage my wife, but I borrowed it.*

We were only allowed to stay in Sudan in the war years for two or three weeks. So I returned to Nairobi thrilled with my first experience of teaching in Sudan.

THE UNWILLING AUTHOR

In our courses for the teachers, English Grammar was a must. They were using a text book called 'Brighter Grammar'. However, the book did not live up to its name and far from being 'brighter' it just made them more confused, with terms such as Definitives and Interrogatives. I grumbled a great deal about this book. One day, after yet another grumble, Lyn turned to me and said, "If you don't like the book, you had better write a new one!"

"I couldn't possibly do that," was my immediate reply. My problem was that at school, English had been my worst subject. I cannot remember ever getting more than 55% in an English exam. So the thought of writing an English book seemed to me to be

totally ridiculous. However, the idea just would not go away. As fast as I dismissed it as 'not for me', it came back, niggling at the back of my mind. So, after praying about it, I began to give it serious consideration. The only good thing about Brighter Grammar was the little cartoon-like illustrations. After more prayer, I decided that if I

was allowed to use the pictures, I would have a stab at writing a simplified grammar. On my return to Nairobi, I

117

wrote to the publisher, explaining the situation. To my amazement – and somewhat to my dismay, they were happy for me to use them, as long as I put in an acknowledgement. As I had made the situation known, I was now trapped! So I set to work and to my surprise I did not find it too difficult.

Having studied Latin and Greek, my knowledge of grammar was pretty good. Also I found I could replace the difficult words with easier ones. The chapter entitled 'Definitives' became 'This and That'. 'Interrogatives' became 'Asking Questions' and so on. Contrary to my expectations, I actually found myself enjoying writing the book. In all the grammar exercises, I was able to use Sudanese names and the names of Sudanese towns and cities. (I later found that the students got really excited if their own name or the name of a local town was mentioned.) A few trial copies were printed by SLC and on our next course we tried it out. Apart from a few hiccups, it went down really well. It soon became a 'best-seller' among other groups who were teaching English in Sudan, so at a later date I needed to write Book 2 for the more able students.

This whole process taught me an important lesson. If God clearly wants us to do something, it is no good saying "I can't" because, with His help, we can. I believe that God has given all of us hidden talents, which are waiting to be used. Then when He calls us to do something unlikely, He empowers us. Another important spin off from this experience is that I cannot take the praise for having written the books, because it is God who gave me all that I needed – so all the praise goes to Him!

MY FIRST CHRISTMAS IN AFRICA, 1995

Back in Nairobi, Christmas was soon to be celebrated. It was a great joy to find that there was none of the Christmas fever that has invaded the west. It was seen to be the religious festival celebrating the birth of Christ. However, I decided to give a party for the sixteen ladies from my Literacy Class. I made some rather makeshift decorations, with the help of some paper chains sent by

118

my daughter Val. Then I tried to think up some good games that did not require language or writing – quite a challenge.

Most of the ladies had never been in the home of a mzungu (white person), so they felt excited but a little apprehensive. However we had a great time and they joined in the games with enormous enthusiasm and a great deal of laughter. Their favourite was Pass the Parcel. I spent ages wrapping up small gifts and sweets in reams of newspaper. When they played, I found they had a strong sense of fairness, for towards the end, when there were still one or two people who had not yet had a chance to open a layer, they all kept their eyes open and made quite sure that nobody was left out. So even if the music had stopped, they kept passing on the parcel until everyone had had their turn.

I made a nice tea for them, with homemade cakes. One was a very rich chocolate cake, which a number of them wanted to take home to share with their families. The pretty paper napkins I provided were carefully wrapped up and taken home too.

ACROSS was running a programme of Christmas Buckets. They bought plastic buckets and filled them with useful items for the home and some foodstuffs to distribute to the poorest Sudanese refugee families. I made an appeal in my prayer letter, with my daughter Alison acting as banker. She was able to send a cheque for £500. The recipients were absolutely delighted to receive such a gift. To them it was a godsend.

At that time, the Kenyan Police had clamped down on refugees who were flooding into Nairobi without any papers. A few weeks before Christmas they arrested about 1000. They came at night, banging on doors, or even breaking them down and dragging the hapless people down to the prison, often beating them for no apparent reason. They would always tell them to pay a fine, demand money and sometimes tear the house apart until they found it. Then in many cases, after leaving a house, they could be seen just sharing out the money between themselves. Sadly the Sudanese had no way of standing up against this treatment. So the Christmas Buckets were all the more welcome.

119

There was another event that underlined the uncertain and sometimes frightening situation of the Sudanese refugees. Just before Christmas Martha, my new housemate had a real blow. During her time in Sudan, she had started work on a translation of the New Testament into Latuko, one of the tribal languages. Now she had returned to do a final revision with the help of a Latuko man called Toby, who had come especially from Khartoum to help her with the work. She had worked really hard to get all the complicated paperwork done for him, and finally he had arrived.

Unfortunately, while Toby was out of the house, he was rounded up in this police crackdown. One of his papers was not in order, so he was told to leave Kenya 'TODAY!' Martha and I had a great rush to try to get a bus ticket (we queued for an hour), then to get the correct Exit Permit, or he would be arrested at the border. We spent two hours in horrendous Nairobi rush-hour traffic trying to get everything done. In the end, we just could not get it all completed, so he had to stay with us over the weekend – but never to show his face, in case the police found him. Uganda was not as fussy as Kenya about refugees, so it was decided that Toby should go there. The upshot of this was that Martha also had to move to Uganda to finish the work.

Happily I did not have to spend Christmas alone, as I was invited to lunch by some American colleagues – and was rather disappointed with my Christmas dinner. In November, they had celebrated Thanksgiving, with turkey and all the trimmings, but for Christmas they produced a splendid variety of salads and cold meats. Sadly I really do not like vinegar or salad dressings, so I was rather disappointed. However they had managed to get a Christmas pudding as well as pumpkin pie, which was delicious. But it was very kind of them and I was very happy to have been included. I was even more aware of missing my family and friends back home.

MORE BOOKS TO WRITE

Some time later, my boss Rev Gordon Tikiba asked me to accompany him to a workshop that was to be held in Nairobi, to put together a new curriculum for the primary schools in southern Sudan. I was to serve with the English Language Group. It was hard going, with very lengthy discussion as to what to put in and what to leave out. Actually being present at a discussion with Sudanese men was a bit of an education, as each person expected to be able to speak at length, not worrying if it was a repetition of the previous speaker. So it could drag on for far too long.

There were already some English textbooks, but the material for the first two years of primary school was entirely oral. The thinking had been that before they could read English, they needed to be able to speak it. I thought that this was eminently good thinking. However, most of the other members in the group thought that the children should immediately be taught both to read and write in English. I said that I believed that this would be too difficult for an average 6 year old, who would also be learning to read and write in the mother tongue, often with a different alphabet and different sounds. They all said that, "That was how we were taught – and look at us now!" I did not quite like to mention that they were among the intelligentsia of south Sudan, while I was more concerned with the average – or below average – child. So they had their way and it was decreed that the Sudanese children should start straight in with both reading and writing in English.

So as you may have guessed, this English 'failure' was given the task of writing a new series of English textbooks, which was no easy task. As the pupils would be learning to read in their own languages, which were generally phonetic, I therefore had to take a different approach, with much more of 'Look and Say', illustrated by lots of pictures. To my mind this is not the ideal way to teach, but in any case a great deal of English is certainly not phonetic – would, through, laugh, taught, and so on. What was more, it had to be prepared in the dreaded Ventura Publisher.

On the bright side, we had an artist, Henry, who worked with us. Henry had the skill of producing simple line drawings that were easily recognisable. In the west, we learn to 'read' pictures from our earliest years. It was very different in much of southern Sudan at that time. There was very little of the written word in the villages, where there are no newspapers, no magazines, no books (unless the pastor had a Bible), no posters on the walls. So the people saw very little writing and almost no pictures. Once, when I was in Sudan, I had with me an illustrated Bible. When I first showed the children some of the pictures, they could not at first 'read' the picture, until I explained it to them. I therefore realised all that was required in my books were simple line drawings.

Once Henry had produced the pictures, I then had to transfer them to the book. To those who are working in Word or Apple, this is pretty straightforward, but in the dreaded Ventura it was a very much greater challenge. Often I had to go to find Rhys, telling him I had once again lost my picture. He patiently recovered it for me, showing me once again how to manage the process. As time went on, I found I could usually manage it myself – but the pictures still had a habit of disappearing from one page and reappearing on another.

My next venture into writing was in the field of Adult Literacy. As some of our students in the Literacy Class began to make strides towards reading, we realised that what they needed was a very easy reader, with simple stories, set in their own cultural setting. This was a different sort of challenge. As the ladies had a very limited vocabulary, I had to tailor the stories to what they knew and gradually add new words – but not too many at once.

At least I could now use phonics as well as 'Look and Say', so the first story was The Cat and the Rat. I was determined to put in - The cat sat on the mat – so I did! After the first story, I had the problem of finding out how many different words I had used.

Here Rhys was again invaluable. He taught me a special programme which listed all the words I had used in each story, as well as the number of times they had been included. Working from this list, and adding one or two words per page, I was able to write the next story. In the next story I would try to use these words again, adding a few new ones, and so on. The first book went down really well. It gave the ladies the concept of the joy of reading and understanding a story. Book 2 followed, working up to more complex stories like The Buffalo Hunt and Fire in the Home. Again Henry and his art work were invaluable. Although I was enjoying my work, I still had a pressing desire to again go to Sudan. My wish was about to be fulfilled.

The map below shows the area where I worked. See also the map at the beginning of the book. When working with the UN, we were mainly in the area north of Bor. Bor was held by the northern army, so we often heard shell fire. Although we were bombed a couple of times, we were never attacked on the ground. Later on, I worked mostly in or near Yei or in the refugee camps in the north of Uganda and the north of Kenya. I was never able to visit Juba, the capital.

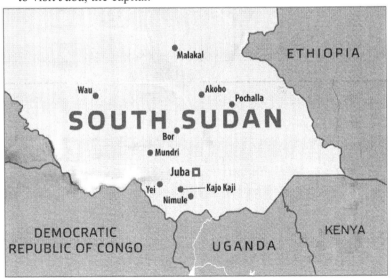

123

CHAPTER 9 MORE CHALLENGES

My next trip into Sudan, in January 1996, was also unnerving. Having recently come from an airport, where you board through a covered passageway and finally find yourself on the plane, it had been rather different at Jomo Kenyatta Airport in Nairobi, where we disembarked on to the tarmac and walked into the terminal. When going to Sudan it was even easier. We usually left from Wilson, a small airport in Nairobi, with little planes dotted about. Your plane was pointed out, so we wandered between the other planes and then climbed up a little ladder into ours. On our way to Loki we were usually on 16-seater planes.

In the morning I was taken to Wilson and was led towards an even smaller plane. On looking into it, to my horror, I saw that there were no seats. I had visions of sitting on the floor without a seatbelt. However, a little pick-up truck appeared, bringing the seats, which were then bolted down.

The lady who had taken me to Wilson was a Kenyan from the Kikuyu tribe. This tribe has a problem with the letters L and R, so when I finally clambered up the steps into the plane, she cheerfully called out, "Have a good fright!" Actually I did have a bit of a fright. I was seated in the co-pilot's seat, right at the front of the plane. An hour or so into our journey the sky turned black. The pilot began to weave in and out of the clouds, hoping to avoid the worst of it, but suddenly we were in the midst of a ferocious hail storm, with hail stones clattering on our windows like machine gun bullets and then making streams of water, so we could see nothing. Then just as suddenly we came out of the cloud and there below us was the great River Nile, winding away into the distance. I was extremely relieved when we finally put down at Lokichoggio (Loki), the gateway into Sudan.

Again we were to teach 40 teachers from 40 local primary schools. I thought that my bumpy ride on the plane had been challenging, but I was amazed at the journeys some of these teachers had undertaken. It was the end of the rainy season and there was still a lot of standing water around. Two of them had walked for four days, sometimes up to their armpits in water. This showed how desperate they were to get some training after all their years of deprivation. By the time they went home, the ground had dried. This was a real blessing, for having come with nothing, they each went home with the UN box of books, which they carried proudly on their heads.

I was still very 'green' in the work and this was apparent on one day in particular. I was sitting in my tukul, marking some homework, when I heard a loud and unusual crash followed by another. I put my head out and found all the rest of the staff huddled in the bomb shelter! They had all heard and recognised the sound of the Antonov bomber, while I had missed it altogether. The crash had been two bombs, which had landed about 100 metres away!

I quickly jumped into the bomb shelter with the others. After we were sure it had gone for good, we went to see the damage. There was none! The bombs are designed so that on impact they send out a hail of sharp pieces of metal, to do the greatest damage. However in much of South Sudan the soil is very soft and very deep, with the result that the bomb had gone deep into the soil with no damage at all. It was then that I learned that the soil can be up to 8 metres deep! Now I am home in South Croydon I often think of this as I dig in my garden, striking chalk, less than one spade deep.

After the plane had gone, we clambered out and there followed a very interesting conversation. While in Sudan, we had only a satellite radio with which to make contact with our base, and when information – such as a bomb being dropped – was sensitive, the operator had to use a code. Unfortunately the code book, could not be found, so the others put their heads together to see if they could remember the code for 'bomb'. One person was sure it was that we had received two green tomatoes but another was equally sure that it was green bananas. After a lengthy discussion it was decided we would just say that we had received two bombs, the thinking being that those in the north probably knew about it anyway, so we only had to inform our own people.

The next day, some of the men set to work to make a big

bomb shelter for the students. As there was nothing like cement available, it was just a large fairly deep hole, where we could all take shelter in case of shrapnel, but it would of course not be of any help from a direct hit.

The building that we taught in was rectangular, with the usual mud walls and thatched roof. It had only one door, near the front. It was so low that even I had to duck to go through, so it was quite a problem for the students many of whom were well over 6 feet tall.

The insecurity continued and Antonov bombers flew over three or four times a day. As soon as anyone heard their special sound (it was always the youngest who had the sharpest ears) we would all evacuate the building. This meant that the 40 students and I all had to hurry out through the low door and jump into the shelter. Several of the tall men ended with bruises on their foreheads, when they had not ducked low enough. When we came back, it was extremely difficult for me to remember where I had got up to in the lesson, and also for the students to concentrate on their work.

It was with a certain sense of relief when the UN plane arrived after a week to take us back to Loki. I never liked Loki. It was very hot, very dry and very harsh and soulless. Once there, my greatest desire was to leave by the next available plane. I was on standby the next day (Saturday) but there was no seat, so back we went to the ACROSS Compound. I was again on standby on Sunday, but was again disappointed.

On Monday, there were still no flights scheduled, so Rhondda suggested that we should take a trip to Kakuma Refugee Camp, about an hour's drive away. It was my first experience of a refugee camp and it was not a happy experience. The camp was run by United Nations High Commission for Refugees (UNHCR) and held thirty three thousand refugees, most of them from Sudan, living in poverty and despair. Other people's words cannot fully portray the soul-destroying suffering. It was only when I could see it firsthand that I could begin to appreciate the sheer misery of it. They had been hounded from their homes and could see the long dark shadow of Islam threatening their religious freedom.

The housing consisted of little tin shanties, which became like ovens in the hot weather. It was located in a desert area where nothing could grow. Water could be obtained from bore holes, but collecting water entailed one or more hours of queuing in the hot sun. Everyone had a ration card and could collect food twice a month, but the amount was barely adequate. One student wrote, 'Our stomachs cry out for nourishing food, but our hearts cry out for our beloved land of Sudan'. Another wrote, 'My land, my beautiful land, my fountain of everything is torn apart by war. When two elephants fight, the grass will suffer.'

Many families had little idea of housekeeping, so when the food arrived they ate it – and went hungry until the next distribution. In their original home areas in Sudan everyone had a good plot of land to cultivate, but in Kakuma there was no spare land available, and in any case it was far to dry for any crop to grow. Thus the people had nothing to do all day except sit around aimlessly. This was particularly hard on the young people who could not bear the inactivity and often got into trouble. What struck me most was the sense of sadness and despair all around me.

Our visit therefore was a very welcome break in the monotony for those we visited. We brought some books and some foodstuffs for the Africa Inland Church (AIC) and had a good time of fellowship with them and tried to encourage them.

THE LOST BOYS OF SUDAN

The Camp was divided into Units. In one of these Units was a group of young men who became known as the Lost Boys. Theirs was an amazing story.

During the war years families were often scattered. Those who managed to stay together were concerned about their children, particularly their boys. This was because the southern army was desperately short of men, so they enrolled boys often as young as 10 or 11. They were toughened up in brutal and inhumane ways, taught to fight, given a gun and sent off to the front, where a good number of them disappeared and their parents never saw them again. They were mostly presumed dead.

In order to save their sons, parents in many areas decided to send their boys for refuge in Kenya or Uganda. For those living near the borders, this was not too difficult a task, but for those further north, from the Dinka and Nuer tribes, this was a much greater challenge. Among these boys, I later had several as my students and they were able to tell me their stories.

They explained that they had set off from their home villages in groups, usually led by their school masters, hoping to live off the land as they went. Because of the threat of being found by the army and from the fear of bombing, they usually travelled by night, sleeping in the open by day. As they travelled in the pitch dark, they were formed into long columns, each boy holding the shoulder of the one ahead. Some of them became sick and too weak to go on, so they were just abandoned and the line joined up again. One student told me how one night they were aware that there was a lion in the vicinity and how the boy behind him was snatched by the lion. He could still remember the sound of the boy's screams. How he praised God that he had been spared! He went on to become a very good primary school teacher.

The walk went on for months until finally they reached Ethiopia and were put into a refugee camp in a place beyond Pochalla. After some time, there was a sudden change of government in Ethiopia and the new leader decided to expel all refugees. One day the army came and told them they must leave at once. Those who lingered were shot, while the others fled for their lives. The soldiers pursued them until they came to a fast flowing river. One of the older boys managed to swim across with a rope, which was fixed to trees on either side to produce a make-shift hand-bridge. The boys, many of whom could not swim, had to make their way, hand over hand, clinging on to the rope. Another of the students told how he watched as his younger brother was swept away.

Once across the river, the Ethiopian army withdrew, and so began yet another long trek to safety. It took months before they finally arrived in Kenya and were taken to Kakuma. It is estimated that about 20,000 set out on this epic journey, but more than half perished on the way, mostly through sickness or dehydration.

During my time in Sudan, I collected many stories. One of these stories was related to me by Martha. She was a Dinka girl, growing up in the war years. Sadly, she was disabled and was hump-backed. Disabled children were considered a curse on the family in those days. Even today, in some areas they are still considered something to be ashamed of. When she was about eight, the elders decided to try to straighten her back, so they made a long cut along her spine (I have seen the scar) and tried to force the spine to become straight. She somehow survived the ordeal and was able to grow up. Most girls were not sent to school as education was not considered necessary for girls. Instead they had to be trained by their mothers to become good housewives. As Martha would clearly not fetch any dowry her father, who was rather more enlightened than others, allowed her to go to school. This was wonderful for Martha, who was very intelligent. She did extremely well in school and later became my interpreter on many of my trips, being fluent not only in Dinka but also in English and Southern Arabic, the trade language of the area. She shared some of her story with me.

129

Martha had a younger brother called Matthiang. One day the southern army came into their village and took away all the boys by force, so they could be trained for the army. Matthiang, who was about twelve, was among them. There was much anguish in the village, as the people watched all their boys being led away, but nothing could be done. Little by little messages came back from some of the boys, but nothing from Matthiang, so Martha and the family became very concerned. What had happened was that one day on a forced march, carrying a gun that was far too big for him, he fell and rolled into a ditch. The officer came and ordered him to get up, but he did not move. The man began to beat him, but still he did not move. His friends helped him up, but there was something very wrong with one of his legs. The army could not do with boys who were unable to march, so they abandoned him in the next village, at the home of a woman who was a distant relative.

Meanwhile, Martha and her family were waiting anxiously for news. Finally a message came through that he was injured and was in that village. His parents were not able to go to go to him, so Martha said she would go. "But you are disabled. You cannot go," they said.

Martha took no notice of them, for she was determined to go. Off she went, just travelling a few miles each day until finally she found him. He was lying on some straw, infested with lice and half-starved. She washed him and fed him for some weeks until he was strong enough to make the journey home.

Martha's comment, after she had shared her story was this: "I may be disabled, but I am able. Although my body is weak, inside my heart is strong!"

Although Matthiang too was now disabled, he was able to go back to school. Then, with money given to me by friends at home I helped to pay the fees for him to train as a teacher.

A HEALTH SCARE

After our trip into Kakuma, we returned to Loki and finally got on a flight back to Nairobi.

I had to go to the doctor for my final injection against Hepatitis B. I mentioned that I had lost about 20 lbs and had chronic constipation. He became suspicious and arranged for me to have a barium enema – not a pleasant procedure. Afterwards I was greeted with some bad news. Firstly that I have an extra loop in my bowel, a condition with the rather strange name – a redundant bowel! But much more alarming was the fact that they had found polypoid lesions and possible polyps, leading to cancer.

Having been through the horror of totally emptying the bowel once, I was now told that I must go through the whole procedure again, but this time to have an endoscopy. You can imagine the feelings I went through as I waited for this. However, the very next morning I was reading Isaiah chapter 14:24, which was one of the verses that had helped to send me out to Africa –

Surely, as I have planned, so it will be; as I have purposed, so it will stand.

I felt much encouraged and knew that God was in control.

Before the endoscopy was done, I had to make sure I had the money to pay for the procedure. It meant phone calls to my insurance company to see if my 'Emergency Cover' would pay for it. Thankfully they said 'yes'. As there is no health service and many people are very poor, hospitals normally refuse to do any procedures until there is certain proof that the money is there. As I did not have enough cash available, I was forced to borrow money from some friends, until I raised enough to pay the full amount. Once the insurance money came through, I was able to repay them.

So after yet another course of extremely strong laxatives, the endoscopy was done, under anaesthetic, thankfully. The result this time was much better news – no polyps or lesions, but they were very sorry that because of the length of my bowel, their tube with its little light was not long enough to reach to the end! I slept very well that night!

131

I have recently been reading my diaries from my years in Africa and was surprised to see how often I had been ill. About every three or four weeks I would note that I had diarrhoea or stomach cramps. In spite of having had all my injections, I had Typhoid twice. This was extremely unpleasant. On the first occasion, I woke up to find the world spinning around, with a raging headache and became incontinent.

Pat urged me to get in the car and she would drive me to the Parasitology Clinic for a test. While I was so nauseous, I could not even think of getting out of bed. However I remembered I had some tablets for nausea, so we managed to get there. We were told that I had an extremely high count of typhoid and must take some very expensive antibiotics. I then recalled that my doctor in England had very kindly given me some medicines to take with me – and yes, it included this very antibiotic. I thought back to the verse in Isaiah 56:11 that had sent me out – *I will satisfy your needs in a sun-scorched land* – and praised God for using my doctor to fulfil this very urgent need.

My other major health problem was caused by sand flies. Although I always slept under a mosquito net, these flies were so small that they were able to penetrate the net and bite me while I slept. It took me some time to work out what was the problem. When I got back to Loki I was able to immerse my mosquito net in Deet (a very effective insect repellent) which did the trick.

These bites became very sore indeed. When I got back to Nairobi I counted 12 bites, all weeping and four of them a good inch across. My doctor was very concerned and put me on antibiotics (the same expensive one, but I had been home and the doctor had given me another course). The sores soon cleared up but for the next two or three years I would have small itching spots that came to a head and then burst, while the poison gradually worked its way out of my system.

BACK TO SUDAN

In February, 1996 I was invited to join a team from the Presbyterian Church of Sudan (PCOS), to teach English once again. For this, I had to get permission from ACROSS. At first they were not very willing, but finally let me go, as long as I kept in touch by radio. I said that as long as there was radio contact, I would ask the operator to send regular messages.

So off we went. We were a small team, just James Kuong, James Kuol and me. This at once caused problems with the radio, as we used our initials to identify ourselves, so although I was known as Juliet Kilo, so were the other two! In the end we decided to use our real names. The operator managed to get a message through to say that I had arrived.

In my letter home, I wrote

This is a very different location. We flew over the Nile then over a vast area of very green swamp which is called the Sud – from which Sudan probably gets its name. We landed in the village of Nyal, which is more like a desert. We walk on sand and are surrounded by palm trees with big round orange fruits, bigger than coconuts. The compound has an outer fence of upright stalks of sorghum and there are two "buildings" made of sorghum stalks and one tukul of sticks and mud. Being the only female, I have a nice roomy tent to myself, but the camp bed I have borrowed is so hard that I have bruises on both hips!

There are four of us – one Sudanese, one American, one Kenyan and me. We come from four different churches - Presbyterian, Seventh Day Adventist, Pentecostal and Anglican. We come from four decades, one in his 30s, one in his 40s one in his 50s and me in my 60s. Perhaps God has a sense of humour in putting such an assorted group together, but we're having a good time together – good fun and good fellowship.

This time we were in a completely different area with very sandy land, with a scattering of palm trees. as opposed to the thick red soil I had previously experienced. Also we were

133

 working with a different tribe, the Nuer, the second largest tribe in southern Sudan. The church had a beautiful compound, with a huge tree, a sycamore fig tree, whose branches spread out to cover almost the entire compound, so giving us shade at all times of the day. It was such a joy to be able to relax in its shade. The major disadvantage was the insects, which arose in swarms as soon as the sun began to set. So by about six o'clock, having taken a shower, we had to take shelter in one of the tukuls. My tukul was fine, except that it had a broken door, so I was unable to shut myself in at night. At bedtime I just had to tuck the mosquito net tightly around me and pray for the dawn! One evening I happened to ask what sound hyenas make, so they made a sort of muffled howl. They told me that they sometimes come into houses and bite people while they sleep. That night, with my broken door, I heard that very sound. I got up to make sure that the broken door was firmly wedged shut!

Another small problem I had to overcome was eating. The Sudanese eat with their hands. Whereas I could manage a piece of chicken with my hands, there was no way I could manage to eat beans and rice without it spilling all down the front of my clothes. When they realised this, they agreed to give me a spoon. For some reason there was only one spoon in the compound. Often as we sat down to eat, there was no spoon. The shout went up – MALAGA – and the spoon appeared. It was one of the first Nuer words I learnt.

I began teaching the next day. The school building we were using was at the other end of the airstrip, so I had a pleasant walk in the early morning and a much hotter walk at the end of the day.

The Nuer are another proud and warlike tribe. For centuries they had been in conflict with the other main tribe – the Dinka. Having learned the correct words of greeting in the Dinka language, I greeted a Nuer man with those words, but this did not go down at all well. I had clearly insulted him and I very quickly learnt the Nuer words of greeting.

In the evening we would have Devotions together. We were reading in Matthew's gospel and came to the passage where Jesus told his disciples not to forgive only seven times, but seventy seven times, I explained that forgiving seven times was pretty amazing in those days and asked what the Nuer culture taught about forgiveness. Moses, one of our team said that they might possibly forgive three times, but certainly no more. When I read the verse saying seventy-seven times, he was silent, so I asked him what he thought about it. He said he definitely could not do this. When I reminded him that this was part of Jesus teaching, his reply was, "But I am a Nuer." I sadly realised that for so many of the Sudanese, the tribe is more important than the teaching of the Bible. This can be a stumbling block for true Christian growth and discipleship

Tribalism is in many ways the bane of Sudanese life for it means that people have more affinity with their tribe than with their country. Governing the country can therefore be fraught

with problems, as each person has the needs of his own tribe in his heart. It becomes a real issue for people in power, for as soon as they have the authority to employ others, they are under intense pressure from members of their tribe or clan to give them a job. "You are my relative, so you must give me a job," is a sentence that they too often hear and find very difficult to ignore. One result is that in any office, you may find that all the staff members are from the same tribe. If someone from a different (or opposing) tribe comes with a request, they may well be refused.

135

This tribal conflict was underlined for me yet again, just today. As I was writing, an email came in from my friends Nicola, a German missionary working in Rumbek. Here is the text:

Currently, security in Rumbek is bad. Today, last week and in December fighting occurred again between different clans among the Dinka, which keeps triggering constant revenge. A number of people were shot dead and even more are injured. Please pray for a miracle to let this spirit of revenge cool down and to keep our staff and their families safe. Having some degree of education makes them a popular target, assuming that their loss will be felt more strongly by their clan. It's a truly vicious circle.

Having said all that, I was actually thrilled to be working with the Nuer, for a very particular reason. At university I had studied Archaeology and Anthropology. Part of the Anthropology course entailed studying a tribe. I wandered into the departmental library and looked for a book that was not too long and came away with a book about the Nuer! So here I was 44 years later actually working with the Nuer. How often have I found that some experience earlier in life was just what I needed as preparation for future service. I'm sure that God had a hand in it and I felt he was smiling down on me! To cap it all, I was asked to preach in their little grass-thatched church on the Sunday.

The course was going well, when disaster struck. When I got up one morning I could feel tension running very high. They explained that a group from a neighbouring village had come during the night and murdered our sub-chief. Now the people from our village were arming themselves to go out and take revenge. As I looked out of the compound, I could see figures moving around, carrying spears and shields. I was told that I must not go out of the compound.

A conference was called between our group and a group of Italians who were also running a course in the area. None of them wanted to pack up and go home – we had come all this distance and wanted to go on with the teaching, provided it was safe. I was not present at the meeting, so when it was over they told me their decision. As long as the fighting was conducted with spears, we were in no danger, so we would stay. If guns were used, bullets could ricochet or stray in our direction, so we would leave. As they were not sure how their various groups back in Nairobi would feel about this, they decided on radio silence. This meant I could not make the daily report I had been told to do.

So next day off I went to teach. It was an eerie feeling as I walked along the length of the airstrip. Instead of the usual movement of people passing by and greeting me, there was not a soul in sight. I was just a solitary figure, tramping up the sandy airstrip to the school. The students were all there except for one unfortunate man who came from the village which had made the attack. He was put in the prison, not as a prisoner but as the only safe place for him.

The fighting went on for two more days. We did not see the fighting, but often saw wounded men being brought back to our village. We could hear much howling and yelling as they confronted one another. I felt no fear, but was very aware of the Lord's presence.

When the local Commander heard of the trouble, he came to put an end to it. He visited both villages separately, telling the men in no uncertain terms that unless they laid down their arms, they would face his firing squad. The meeting in our village took place on the airstrip. The men realised that they had no alternative but to lay down their arms – but they did it with a flourish. They massed on the airstrip, with much posturing and aggressive behaviour. They leapt into the air, fought imaginary enemies, pranced and waved their spears in a most alarming way. Then they charged down the path, just in front of our compound, to lay down their arms. I had my camera with me, but they were running too quickly. However, when the last few came along I bravely stepped out in front of them, holding up the camera. They were delighted and posed for a photo-call!

Almost at once, the village came back to life and that evening there were all the usual sounds and happy laughter. There were ten dead and several injured. The two worst cases were sent back on the same plane as I was, to a hospital in Loki. The murderer was found and sentenced to be executed and his family had to pay a very substantial fine, between 500 – 1000 cows. (Cows are the major form of currency in this area.)

This time, instead of the usual small planes I was used to, we flew in a Buffalo, a much bigger plane that often carried cargo. With us were the two casualties from the fighting. They were carried in on stretchers and laid on the floor, each one covered with a white sheet that looked more like a shroud. They were groaning and I wished I could have done something for them. The door of the plane did not fit properly and as we gained height, it got colder and colder. Both the wounded men were shivering wildly – and so was I. When we finally landed, I found that my legs were so cold that I could not easily climb down the ladder. I clung on to the handrail and staggered out into the wonderful warm air of Loki. Usually I grumbled about the heat, but not on that occasion.

My return to Nairobi was a difficult time. I was summoned to the main ACROSS office and asked why they had not been receiving radio messages from me. I told them the whole story, thinking that my part in it had been positive and that I might be complimented on a job well done. Quite to the contrary, I was roundly told off for not getting messages through. I explained that there was no way I could have forced myself into the radio room, and in any case I did not know how to send radio messages. I was still considered to have done wrong, so I was told that I was now grounded and could no longer go on any trips to Sudan. I made no reply and left the office, but I was seething inside. My greatest joy had been my trips to Sudan. However, I pulled myself together and poured out my troubles to the Lord. That evening I shared it with my housemates who tried to console me, saying that I had many more books to write.

SUDAN AGAIN

I believe it was then that the mission labelled me as a risk-taker! I remained grounded from February until July, working every day in the office and continuing to teach literacy on three afternoons. In July ACROSS was again contacted by the group working in Nyal. I think that the management had realised that I had not actually done anything wrong, so they sent for me. They said that they realised that my teaching skills were not being used. I at once broached the subject of going back to Nyal for another course. My boss said that provided I did not get involved with any more bombs or spear fighting, I might go back. I promised that I would do my best! Now at last I was free to go. You can imagine my delight!

I was to be accompanied by an American lady called Penny. This time the course was uneventful and we enjoyed the work, although it was so hot that it drained us of energy, and the insects were a constant problem. When I returned and had a bath, I counted 58 bites, mostly on my arms and ankles. In the evenings we sat in the shade, enjoying the palm trees which were silhouetted against a red sky. However, there were snakes and scorpions around, so we had to go carefully and check our shoes before we put them on.

One evening we were relaxing under the beautiful spreading branches of our sycamore fig tree, when something fell on to my neck. I instinctively brushed it off and then felt a burning pain. It was a caterpillar with poisonous hairs. Afterwards I was told that when it is crawling along, if you brush it in the direction it is going, there will be no harm done. If, on the other hand you brush it in the other direction, it will leave its hairs in your skin. So guess which way I pushed it? It was extremely painful and I had a big red weal on my neck for the next few days. I was told on my return that if you make a thick paste of flour and water and allow it to dry, then pull it off quickly, it will remove the hairs.

139

Thankfully it never happened again, so I never had the chance to put that theory to the test.

It was a very peaceful place to be, falling asleep to the sound of a chorus of frogs. I had a comfortable bed and was in a tukul, sharing with Penny. The only snag was the lack of furniture, not even a box to put things on, so everything had to be laid out on the floor. I said it was peaceful, but one night we were woken by strange animal noises. Next morning they said it was a pack of hyenas, chasing off a lion – but not in our direction, thankfully..

On Sunday I again had the privilege of preaching in the church (picture 13). After the service we came across a group of about 20 women doing a traditional dance, with lots of stamping and jumping and rushing from side to side of the airstrip, waving green branches. We discovered that they were rallying their supporters for the election of a new chief. After a while, the two candidates appeared – the old chief and the new contender. Each of them was followed by their supporters, who were waving flags and cheering lustily. They stopped a good way apart. Once they were settled, their supporters sat in orderly lines behind each of them. Then the Commissioner arrived with his guard, consisting of a motley group of soldiers in a variety of bits of uniform, carrying machine guns. They walked up and down, occasionally pulling out one of the people who had sat down, as they did not come from that village and were not eligible to vote. Finally they were carefully counted. There were 835 for the old chief and 709 for the contender. So the old chief was carried around on the shoulders of his supporters. There followed a number of lengthy speeches, the whole affair taking about five hours. It was not exactly a secret ballot!

We finished the course and packed up to return on the Saturday. I was returning to Nairobi, but Penny was going on to another location where her husband was working. That morning, we both had Bible verses that appeared to have a warning. Mine was from Psalm 35, which spoke about people plotting my ruin, and enemies casting a net for me and digging a pit for me. So we prayed about our journeys. When my plane came in, it made a very unbalanced landing and it was seen that one of the wheels was loose. They mended it and I boarded for my return. We were both relieved that although there had been danger, nothing had come of it. So off I went, but Penny was to leave later on.

After I was back in Nairobi, I heard some terrible news. The plane that was carrying Penny was in a crash. On landing, it overran the airstrip, plunged into the bush and overturned. Penny and her friend Karen ended up hanging upside-down from their seat belts, which they could not undo, because their bodies were weighing them down. They were terrified that the plane might catch fire, so after a tremendous effort Karen wrenched herself free and freed Penny too. They were quite disorientated, and struggled to find the emergency door.

To add to all the horror, both of their husbands were on the airstrip to welcome them. When they saw what had happened, they raced down the full length of the airstrip, forcing the door open to get their wives out. Penny and Karen were put on stretchers and carried into the shade of some trees, while urgent messages were sent to Nairobi for another plane to come and pick them all up. It was some hours before help arrived.

I later visited Penny in Nairobi Hospital. Her injuries were not too awful, but she had suffered quite bad whiplash. It was the trauma that was her greatest problem. Every time she closed her eyes, the whole drama was played out in her imagination. It took some time before she was fully recovered. We talked about it and realised that our verses had in fact been a warning, but not just for the loose wheel. We also realised that the powers of darkness were working against us, trying to stop the good work we were doing, in bringing the light of learning and the light of the glorious gospel of Christ to the Sudanese people.

IN MARIDI

In August I was approached by ADRA (Adventist Development and Relief Agency) expressing an urgent need for an English teacher in Maridi, a comparatively safe area, not very far from the Uganda border. I knew very little about Seventh Day Adventists. I was told that their theology is similar to ours, but

141

that they insist that the day of rest is Saturday, not Sunday. So I agreed to go with them. They were a very pleasant group of people and we got on well. On the first weekend, we decided that we would have two services, one on Saturday and one on Sunday. I was asked to speak on the Saturday, so I invited one of them to speak on the Sunday. I gave a simple gospel address, which was well received. However I was rather annoyed that their Sunday address was all about how we should be worshipping on Saturdays. Not very tactful, I thought.

I started teaching a group of 40 student teachers and the course was going well. It was very hot, so one day I decided to go for a walk in the cool of the evening. As I was walking beside fields of tall sorghum (the local staple diet) I heard a strange noise on my left. Something was approaching through the tall stalks. It went swish, swish, swish. HELP! I thought. Do they have lions in Maridi? Or is it a group of marauders? I began to run, or to hobble, as my knee was in a poor state, a real sense of fear driving me on. You can judge my relief when out of the field there emerged a woman, pushing a wheelbarrow! You can imagine how I laughed at myself and my unfounded fear. This experience did bring home to me that Sudan was not like London, and there were real dangers lurking around us.

On the Thursday we received some very bad news – a local village called Kotobi had been bombed. We immediately began to pray. Gradually more details came through. The people had been attacked from a helicopter gunship, which is a terrifying experience. When I had been bombed, it was by an Antonov bomber, which flies at a very high altitude, so their accuracy is very poor. Being attacked by a helicopter gunship is a very different matter. The helicopter comes  down and hovers, just out of range of the light guns the villagers might have. The crew have a very clear view of the village. First they look for any long roof. All the people live in round tukuls, so a long roof must belong to a church, a school or a clinic. These are the three targets they will go for.

On this occasion, they could see two long roofs, which were the two churches, one Catholic and one Protestant, so they sent rockets, destroying both of them. Then they hovered over the market place, where the women were running around, looking for shelter. The people had dug some small foxholes, so some of them were able to hide in them, but there was no room for everyone. In the picture you can see Boutros demonstrating for me how he hid. The helicopter crew opened the side door and fired on the women below, killing fourteen of them. It is hard to understand such senseless slaughter.

Our course had finished but I lost my seat on the plane as they took injured people out. Next day a team arrived to assess the situation. My colleague Arkanjelo was leading the team, so I begged to be allowed to go with them. I said I wanted to take photos to take back to the West to show them what was going on. They agreed to allow me to accompany them. It was a sad scene that confronted us. Many women were mourning. This they did by 'keening' – crying out in loud shrill voices, over these unnecessary deaths. The churches were totally devastated and many people were just wandering around, looking dazed by what had happened. I felt a real sense of anger stirring in me against the fanatical regime in the north that would do such a terrible thing to the innocent people in the village.

THE END OF THE YEAR

All too soon, my year was coming to an end. Although I had a contract for just one year, I knew that there would be no problem if I wished to extend it. I contacted AIM and they were only too happy for me to continue. Then I had to break the news to my family, but I think they already had strong suspicions that one year would not be enough. The person who was particularly pleased was Peter, my lodger, who could now stay for a further year. I booked my flight home. As I did not want to turn Peter out, my daughter Alison very kindly made room for me in her home, just up the road from my house and our church.

On my return, the Croydon Advertiser again interviewed me and published another article taking up over half a page. It also had four of my photos attached. The headline was:

FAITH PUTS BOOKS BEFORE BULLETS

Jan King returned from a year-long mission to train teachers in war-torn Sudan earlier this month. While there, she had one training course abandoned because of a security alert, witnessed the destruction from a bombing campaign and stayed in an area where a village clan had gone off to fight after their tribal chief was murdered.

She said, "A lot of this year was been a learning experience and it has been very rewarding. It is so positive because the people want to learn."

On the less positive side, Mrs King was forced to sit in primitive bunkers – holes in the ground – as bombers flew overhead.

CHAPTER 10 BACK TO AFRICA 1996-1997

As ever, leaving England was very difficult, but at least this time I knew where I was going and there was a house ready for me. I also knew what things to take with me, so I went with reading glasses, pocket calculators and Ladybird reading books. There was no problem about the extra weight I was carrying or with the customs checks, for which I was very grateful.

I wrote home to Alison saying:

I had such a beautiful time with you – it was such a joy to be with you and see so much of you, particularly James. I feel very bereft with no little 'pyjamaed' figure, clutching his drink and Thomas book, climbing on to my bed in the mornings. I have to keep reminding myself that the year will pass even more quickly this time.

Pause – I have just disposed of a cockroach that I found in my desk drawer. We have rats in the garden trying to get on to my bird table. Perhaps I should buy a rat trap, but I don't fancy disposing of the body.

Having unpacked I plunged back into the work at the Office. I was very warmly welcomed back by the staff at Sudan Literature Centre (SLC), particularly as I had brought some chocolates with me, three each. One of the men tried to persuade me that in his culture it should be three for the women but four for the men. I was not falling for that!

My second day back was Kenyatta Day (named after the first President of Kenya) so it was a holiday. I went with some English friends to Fourteen Falls. It is a beautiful area, dotted with flame trees, but sadly they were not in bloom. However the jacarandas were at their best, with their spectacular blue/lilac flowers and, where the blooms had fallen, a carpet of blue around each trunk. We had a picnic near the water then wandered along beside the swift running river. It was idyllic!

Public transport is very cheap, but really rather dangerous. There are a few buses, but most passengers travel in matatus.

These are privately owned minibuses, with seats for sixteen, but often have far more than that on board, as well as others hanging on, with one foot on the footplate at the rear of the vehicle. The drivers are utterly reckless - people told me that many were on marijuana, which they chew all day. As their pay depends on how much money they get each day, it is a huge challenge to pick people up before any of their rivals can do so. You see them driving on the pavement (where there is one), driving on the wrong side of the road and cutting in, in front of other vehicles, in quite an alarming way. When I was driving my little car, I had to make sure there was never any space in front of me, or a matatu would cut in. They are brightly coloured with exotic names, such as Palm Springs, Arsenal, God's Peace, and so on.

HOSPITALS

Soon after I returned, I heard that one of my AIM friends had been in an accident. The matatu had left the road and Bridget had been thrown out of the back of the vehicle. Three people had been killed, Bridget was rushed to 999 ward, as that was the only spare bed. As I entered I was nearly overpowered by the stench of urine and the groans of the patients. There were no staff members to be seen. Rosemary was sharing a bed with another lady, head to feet. (There were fifteen beds for twenty-seven women) I asked her what treatment she had had. Over the three days, she had been given two aspirins. I have never felt such an atmosphere of despair. One man had managed to buy the medicines for his wife who was there, but when he came back next day, they were all gone, having been shared out amongst all the patients.

I later found out that although it was the national hospital, it was not being provided with medicines. New nurses arrived, full of good intentions to serve the patients well, but when there were no medicines or pain killers to offer, they did not know where to turn. If they went into the ward they were greeted by desperate demands from the patients, but they had no means of helping, so they very soon lost heart. I felt a great sense of the injustice of it, and yet unable to do anything to help.

Rosemary told me that during the night, one of the women called out, saying that she was giving birth. No-one came to help, so she squatted on the floor and gave birth to a stillborn child. She climbed back into bed weeping inconsolably. When the staff came on duty in the morning, they told her they would not clear up the mess, in case she had AIDS, so she would have to do it herself. Happily we were able to move Rosemary to another hospital and she finally made a full recovery.

I walked out of that hospital feeling moved to despair and then drove on to Nairobi Hospital to visit Bridget. This is a private hospital and there could not have been a greater contrast. As I entered its spotless corridors, to visit her in a small private room with flowers in a vase and get-well cards on the wall, I was again angered at the injustice of it and of my powerlessness to do anything.

Over the next few weeks things went according to routine. I was hard at work at the office and also teaching literacy to the Sudanese ladies. It was still a secular job and I hoped for some Christian work to do, but that did not materialise. I knew that I was in the place that God had planned for me and was doing work that would bless people in many ways. Looking at my diary I see that I had a varied social life, including sharing a meal with friends three or four times a week, which was very pleasant.

TO SUDAN

In December 1996, I was invited to teach English with a group called Med-Air, an offshoot of YWAM (Youth with a Mission). They were working in a village called Atar, in a very remote area, in the east and far further north than I had ever been before. The lovely team were mostly young Dutch nurses who made me very welcome. They were involved in a programme of immunisation, going out in different directions each day, carrying their precious drugs in insulated bags. This fulfilled a desperate need among the population. Much of Sudan is very beautiful, but it is home to so many diseases that are hardly known to us –

Typhoid, Bilharzia, guinea worm, Ebola – the list could go on, but the major killer is still Malaria.

Med-Air was very well equipped compared to the Sudanese groups I had worked with. For the first time, I was given a mosquito tent to sleep in. This is a domed tent, made of mosquito netting, with a strong plastic base. There was room for my mattress and a few other items. There was a zip right the way round, giving great security. It was a fabulous experience, sleeping under the velvet dome of the sky, sprinkled with stars. If the moon was full, it could be almost as bright as daylight. One morning I woke up feeling something wriggling under me – it was a snake, but it could not get to me, so it slithered away. I made quite sure that the zip was done up tightly both day and night! Another problem was getting dressed, as people could easily see through the netting.

We settled in, and the following morning I was taken to the school building to meet my students. The room this time was simply a roof, supported by poles, but with no walls at all. There were 42 very eager students, so I began the lesson. After half an hour or so, we heard some strange noises and shouting. Then we heard gunfire! I wondered what I should do, but kept on with the lesson, although the students naturally became very restless. After a few minutes one of the Med-Air staff came running and told me to return to the main compound as fast as I could. In spite of my painful knee, I made it in a very short time! All that day we were confined there. By the evening we were informed as to what had happened.

It appeared that, during all the war years there had been no training of any sort in Atar. When the news of our planned arrival was announced, there was a great rush of people who were desperate to come on the course. The local Education Co-ordinator was Henry, a little man with a very forceful and unyielding personality. Out of all the applicants, he had selected forty and told the others, in no uncertain terms, to return to their homes. They were very angry, and having grown up in such turbulent times, they were totally lacking in self-control. Rather than returning to their homes, seven of them decided to come back and kill Henry. He at once went into hiding. When they could not find him, they became very aggressive, so a messenger was quickly sent to the local Commander. He arrived with a small detachment of soldiers, who fired their guns into the air to restore order.

The seven men were rounded up and the Commander spoke to them. He was a very good and sensible man, much respected by the rest of the community. Rather than being angry about the incident, he discussed things with them and it was agreed that there would be another training course in the near future and they would all seven be included. After the meeting, the Commander came to have tea with us and told us about the area, which had been dogged by cattle rustling and inter-tribal fighting for years. The young people knew of nothing but war and were brought up to be tough and aggressive. As with Moses, the Nuer man I wrote about earlier, they had next to no concept of forgiveness, but when wronged demanded vengeance and retaliation. It made us sad to hear how war had shaped the character of these people, who could in other circumstances be so kind and helpful. Some weeks later we heard with great sadness that this humane man had been murdered by a group who felt that they had not been fairly treated.

The local tribe is called the Shilluk, another group of very tall and very black people. Their neighbours, with whom they are in constant trouble are the Murle. For some reason, in the past the Murle had had problems with producing children, so they had resorted to raiding neighbouring tribes and stealing their children. This still goes on today and I remember a dear man called Zachariah, who was a wise and mature man who had attended one of my courses. He was also a gifted teacher and had been made Headmaster of his school. Sadly his daughter was stolen by some

149

raiding Murle. He was totally devastated. He gave up his post to search for his child. Some years later I heard that he was still looking and had become a broken man. What a tragic loss.

To get back to our course in Atar – the next day we thankfully returned to work. During the afternoon I was more than a little surprised when the Commander and some of his men decided to join the class, sitting at the back. I welcomed them and explained that no guns were allowed in my lessons, so they trooped out again, leant them up against some trees and came back for the lesson!

Later that week, I had decided that a good way to get the students to pronounce English was by singing English songs. They enjoyed it very much. One of the songs was Old Macdonald had a Farm, which went down extremely well. When we came to the lines, A moo moo here and a moo moo there, they all waved their arms in the air to demonstrate. Now it so happened that a very poisonous snake was lurking in the grass roof of the school. Perhaps it was the 84 long black arms – and two short white ones – that were waving that did it, but the snake suddenly fell from the roof, slithered down the outside of the back of my dress and landed behind me. They all yelled and I executed a tremendous leap for safety! They soon killed it, and told me that it was a burrowing viper and it was very deadly.

How I praised God for protecting me throughout my time in Atar. It was with a certain sense of relief that I left this very insecure area and returned to the relative security of Nairobi.

TO PALUER

In February I was invited to teach English at a village called Paluer, where there was an ACROSS base. As well as the Teacher Training, there was a group of nurses running a Community Health Project. There was a large compound with a good number of tukuls, a dining room and other rooms. It was very close to the School Compound, where we were teaching. The picture on the next page shows the school compound at the front of the picture. This is where the teaching took place. Behind is our compound,

150

where we lived. During the 6 week course, they killed over 50 poisonous snakes! This time the course went well, with no great

dramas, although the Antonov bombers often passed over us, high in the sky. We also heard distant shelling, but thankfully nothing came near us.

We had the usual 40 student teachers, who had come for six weeks. During the first week, which was an introduction, Russ and Lyn had chosen the best ten students so that they might become Trainers of Trainees (ToTs). I came for week two which was Intensive English and brought with me copies of Grammar Book 1, which I had recently finished. It was very well received by the students. When the Education Co-ordinator received a copy, he was delighted. He too had had serious misgivings about Brighter Grammar, so was very pleased to have a more user-friendly book for the students.

I said it was intensive English and it certainly was. I had recently had a letter from a teacher at home, grumbling about having to work 20 hours a week. I taught 34 hours in that week, in temperatures of about 40C. But it was only for one week and I really enjoyed it. Although it was so hot, it was dry heat, so we did not have to put up with humidity. Dehydration was more of a problem, so we all had to carry water with us and keep drinking. Another problem is a lack of salt. When people sweat a great deal, they lose a lot of salt. For me the warning sign was when I began to get cramp in my legs, particularly at night. One of our group woke up one morning feeling tired, with a mild headache and slight nausea. I suggested he took some salt, dissolved in water. The result seemed miraculous. Within an hour or so, he was back to full strength, with all the symptoms having disappeared.

Diet is another problem. Every morning we were up very early and ate some crackers with peanut butter. The peanut butter here is absolutely delicious. The ladies make it by kneeling down grinding it between two large stones, with nothing added. The result is heavenly! After our meagre breakfast, we went to Devotions at 7.30 am and then off to class. At ten o'clock the students have their breakfast. This is often something called kisera, made from sorghum, the local staple. It is very large pancake of a pinky-brown colour and I find it sour and unpalatable. It is folded up like a parcel and generally served with beans and sometimes lentils. I just ate the beans and lentils. Then it's back to class until noon.

When we return to our compound, it is the students' lunch time – but we have already had ours, so we do not usually bother to have any. Siesta, during the hottest part of the day, lasts until 3 pm, then we return to class until 5 pm. The afternoon activities are good fun, as we teach them games to improve their English and also lead class activities, like singing games, to enable them to teach to their own classes. It is so funny to see these tall men learning to play Here we go Looby Loo and teaching them to skip, using a long rope. By five o'clock I'm usually pretty exhausted, so we return to the compound for a much-needed cup of tea. The evening meal is at six o'clock. It is often food brought in from Kenya and is more than welcome.

The result of this unusual diet is that my body clock (and bowels!) got pretty confused and I generally lost between ten and twelve pounds on each trip.

My knee was getting progressively more painful. The walk from the airstrip took 30 minutes, so I just about managed it, but the church was even further away – and I had been invited to preach. As I was wondering how to get there, one of the students, realising my dilemma, came and offered me his bicycle. Of course it was a man's bicycle with the saddle very high. We managed to lower the saddle and I rather tentatively mounted, wondering how I was going to get off again. After a couple of tries, I felt reasonably confident. So on Sunday morning, off I went, wearing a dress and wobbling my way to the church. I got some very funny looks as I arrived rather precipitately and then tumbled off, just managing to land on my feet. It may have looked odd, but at least I had made it.

It was an Episcopal (Anglican) church, using the Book of Common Prayer in Dinka. They followed it

– every word of it! So it was a long service, but I could follow a good deal of it, as I had brought my 1662 prayer book with me. The music was superb. They sang some of our old hymns, translated into Dinka, but the tunes were barely recognisable because they sang them with their own lovely lilting rhythms, accompanied by their local instruments. Apart from drums, which were played quite quietly, they had an instrument called an adungu. In fact they had a number of them of various sizes and they were able to harmonise beautifully. An adungu is made from a curved stick attached to a sound box made from calf skin, with ten or more strings. The smallest ones give off a very pretty high sound. The base adungu is so big that the player sits on part of the sound box and also uses it as a drum.

It was a huge church, with no amplification, so when it came to the time for me to give the message, I really had to shout – and then wait while the interpreter translated it into the Dinka language. He was very good and as well as translating my words, he copied all my gestures too. I was speaking about faith and I used a chair as an illustration. I walked round the chair, saying what a good, strong chair it was and how much I trusted it. Then I explained that the only way to prove that I had faith in it, was to sit on it, which I did. The translator had also been walking round with me, translating. When I sat down, I thought to myself, 'Help! What is he going to do? Is he going to sit on my lap?' I had to repress a smile. Thankfully he just pointed to me sitting on it.

After the service, which lasted two and a half hours, we all filed out of the church, standing in a long line. As each person emerged, they shook hands with those already outside and then joined the end of the line. As I did not know any Dinka I could

153

not greet them, but I did want to know how many had been in the church. So as each one passed, I smiled, saying 45, 46, 47 etc. The total was 431, including children.

It was altogether a wonderful experience, worshipping with so many Sudanese Christians. The following Sunday I was back in Nairobi and attended Matins in the Cathedral. What an extraordinary contrast it was - the Sudan service almost seemed like a dream. The Cathedral service was also based on the prayer book, but the congregation lacked the joy and exuberance of the Dinka service. As soon as it was over, people jumped into their cars and made for their homes.

My next trip was going to be very different indeed.

CHAPTER 11 SHOOTING IN KAKUMA REFUGEE CAMP

Much to my disappointment, a proposed visit to Sudan in May was cancelled due to insecurity, so I asked my boss if I could go and teach in Kakuma Refugee Camp. He refused, saying that he wanted me to get on with writing the English textbooks. However, I was due some holiday and I had had an invitation to Kakuma, so in August 1997 I decided to spend my break there, teaching English. The following account may show that this was possibly not a good decision of mine.

I managed to get a free flight with the Lutheran World Food programme and with some difficulty found my way to the Episcopal Church compound where I was to be based. Quite a large group from Christian Aid had also arrived, so all the accommodation within the compound was full. They found a small tukul outside the compound, with a bed and a chair, so I tried to settle in. It was a bit unnerving to be out in the open, particularly as the windows were merely holes in the wall, so anyone could look in, or even try to pick up some of my belongings with the aid of a hooked stick. I put all my things in the centre and tried to sleep.

The next morning, messages having been sent round with news of my arrival, I soon had a good group of very eager students, so we went to work on the English Course. For the first few days, all went well. Although I was sleeping outside, I was welcomed into the compound for my meals and for fellowship, but the latter was difficult because of language constraints. I made friends with a very delightful young man called John who had gone blind as a child, due to some sickness. Thankfully, he was fairly fluent in English, so we were able to communicate.

Here is the account I wrote after the event, of what happened one evening–

Early in the morning I was sitting alone in my small tukul with the terrible sounds of grief rising and falling around me, Why Lord? I ask myself.

155

It had all begun the previous evening, just a dozen or so of us sitting in the dark in the compound of Bishop Nathaniel Garang. It had been a long hot day and now we were relaxing in the cool of the evening. We had no lamp and there was no moon, so we sat with only the stars to give a little light. We were talking in small groups, one group singing hymns quietly. It was a peaceful scene.

Daniel, a young evangelist, was walking just behind me towards the gate of the compound when it burst open and a gunshot rang out. We heard a terrible cry from Daniel as he fell to the ground, then silence. We all leapt to our feet and ran for our lives.

I seized the hand of John Kuol, the young blind man and we ran together. We were brought up sharply when we ran into a chain-link fence. Young John managed to lift the bottom and wriggled under it, then through the thick brushwood outer fence.

I had thought that at 64, with an arthritic knee, my wriggling days were over, but I too was soon on my stomach, wriggling for dear life. However, the challenge of wriggling out through the thick exterior brushwood was too much, so I curled up into a tight ball in the thick dust, trying to hide my white face and prayed – a wordless prayer, but perhaps such as I had never prayed before.

During our flight, we had heard another shot within the compound. It later transpired that the bullet had penetrated the side wall of one of the pastors' houses, but happily that pastor was not in the line of fire.

There seemed to be two attackers, one with a gun and one with a torch. I curled up even tighter and remained motionless, listening to the footsteps. I was aware of a presence, a menace in the dark. After a few minutes I heard the squeak of the gate, which hopefully meant they had gone. Then I heard a final shot, clearly from outside the compound, near the dry river-bed.

After some time, I could hear people coming back into the compound. I found that all that time, I had been clutching a torch, so I shone it on my face to show who I was and a kind woman helped me to my feet. We stood together in a small knot, holding each other. Very soon other people came into the compound and a Police ambulance came to remove Daniel's body. Thankfully he was still alive. Next day some relatives gave blood, and then he was transferred to the hospital in Loki. He survived, but remains disabled and in a wheelchair.

We were all dazed and of course there was no supper, so we gradually dispersed to our sleeping places. I felt extremely vulnerable, outside the compound. The problem was that nobody knew why we had been attacked. Was it me they were after – the only white person? I lay in my bed, very aware that my door was held only by a bent nail and the windows were just open holes. I was still too bewildered to pray intelligently, so I just lay there in the stifling heat, which is so much part of Kakuma camp. I kept asking myself, Why, Lord?

In the small hours of the morning, a strong wind arose, coming straight towards my door. It brought clouds of dust and even the occasional small stone. As each stone hit my door, which was made of flattened tin cans, it gave a loud crack, causing me to jump out of my skin!

The night passed slowly. Very early next morning I heard the ear-tingling sound of women wailing and keening. It seemed that the third shot that we had heard outside the compound had hit a pastor. It had entered his thigh and cut through an artery. We could see in the sand the impression of where he had dragged himself towards a hedge and had collapsed. During the night he had bled to death. It was only with the coming of daylight that his body was found and his family was informed of the tragedy.

The pastor, John Majok, was a well-loved man and a key figure in the Episcopal church. He had an extensive family, who all depended on him – and now he was gone. So they gathered

157

together to pray and to mourn. Someone erected an awning to shelter us from the sun and together we sat and sought to comfort one another. The Sudanese are a strong people. One of their inner strengths is the ability to gather together and come to terms with their loss and to comfort one another in times of sorrow and bereavement. I felt it a great privilege, as the only white person, to be able to be a small part in this process.

Next morning I talked to pastor John Machar, who had originally invited me to come. The English course would certainly not continue, so I had somehow to get out of Kakuma and back to Nairobi. Pastor John made enquiries, but there were no flights to be had. I told him I could not spend another night in that unprotected tukul, so he found a place for me in the John Bosco Catholic compound. There was a wonderful metal gate to the compound with a very large padlock. I transferred, with all my belongings, but I must have looked a sorry sight. I was rather bedraggled and had had nothing to eat since a light lunch the day before. They were wonderfully kind to me, and gave me some very welcome porridge, which began to revive me. They suggested that I should go and lie down and in a very short time I was fast asleep.

Meanwhile they were looking for a way to get me back to Nairobi and finally found that there was a Shuttle Bus, all the way back. I got the last available seat, a small seat with almost no leg room, over the back wheel, which became hotter and hotter. There appeared to be no springs in the vehicle, so I was shaken around like a rag doll. The trip took a full fifteen hours, but at the end the driver could see what a condition I was in, so he took me all the way home to my own compound. When I got out, I could barely walk. My feet were so swollen that it felt as though I was walking on pins and needles. I staggered to my door. Rhondda opened it, took one look at me and called for Pat to help. Together they got me to bed, with a wonderful cup of tea.

Back in the safety and security of my Nairobi home, I found it hard to believe that it had really happened, but my jumbled emotions left me in no doubt. I realised that my initial question – Why Lord? – was not a question that we can put to God. If we try to penetrate God's intentions, we are sure to beat our heads against an impenetrable wall. The ways of God are not ours to know. We can only invite Him into our situations and cry to Him for comfort and his sustaining power. Although our voices may be trembling with pain, let us still declare, Our God reigns!

After my return to Nairobi, AIM suggested that I should go for counselling, so I made an appointment. I was still very emotional about the whole event, but they were sure that I was not traumatised, because I was able to sleep well, without going over the whole event in my mind.

Then my year was up, so I made plans to return again to the UK, arriving in the autumn. Just before Guy Fawkes' night, I was driving alone in the dark, when suddenly someone let off a firework with a very loud bang, sounding just like the gunshot in Kakuma. When I heard it, my head actually hit the roof of the car! During my stay at home, I was able to tell my story to several churches and groups. At first, I could not tell it without a few tears and fairly raw emotions, but as I repeated it at other meetings, gradually the memories faded. Even so, as I am writing this 16 years later, I still found myself living through it again.

After such an emotional time, it was good to get away sometimes for holidays.

CHAPTER 12   HOLIDAYS

One of the joys of being in Africa was that you could go to exciting places without the heavy travel costs from the UK. During my years there I was able to have some splendid trips.

My first longer journey was in November 1995 and was only about 35 miles from Nairobi to a place called Kijabe, where the annual Africa Inland Mission Conference took place. This is an important AIM location where the Rift Valley Academy, their boarding school is situated. Martha and I decided that I should drive the old car. This was not a good decision. After only a few miles, we broke down – for the first time! We managed to find a mechanic, who did a temporary repair. That however turned out to be very temporary indeed and in no time at all we had broken down yet again. After a very lengthy wait, another so-called mechanic got it going again, but with very little power in the engine.

By then we were getting rather concerned as neither of us wanted to be out on the road in the dark on an unknown highway. Kenyan roads are extremely challenging, particularly in the dark. There are no street lights, no white lines in the centre of the roads, no luxuries like cats' eyes, no marking at the edge of the roads. What is even more alarming is that at the edge of the road, there is often a sheer drop, which can be up to several inches deep. This is because when the road is resurfaced, the workers just add another layer of tarmac on top of the existing one, so the road surface rises over the years. The final driving hazard is that other drivers do not seem to have any concept of dipping their headlights when approaching another vehicle. Put all that together and you have a truly Kenyan experience. Hence our desire to arrive at Kijabe before dark.

We struggled along painfully slowly, with the engine losing power all the time. Finally to our great relief we saw signs to the school. Fortunately the rest of the journey was down hill, as the engine finally failed and we coasted down the road. We just kept on going until the car finally came to a standstill. Clambering out, we looked for signs of activity. There seemed to be a lot of people in the dining room, so we joined them. Supper was over, but thankfully there was a little food left. We were tired, hungry and extremely cold! Whereas Nairobi is about a mile above sea level (5298 feet) Kijabe is over 7500 feet.

We explained our predicament and asked for help in taking our luggage to our room – but there was no room! As we had not arrived, the management had given our room to someone else. Finally they found a place in a dormitory and we collapsed wearily but gratefully.

The Conference was an eye-opener for me. For some reason I had not taken in the fact that AIM really is an International Mission, so I had fondly imagined that at the conference I would be meeting quite a number of other British missionaries. This was very far from the truth. In reality the vast majority of AIM members are from America and Canada. So for me it was a bit of a culture shock – American food, American hymns and Christmas carols, all sung to American tunes! I finally found a small group of British people. One evening there was a concert, so we Brits dressed up in bobble hats, carrying lamps on poles and singing carols to English tunes! It was all taken in good part.

The Conference was fascinating, with so much information about the different locations where members were working and the different ministries they were involved in. I began to understand in a small part some of the problems that were to be met on the mission field. We had really good prayer and worship sessions.

We had to choose which workshops we would attend. One was announced as Car Maintenance. I found the man who was to teach it and offered him my car to use for demonstration purposes. To my great delight he agreed and showed us what was wrong and, joy of all joys, he repaired it for me. Our journey home was trouble-free and this time we were able to take time to enjoy the beautiful scenery as we drove along the edge of the Great Rift Valley.

161

We stopped at a viewpoint and stood spellbound by the fantastic panorama set out before us. The ground dropped away beneath our feet, an almost sheer drop down to a green and fertile valley. Below  us we could make out small homesteads and cattle grazing nearby. As we looked up we had a spectacular view of Mount Longanot, a volcano, rising to over 9000 feet. Our friend explained that the volcano was still active down below and that a good proportion of Kenya relied on its geo-thermal power. We found it hard to drag our eyes away from the sheer beauty of it and drive on. We kept getting further stunning glimpses as we descended towards Nairobi.

THE GREAT RIFT VALLEY

The Great Rift Valley is one of the wonders of the geological world. Geologists tell us that it was formed in pre-historic times. The surface of our world is formed from vast areas called tectonic plates, which are moving about 2 centimetres a year. This remarkable fact can be seen on geological world maps. Indeed, South America and the west coast of Africa were once joined. But over millions of years the plates have moved these two huge continents apart. When two plates collide, there are tremendous earthquakes. When they move apart, the earth's crust cracks and magma erupts, causing volcanoes. So this latter was responsible for the creation of the Great Rift.

It is over 3,700 miles (6000 km) long, stretching from Syria, through the Jordan Valley and Dead Sea, along the Red Sea then into Africa, through Ethiopia then splitting Kenya in half and finally ending in Mozambique. It varies in depth, but in Kenya is 6,000 feet (1,830 metres) deep. Along the base in Kenya there is a

162

series of soda lakes, most of which I had the privilege of visiting on different holidays. I'll write more about them in later chapters.

NEW YEAR

My next short break was less eventful. Every year a group of Christians organise a mini-convention on the lines of Keswick Convention, an annual event in the Lake District in England. The  Kenyan one takes place in a beautiful area about 15 miles from Nairobi. What a wonderful scene greeted my eyes when we arrived at Brackenhurst Convention Centre. It is set out like a little piece of England with lovely lawns and flower beds. Christians come from all over East Africa for a well-earned rest. There is good teaching from a guest speaker, times of worship, seminars and times of fellowship. In the afternoons we are free to go on organised walks in the area, or perhaps play tennis on their courts or just relax. It is a haven for those who have been going through hard times. I travelled in a friend's car and really enjoyed seeing in the New Year there.

MOMBASA

While I was on orientation in England I had made friends with Jackie Atkin. She came to Kenya rather later than I did and worked as receptionist and assistant manager at the Nairobi AIM guesthouse, called Mayfield. We decided that we would like to take a five-day break and go to Mombasa, where we relaxed for three blissful days between two extremely gruelling days travelling. We decided to go by minibus, a six-hour journey on very bumpy roads. On the way down the vehicle broke down four times and we finally were transferred to another vehicle. This meant that we arrived after dark – not to be recommended in many African cities. However God was good and we had made friends on the bus with a very helpful Indian man. He found a

163

'safe' taxi for us and after twelve hours we finally arrived at our hotel, Whispering Palms. Jackie teased me that after my terrible journey to the AIM conference, I was already getting a reputation for disastrous journeys.

The hotel was lovely and served excellent food. There were extensive grounds with a good scattering of seats. We were amused by the signs saying Beware Falling Coconuts, but realised that we would be wise to take them seriously as a falling coconut can do a lot of damage. There was water aerobics every day in the pool. They offered wind surfing lessons, but the wind was blowing very strongly off the shore and out to sea. I had a fear that if I did get going, I might never be able to come back again. In the event, I did not get going at all, but just kept falling off. So I decided to try Scuba Diving, as they were offering free lessons in the swimming pool. With lead weights fixed round my waist, a big heavy bottle of air on my back and large flippers on my feet I went very clumsily down the steps and sank quickly to the bottom, wondering if I would ever manage to get up again. As I reached the bottom the strap on my goggles snapped and they fell off, pulling the air-pipe with them. After my initial panic, I managed to retrieve the pipe and jammed it back into my mouth, clamping it between my teeth. Then giving a few kicks of the flippers, up I came. The staff helped me out and suggested I should try again with a new set of goggles. But I decided that I had had quite enough and surrendered all the gear, slipped back into the pool and enjoyed a leisurely swim.

On the second day we hired a sailing dhow, complete with crew. They took us out to the reef where we were able to swim and enjoy the beautiful variety of colourful fish and fantastic lumps and fronds of coral. After our swim, we were given fishing lines and told that they would make lunch for us, but first we had to catch our fish. In spite of all our efforts, using bait they had given us, we only landed a couple of very small fish. Next they landed on a small island and told us to relax, leaving us wondering if we would get much of a lunch. All was well, as they had clearly come prepared for such novice fishermen and soon the wonderful aroma of frying fish reached us. They spread out rugs for us to sit on and umbrellas to give us shade while we tucked in to a delicious meal.

As we set off to return to the beach, our crew began to race another dhow, but were slipping back. I asked if I might take the tiller, but they were very reluctant to let me take over. Finally they allowed me, with one of  them squatting near in case of emergencies. Here my previous sailing skills with variable winds on winding rivers stood me in good stead and we managed to catch up with the other dhow. They were utterly amazed to see a white woman at the tiller!

EASTER

I had been invited by my friend Edith to spend Easter with her. I was particularly keen to go as she was teaching at the girls' boarding school where AIM had first assigned me to work. The invitation had not been confirmed and as so often happened, our phone was not working. So I decided I would just get up and go. The journey was by bus and went reasonably smoothly. The main problem was that the driver took impossible risks, overtaking near the crest of a hill, not to mention ploughing through potholes instead of skirting round them. It was with my greatest relief when the driver told me that I had arrived. I looked around and appeared to be in the middle of nowhere, until I spotted a small sign pointing to the school. It was a long haul up a very steep hill with my little case on wheels (a leaving present from the staff of Old Palace School). I finally saw the school. On enquiry, nobody knew where Edith was, until she appeared, looking very surprised as she was not actually expecting me. However she made me very welcome and we had a good time over the Easter period.

The setting of the school was lovely, with lots of exotic birds. It was here that I first saw a turaco, with its beautiful colours shining in the sun. I had by then bought a copy of the

Birds of East Africa and was able to write down the sighting. Before I left Africa, I had seen over 340 different birds. In spite of this, I realised that I would not have been happy working in the school, in an enclosed compound with just the staff and girls and no other attractions. God always knows best!

The time went quickly and I needed to get back to Nairobi. Edith accompanied me to the 'bus stop'. This actually meant standing on the road side and hailing the next public vehicle that came along. It could be a Peugeot or a matatu. A few went by full, but finally a very run-down looking matatu pulled up. I could not see an empty seat, but the driver was determined to squash one more paying passenger into his vehicle. I had my case and also a carrier full of plants from Edith's garden, hoping that they might grow well in our garden. The driver threw my case on to the roof, fastening it in what seemed to be a pretty insecure way and then I had to struggle past all the other passengers, carrying the bag of plants to the very back seat. There was no room for the bag, so I had it on my lap, with the leaves tickling my face. After about ten miles, we swerved wildly and the driver came to a halt. It was a flat tyre. He managed to drag out the spare – and guess what? It was also flat.

The driver told us to get out and wait on the roadside. Then he bowled the two tyres across to the other side of the road. He – and the tyres were picked up by another matatu and we waited in the hot sun. One or two passengers managed to get on to another passing vehicle, being able to pay another fare. The rest of us waited. After a very long time, the driver reappeared with two mended tyres and we were again on our way. This time I was able to get a better seat, beside a man who spoke English. I asked him what job he was doing. He quite proudly informed me that he was the rail-traffic controller for the whole of Kenya. This sounded like a very responsible job, until I asked him how many trains there were in Kenya. "Seven," was his reply. I managed not to make a comment, but thought of our local station at East Croydon. I remembered taking my grandchildren Samantha, Annie and James to watch dozens of trains go by.

Having told us that he was going all the way to Nairobi, the driver now announced that he was only going to Eldoret, so we would have to change. We arrived at a ramshackle bus station, with matatus all over the place, all shoving to try to get around each other in the mud. The driver took down my case and pointed in a general direction to a place where I could find a matatu to Nairobi. I wondered around disconsolately, wondering which one to choose. As I stood there, a very nice Kenyan lady took pity on me. She was also trying to get to Nairobi, so we went on together. As it was the end of the Easter holidays, all the matatus were full. She was a very forceful lady and after a while, she asked me to look after our luggage while she went off on her own. I stood there feeling lost and wondering where I might spend the night if the worst came to the worst. Then I saw her waving wildly. I grabbed all of the luggage – and the plants - and hurried after her. She had found two seats for us. As Kenya is a country where so many workers depend on bribes, I did not like to ask her how she had managed it! We squeezed in and settled down for the long and bumpy ride back home. This added to my reputation for having problems when travelling.

THE ARK

Jackie and I decided that we would like to explore some more of beautiful Kenya and one of her friends had offered to lend us her small Suzuki car. They had recommended a trip to the Aberdares, a mountain range on the eastern rim of the Great Rift Valley. Three places had been mentioned: Tree Tops, where Princess Elizabeth learned that she had become Queen, the Aberdare Country Club and The Ark. These last two belonged to the same group, so people can go the Country Club, leave most of their luggage there, and then be taken for one night to the Ark. We set off with great excitement.

It was only about 125 miles (180 km) so we were able to take our time and enjoy the views (but not the potholes), but soon the car began to make a strange noise. We were very near the Ark, so we drove into the car park and jumped out to see what the matter was. All the petrol was leaking out! I rushed around trying

167

to find some sort of receptacle to catch it before it was all wasted. Then we examined the damage. The hotel sent for a mechanic who soldered it together again. "Oh dear," I thought to myself. "Will my journeys ever go smoothly?"

We left most of our luggage and boarded the bus to take us to the Ark. It is built in the shape of Noah's ark, set in an area that is teeming with wildlife. It is located very close to a salt-lick and a major water-hole where the animals come to drink, usually at night. There are four viewing areas from which to watch the animals, all clearly floodlit. As much of this goes on at night, each room is furnished with a buzzer, two buzzes for an elephant or rhino and three for a lion or a leopard. Bath robes are kindly provided, so we can get up and enjoy the sighting. We saw some animals in the evening and then went to bed – and both of us slept through the noise of the buzzer. This was a little disappointing, but there were plenty of other opportunities to see the amazing Kenyan wildlife.

The next day we travelled on to the Aberdare Country Club a beautiful, if rather expensive, lodge. We had a good supper and went to bed. In the night, Jackie had a terrible bout of sickness and was quite unable to get up the next day. I went to speak to the manager, who turned out to be yet another forceful Kenyan lady. I explained our predicament. We had very little money and could not possibly raise enough for another day. We were stranded, probably as a result of Jackie's supper the night before. She said she would do what she could. We knew that they offered 'missionary rates' which were a little cheaper than the regular rate. Even that was too much. I explained that Jackie would not be eating anything, although I would have to eat. She was very sorry and said she could just charge us for one person. It was still too much, so I turned to go, head down, feeling very hopeless. She suddenly called out, "Army Rate". I turned back to see what

168

she meant. She said that the local army were extremely good at looking after the Ark and the gangway leading up to it, so they offered a very cheap rate for the soldiers. So it was agreed that I would pay 'Army Rate' which was less than a third of the actual price.

Next day Jackie was fit to travel, so on we went. We were warned that on the 'road' through the park there was often a rogue elephant, which stood in the road and refused to let cars go past. So, with my reputation, guess what? We came round a bend and there was the elephant. It was not right in the centre of the road, but over to the left and was swinging its trunk rather threateningly. I stopped the car and we sat and watched. After a while, I inched forward, but it also moved forward towards us, so I reversed back. This happened two or three times, It was a huge beast and we were in a very small car and aware that it could easily tip us over. After a few more minutes, it moved slightly further to the left. I said to Jackie, "I'm going – hold on!" I revved up the engine and shot forward. She closed her eyes but I thought it better not to do the same. When we were past, I told her to open her eyes and we slowed down for me to regain my composure.

We had booked the next two nights at an AIM guest house in Eldama Ravine. It was in a lovely situation, with small wooden cabins set among some trees, with wonderful birds to be seen. The AIM folk, the Barnetts, who were running it, were extremely welcoming and we had some lovely peaceful days there. The journey went surprisingly well until we had a puncture. Fortunately we were very near a garage so we limped in. They removed a nail from the tyre, mended the puncture and charged us about 50p (75c) and on we went.

Our next stop was Lake Baringo, which meant crossing the Equator. The picture on the next page shows us atanding at the Equator. This is one of a series of lakes scattered in the Great Rift Valley. The highlight for me was an organised bird-walk in the evening. We saw so many beautiful exotic birds, with plumage in all the colours of the rainbow. I had my Bird Book with me so I could mark down what I had seen, but could not keep up. The

169

guide explained that next morning I would find a list of all that we had seen during our walk. I checked the list and there were 57 birds which I had never seen before, taking my total up to 107.

Our final stop was at Lake Bogoria, a soda lake (like the Dead Sea) with a particular kind of algae that flamingos love. As we approached the whole lake was festooned with pink, made up of hundreds of these amazing birds. It also has hot springs and geysers spurting boiling hot water and steam into the air.

The hotel also boasted a swimming pool with warm water from the geysers. It was such a joy to be able to swim at night, looking up at the stars. The next morning I went in again and as I was swimming on my back, I saw one of Kenya's beautiful kingfishers, just sitting quietly on the branch of a tree. I swam quietly, with as little movement as possible and it stayed there for some minutes, so I was able to see details of its fantastic colouring.

It was with some sadness that we set out next day to return to chilly Nairobi, with its noise and pollution. But we came back with many wonderful memories having seen just a fraction of Kenya's richness – and no car problems all the way home!

LAKE NAIVASHA

Writing about the kingfisher reminded me of another holiday. I had become friendly with an older lady called Evelyn. She had been widowed twice and lived alone. I would often get a phone call asking me to come for an evening meal and we had some good times together. She very much wanted to visit a friend called Diana, who lived on the shore of Lake Naivasha. I was more than happy to drive her there and stay for a few nights.

Lake Naivasha is another of the lakes situated in the Rift Valley and is the home of wonderful bird-life. One morning I decided to make my way down to the shore of the lake with my camera and binoculars. The area below the house was a tangle of thick pampas grass, so it was quite difficult to get through. After a couple of hundred yards I was assailed by a very strong animal smell and spotted a circular tunnel, about the size of a hippo. Hippos are actually very dangerous animals and more people are attacked and killed by them than by any of the other animals, so I proceeded cautiously, keeping well away from the tunnel.

I finally reached the shore and scanned the area for birds. There, not far away was the most beautiful Malachite kingfisher, a rarer bird than the one I had already seen. I was transfixed by the sight and was yet again amazed at the vivid colouring. Suddenly I heard a sort of snorting noise behind me, to my left. I had been told that the most dangerous place to be was between a hippo and the water. And where was I? I was between the hippo and the water. I stepped back quietly, step by step, walking backwards. I think I was too scared to turn round and face it. Step by step I proceeded very cautiously, until I reached the shelter of the pampas grass. Then I fled and arrived panting back at the house.

A wonderful sight greeted me. There was Diana, sitting on a chair with a baby's feeding bottle, feeding the smallest deer I had ever seen. She motioned to me to keep quiet until the feeding was

over and the dear little creature had gone out. She told me it was a dik-dik and she had found it as a baby and adopted it. Now it came into the house, its tiny hooves tap-tapping on the wooden floor, to feed two or three times a day. I begged to be allowed to feed it myself and she agreed. What a thrill it was to feel the strong sucking from the dik-dik! Diana later told me that they grow to a height of only 12-16 inches (30-40 cms) at the shoulder.

The other short break I took in 1997 was a three day safari to visit the Masai Mara Game Park, to celebrate my birthday. The journey was pretty uncomfortable, as there was a huge rut in the middle of the road. Our minibus kept two wheels on the road and two on the grass verge, so the whole vehicle was at a strange angle with the possibility of toppling over. When the driver had had enough of tipping one way, he changed sides and drove on the wrong side of the road, but with the other two wheels on the road. We were extremely relieved when we finally arrived at the Lodge. There was a game drive that evening, followed by two others the next day. This was my first real view of the fantastic wildlife of Kenya. We saw so many animals that it was almost overwhelming. On the horizon we watched a long procession of elephants marching purposefully, silhouetted by the bright colours of a beautiful sunset. We stopped very near groups of cheetahs, admiring their sleek bodies and their playful cubs. The safari vehicles were in contact with each other by satellite radio and we suddenly got news that lions had been sighted. Off we went at an alarming rate, then slowed down and inched our way towards the site, where there were some other vehicles – and there they were, two lionesses and their cubs, It was a magical moment.

The area was teeming with other animals, water buck, zebra, and gazelles to name a few. When we spotted some buffalo, our guide warned us. "These are one of the most dangerous animals, as they will attack for no apparent reason. They often hide in the bush ready to charge any intruders." I had been thinking of getting out of the vehicle to get a good picture, but very quickly changed my mind! Then came my first sight of giraffe in the wild. What amazing creatures they are, with such long necks and such an ungainly way of walking. We feasted our eyes on them watching them effortlessly reaching to the top of some of the trees, to feed.

ZANZIBAR

Just the name Zanzibar has such an exotic ring about it. My friend Linda and I decided that we must go there. The flight from

172

Nairobi was beautiful, passing very close to Mount Kiliminjaro. (As I write, James, my eldest grandson, has recently had the joy of climbing the mountain.)

Zanzibar was hot and sticky, but blessed with a good wind off the sea. We enjoyed wandering around the old Stone Town, with beautiful carved doors and its many alleys. There were two sizes – a one-donkey alley is just wide enough for one donkey with its load, then there are two-donkey alleys, but no room for a car. Being narrow, there is plenty of shade in the alleys.

Our first trip out was by boat to Prison Island. Zanzibar had been a big centre of the slave trade and we saw plenty of evidence of it. There was the site of the Slave Market, near the Cathedral and an underground prison on the island. The slaves were kept in appalling conditions, so that once the weaker ones had all died, the others were deemed fit enough to be sold and sent off to other countries. Apart from that, it is a beautiful island surrounded by

 the multi-coloured sea, which gets its colours from the clear water above pure yellow sand below. As the water becomes deeper, so the blue becomes darker. The other attraction is the giants. It was such fun feeding them. As we held out bunches of grass they snapped them up greedily – we were particularly careful not to have our fingers snapped up too!

The next day we were taken on the Spice Trail, seeing how all the different spices were grown. On the following day we went out in a dhow to see the dolphins and to swim with them. I was all kitted up with goggles and flippers and off we went keeping our eyes out for these amazing creatures – and there they were! I was really excited and tried to scramble out of the high-sided boat and swim with them, but I was impeded by the flippers, so each time I was just too late. So my claim is not that I swam with dolphins, but that I swam where the dolphins had recently been!

MOMBASA AGAIN

Another holiday was in March 1996. Four of us arranged to stay in the AIM guest house on the coast south of Mombasa. It seemed like paradise after the rush and bustle of Nairobi, as well as its noise and smells. The guest house was set in a quiet spot, with a big lawn dotted with palm trees. A gate led us straight out on to the beach, with the vast rolling waves breaking gently on the shore. I was entranced by the scene.

The greatest attraction was snorkelling in the extraordinarily clear water. Towards low tide, we could walk out and enter the water quite near to the edge of the reef. It was teeming with brightly-coloured exotic fish, against a backcloth of huge deposits of coral scattered on the golden sand below. With the greatest excitement I fitted on my mask and snorkel tube. First I checked if I could breathe easily and soon found out how deep I could go without submerging the end of the tube and breathing in sea water!

We wore light shoes, as the walk on the coral would have torn our feet to ribbons. I began my first ever swim using a snorkel and was spellbound. It was a staggering sight, with the fantastic fish swimming in and out of the coral. Then I saw a fairly large triangular fish below me, so I put my foot on it gently, watching it swim off at speed. My friend tapped me on the shoulder, so we put our heads above the water. "Jan," she said, "That was a sting ray. It is very dangerous." I thanked her and began to go more carefully. Next I spotted a big lump of a fish, sitting on the seabed. This time I called my friends to have a look. They joined me and looked down. "Jan," they exclaimed, "That is a stone fish, the most deadly of all!"

The next day, I could not get enough of snorkelling and stayed out for a long time. As I came out of the water, I felt a pain on the back of my legs. I had been told always to wear a t-shirt, to protect my back from the intense sun but had never thought about the tops of my legs. When snorkelling, my head was under water but I did not realise that my legs were still on the surface.

174

I had never before suffered from sunburn, but this time I found that I had second degree burns and could not sit down comfortably. Happily, with the application of various creams I soon recovered, but I had learned my lesson. The tropical sun is really intense compared with the sunshine we get at home.

As we were relaxing, they teased me about finding the most dangerous fish of the area. They reminded me of our car problems going to Kijabe. They asked if it was safe to be with me when I travelled. My reputation of being a disaster centre was on the increase!

A NEAR THING

I had yet one more holiday in Mombasa and it could quite well have turned out to have been my last. It was a very frightening experience.

My friend Pat and I were staying in Mombasa and decided that we would like to go snorkelling, so we hired a taxi. The driver agreed to take us to the beach, wait for us and then bring us back. When we arrived there were already a good number of people on the main reef. Pat was a seasoned snorkeler, as she grew up in Kenya, so she suggested that we should go out on another reef nearby, where there were no other people.

She explained that we should go during slack tide and warned me that as soon as the tide turned and began to come in we must return to the shore. She explained that when the baby starfish began to wave their arms, it meant that the tide had turned. So off we went and had another glorious time in the beautiful clear water.

We were a good way out by now, having walked along the coral pathway, and the starfish began to wave. I had just seen a really lovely spider shell which I felt I must have. I dived down and managed to get it. When I emerged we were rather concerned because the water seemed to be coming in much more quickly than usual. The coral pathway was still visible so we hurried along as quickly as we could. The pathway became more and difficult to see and suddenly we were in deep water and had to

175

swim. By now the beach was a long way off. I am quite a strong swimmer, but better at short rushes than a long sustained swim. We swam along together, but I began to tire. The beach seemed to get further and further away. Pat was stronger and younger than me and was able to make better progress. She realised that although she felt she could reach the shore, there was no way she could help me, so she went on ahead.

I was still wearing my shoes, which of course were full of water, so I longed to take them off, but this meant putting my head in the water and fighting with the laces. I knew I could not do that, so I ploughed on. Suddenly she called, "Come over here. I can stand, so we can have a rest." Sadly, when I got there, I found that although she could stand, I was not tall enough. So I motioned her to go on.

I lay on my back for a while, but the waves were breaking over my face making it hard to breathe. "Lord," I whispered, "If this is my time, please let it be painless – and please comfort my family back home."

As I lay there on my back, the moon came up and its beam shone in a line straight towards me. I somehow felt that this was God, telling me that I was in His keeping and that this pathway of light would lead me back to the shore. So I began once more to work my weary arms and legs, keeping in line with the moonbeam. After what seemed an eternity, I felt arms pulling me and a voice telling me I could put my feet down. I staggered up through the shallows and collapsed on the beach, shivering violently.

Put urged me to get up at once and keep going until we reached the car. What a blessed relief it was to climb into the back of the car and wrap myself in a dry towel. I was relishing its dryness and comfort, but even more I was rejoicing in my God, who holds my life in His hands. It seemed that He had not finished with me yet! I remembered some lines from my favourite hymn -

176

From life's first cry, to final breath

Jesus commands my destiny.

No power of hell, no scheme of man

Can ever pluck me from His hand.

Till he returns or calls me home –

Here in the power of Christ I stand.

That's enough about holidays for the rich. It was very different for the Sudanese.

CHAPTER 13 WORKING WITH REFUGEES

I returned to the UK for six weeks and was once again interviewed by the Croydon Advertiser. After a rather astonishing headline, they wrote some good things. We sometimes grumble about the way the media report stories, but my experience was just the opposite.

In 1997 the double headline was

GIRL'S OWN ADVENTURES OF MISSIONARY JAN

Former schoolteacher swaps the classroom for the warzone while armed only with her battered copy of the Bible.

Typhoid, gunfire and poisonous snakes are not the run-of-the-mill constituent parts of normal retirement. But under no circumstances could Jan King's retirement be described as being normal.

In a few weeks' time Jan, a committed Christian, will be setting off on her third year-long contract as a missionary worker in Nairobi and war-ravaged southern Sudan.....

"I read my Bible every morning and there was a period in 1993 when I read verse after verse about getting up and going and God said He would be with me," said Jan.....

On returning in October I soon got back to work on writing the English text books. We also started a new Literacy Class. Our first group had progressed well, so we had a Graduation Ceremony and gave them certificates. The Sudanese love their certificates and expect one at the end of any course. Sometimes we were hard put to find what to write on the certificates of students who had really made little or no progress, so we produced fancy-looking certificates stating that the student had attended a course. Our current students were sad to have to leave and begged to be allowed to continue. On reflection we could see that they were now able to communicate, although at a fairly low standard. But in Nairobi there were hundreds who were still totally illiterate, so their needs had to be put first.

The Graduation was a great event, with speeches from various VIPs. Class 1 prepared a choral reading from their Reader and Class 2 read a story about Jesus. The top class presented a story, partly in chorus and partly by a narrator. This was greeted with enormous pleasure by the visitors, their husbands and their friends. We all realised just how far they had come, considering that most of them had been totally illiterate and had known very little English. This was followed by a real Sudanese feast of cake, groundnuts, bananas and fizzy drinks. It was altogether a memorable day for all of us.

CHRISTIAN WRITERS' WORKSHOP

My next trip was rather different. Instead of travelling into Sudan I was to teach in a refugee camp for Sudanese in Uganda. We were looking for talented Christian writers. Rhondda had already taught one Course for Christian Writers and now invited me to join her. I explained that I had never done anything in that field, but she assured me that she had the materials all prepared on sheets, so I could just follow her syllabus. She had other business in Kampala, Uganda, so she went ahead and I was to join her later. We were to meet at Entebbe Airport on a certain date and she helped me to book my flight with Missionary Aviation Fellowship (MAF), who had a small fleet of twelve-seater planes. But of course my journeys seldom went smoothly and this was no exception.

First I had to go by long distance bus to Kampala, which was an experience in itself. It was a twelve hour journey, following roads that varied from mediocre to appalling. I was travelling with Anthony, later to become a Bishop in the Episcopal Church

179

of Sudan, who was going to stay with the current Bishop. I had booked into the AIM guest house. The journey was fascinating, as we passed endless villages and bustling small towns. I noticed a large number of churches of a multiplicity of denominations, with names such as Christ the Lion, and the Band of the Born-again. Crossing the border from Kenya into Uganda was an interesting experience. While still in Kenya, we were told to take our passports, get out of the bus and walk across to Uganda. The driver promised to meet us at the other side. I wondered if I dared leave my luggage on the bus, but all the other passengers seemed happy to do so. We queued to have our passports stamped in Kenya, walked a few hundred yards into Uganda and queued again to have a Visa put into our passports, for $30 US. Happily the driver was there with all our things, so we climbed rather wearily aboard and went on our way.

I had noticed some bicycles carrying travellers along with their luggage. One of the other passengers told me that these bicycles were called boda-boda, because they took people from border to border! Later on I was to travel on a boda-boda and I can say with great conviction that it feels extremely unsafe to be sitting side-saddle on the small rack behind the cyclist.

Ugandan roads at that time were far better that those in Kenya, so we set off at a great speed. As we were bowling along a small boy on a bicycle that was far too big for him came off the pavement and wobbled into the road. He saw us coming and managed to throw himself clear, but the driver did not have a hope of missing the bicycle. We had thought that we were in a nearly deserted part of the road, but a small crowd appeared seemingly out of nowhere, and began threatening our driver. He was clearly terrified. My friend told me that in such cases the driver was always blamed and in some incidents drivers had been dragged from their cabs and beaten to death. The driver did his best to pacify the crowd. The boy was unhurt, but the bicycle was badly damaged. The father arrived and demanded a large amount of money to repair the bicycle. Although it was far too much, the driver wisely handed the full amount over. Next we had to go to the nearest police station to make a time-consuming report of the incident.

It was getting late, so I began to feel a little concerned. The driver was to take each of us to our own destination and it seemed that I was to be last. One lady did not quite know where she was going, so we wasted a good half hour looking for the right house. It was getting dark and Anthony was due to get off next. However the dear man insisted on staying with me to make sure that I arrived safely. But I never arrived at the AIM guesthouse. I had instructions, but none of us knew the place and after several attempts the driver gave up. Anthony kindly invited me to come with him and assured me that I would be made welcome. When we arrived at the Bishop's house, it seemed that even Anthony was not expected. Nevertheless, with typical Sudanese hospitality, we were both ushered in. They very kindly gave me a small bedroom but I found out later that Anthony had slept on a chair.

Next morning they sent me on my way to Entebbe airport to catch my plane. The weather was atrocious, with high winds and lashing rain. I arrived at the airport, went through security and sat down in the departure lounge. Nothing happened. Finally some flights were called, but only on international journeys, with big jet planes that could cope with the elements. After a long time a man came out and told us that the plane was too small and could not take off. As it was Saturday, we would have to wait until Monday, because MAF prefers not to fly on Sundays. I was feeling rather lost, wondering what I should do. However, someone helped me to book into a Christian Guest House and then organised a taxi for me.

On Monday off I went, again checking in at 6.00 am. By now I was wondering what had become of Rhondda, who was meant to meet me on the plane, but as I had no choice, I boarded the plane and away we went. It is spectacular, flying over Uganda as it is so green and fertile. Winston Churchill had called it the Pearl of Africa. I was going to a place called Adjumani and was slightly worried that there would be nobody there to meet me. After we disembarked, I stood rather disconsolately wondering what to do next. Various vehicles arrived and picked up their people, but no-one came for me. When the last passenger was about to be taken away, I asked the driver if he could possibly take me to the Refugee Camp. "Which one?" he enquired. "There are twenty different camps here." I was dumbfounded as I had no idea. Rhondda had just told me we were going to Adjumani. The driver said he would take me into the town and leave me at an office where they might be able to help me.

There was a very kind Ugandan lady in the office, who tried to help. I felt utterly foolish to have travelled this far without knowing my destination. She started talking about the different camps and finally mentioned Transit Camp. That rang a bell with me and I said that was where I was meant to go. The driver was still around, so I begged him to take me. He explained that it was 15 km over very rough ground. I gave him some money and he finally agreed, although he was not too happy about it. To add insult to injury, we had a puncture, so he had to stop and mend it. I sat under a tree feeling very bad about the whole situation.

When arrived at the Transit Camp, some people came out to see who was in the vehicle. They were delighted that I had come and ushered me into a completely empty tukul. I looked around in dismay – no bed, no mosquito net, nothing. However in no time some young men appeared carrying the different sections of the bed and fitting them together. Then some nice young women arrived with mattress, sheets and a net. I asked them where Rhondda was sleeping. "She isn't here," they informed me. "But now you are here, we can begin." And off they went to tell the other Christian writers who had come for the course.

"Help!" I thought to myself. "I know nothing about teaching writing skills. Rhondda has all the materials, what on earth shall I do?" Fortunately I had brought a complete set of my English Grammar books, so we got to work on them. I was praying rather desperately for Rhondda to come. I was also feeling rather hungry, but no food arrived. Finally I was given a few fried sections of cassava, a new experience but quite tasty. I later found out that there was no food because there was no money. There was no money because Rhondda was bringing it with her.

Next morning we ate some more cassava, then wonder of wonders, a car drew up and Rhondda appeared! I rushed over and gave her a big hug. She gave the cooks some money and unloaded all the materials. After a somewhat better but rather late breakfast, she took over the teaching. By the next day I too was able to do some of the teaching, using her notes.

Each day began with Devotions, which consisted of a couple of songs, a time of prayer and a short devotional by one of the participants. We had a Bishop and various archdeacons and other clergy on the course, who were invited to give the talk. Sadly I found the talks far from edifying, just a lot of church jargon and no gospel message. I was longing to be able to give one of the talks, but as the days went by, it was always given by one or other of the clergy. Finally on the last day I was invited to speak and gave a very clear gospel address. I noticed how this really caught their attention and they listened almost hungrily.

I was desperate to know what impact this had had. Happily it was the last day and one by one they had to bring their work to me to check. After each check I casually asked how they had found the talk. The response was amazing. Two of the men just gave their lives to the Lord there and then. One archdeacon confessed that he was now a back-slider so we prayed together and he promised to put his heart into his ministry. One pastor said he was thinking about the message. He said he had never before heard the gospel presented clearly. What a sad situation, underlining the danger of 'churchiness' rather than a clear explanation of the gospel. This particular man said he needed time to think about it. About two years later I met him again and could at once see a real change in him. He told me that after some days of spiritual struggle he had opened his life to the Lord Jesus, who had transformed both him and his ministry.

183

As I taught there and in different places, I usually asked the students to write an article entitled "How the war has affected my life". Here is one of them, written in his own words, with minimum editing.

HOW THE WAR CHANGED MY LIFE by Dominic

I was born in a small village. My father is a farmer and we have cows and goats. In 1978 raiders from the Lord's Resistance Army in Uganda came and raided all our cattle. I was very young. In those days, they came with the motive of killing the men and the boys. They always came at night and surrounded the village.

One night they came and besieged our village. It was at 4 am that we heard gunshots. When my father came out to see what was happening, they had already made an ambush at the door. He came back and told us. So my parents decided to put a small skirt on me. If they saw I was a boy they would kill me or take me along with them.

At that moment, the enemies started to open the main gate of the compound, so my father decided to break out of the window and run into the bush. So I was left alone with my mother and two sisters. The enemies finally broke into the house, so we all tried to hide in the corners. O God. I promise that I will trust and remain in Him until the end of my life, because he rescued me and has taken care of me up to now. The enemy came and laughed at us and sent us out into the bush. After we had gone, they looted all our property in the house.

I really thank God for his kindness that he saved me and removed me from the bondage of darkness.

OTHER REFUGEE CAMPS

Over the next few years I had the privilege of teaching in a number of Refugee Camps in different parts of Uganda. Generally speaking the journeys were difficult, but this was far outweighed by the joy of being able to serve the various Sudanese communities.

Several memories stand out. One such was when the Lord's Resistance Army (LRA) was active in the area. The LRA is a group of terrorists led by Joseph Kony. It began when a Ugandan woman called Alice Lakwena claimed that the Holy Spirit had told her to overthrow the government of Uganda because of the evil way in which the people of the Acholi tribe had been treated. Many Acholi people flocked to join her, particularly as she said that she was invulnerable. However, she was exiled and most of her supporters dispersed. Joseph Kony, who claimed to be her cousin, took over the leadership. When most of the men deserted him, he began to use thousands of children, by abducting them from their homes, brutalising them and training them to fight and kill.

Kony lost sight of the original aim of overthrowing the Uganda government and his so-called army became a terrorist group, ranging between Uganda, the Democratic Republic of Congo and Sudan. They live off the land, by stealing and looting. One of the pastors I was teaching told me, with tears in his eyes, that he had had a good harvest and had several sacks of grain put by for the dry season, but the LRA attacked and stole the whole lot. Then they set fire to the one field that he not yet harvested. He and his family now faced a very hungry period.

When the threat of the LRA was at its highest, children would come every night to sleep rough in the towns, for fear of being abducted, and then return to their schools and villages by day. Those who were taken had an appalling time. The discipline was unbearably harsh. If any child tried to run away he would be dragged back and the other children were forced to kill him. Gradually they became brutalised and were even able to kill for the pleasure of it.

On one occasion, when I was in one of the camps, we knew that the LRA was in the area. One Friday, while I was teaching, a child rushed in asking to speak to Pastor Francis Otto, so he went out to hear the news. When he came back, his face told it all.

185

Although a Sudanese cannot turn white with emotion, it was written all over. His nine-year old son Emmanuel had been abducted. We stopped the lesson and all turned to prayer then and there and over the weekend, crying to the Lord for the boy's return. On Monday he reappeared! He was dirty, his feet were lacerated, but he was home. What a time of praise we had! It seems that he was so miserable and just kept crying and crying, so they gave up and just abandoned him in the bush. Somehow he had managed to find his way home again.

TEACHING ENGLISH

One of the world's greatest problems began at the Tower of Babel. It was there that God reacted to the pride of the people by 'confusing their language'. How much easier it would be if we all spoke one international language.

As I taught in various refugee camps and in Sudan itself, I came to realise how difficult it had been for the Sudanese to go to school and learn English. In most of my classes, I found that about a third of the students had remained in Sudan, hoping to be able to get some education. Time and time again, their villages were bombed and the school destroyed. So they would relocate and try once more to find a school. These were often just with the children sitting on the ground under a tree. So they were years behind in their education.

Another group had been forced to attend Islamic schools, which were conducted in Arabic. They had great problems when learning English, as Arabic is in a different script and is written from right to left. I remember giving a boy who had been living in Khartoum a book to look at and seeing him beginning at the last page rather than page one.

The third group were the most fortunate academically as they had fled to Uganda or Kenya and had been able to attend the local schools. There Primary Education was free. Secondary schools demanded fees, but a good number of Sudanese were able to get sponsorship and could go on to take national exams. However they faced the problem of getting jobs in Kenya, as they would require a Work Permit. Many able men and women were able to work for non-governmental organisations. They, however, were the exceptions.

Here is another account of how the war affected one of our students and how it had impacted on his education.

HOW THE WAR AFFECTED MY LIFE by Data Peter

I was born in 1980 and when I was five, the war came to our area. At first we were hiding in a big cave and taking cover under big trees. We experienced robbery, killing, raping and misuse of resources. Eventually we lost all our belongings and were only thinking of how to rescue our lives for the future.

In 1989 we went to Uganda for refuge and I joined Primary 1. We met under trees, no blackboards, chalk, books, pens or text book for the teachers. Next year the Jesuit Refugee Service took over the schools, so all was OK. Our parents put up a school structure. But the health section was not in place, so this led to a great number of deaths recorded. Also there was a food problem as there was not enough food for almost a complete year. We went on, only eating cassava and beans.

Everything became harder and harder, but in 1994 we were transferred to Rhino Camp in Uganda where we were able to cultivate. In 1997 the rebels in the Lord's Resistance Army broke into our camp and vowed that they would finish off all the Sudanese. This was the year when I was to join Secondary School. My aunt told me not to go, but I told her, "It is better to die at school than to wait in the camp." The LRA continued with bad activities like cutting off the ears of people or taking out their eyes.

I joined Senior School and struggled until I finished my O levels in 2000. Due to poverty, my friends and I decided to join the Uganda Army to earn a living. In the process, God changed that vision and rescued me from critical situations.

In March 2001 God touched my heart and I was born again. I had become helpless and hopeless of my life, so I committed my

187

life to Christ. I was by then running after the things of the world, but God changed that. That is why you see me now enjoying life in God.

'I CAN NEVER FORGIVE'

While I was working in one of the camps, I had a similar experience to that with Moses, the Nuer church leader in 1996. I was teaching English for two 45 minute sessions, but was free for the rest of the day. So I invited any church members to come for extra English. One of the groups was of women only, including a lovely lady called Mary, who often looked very sad. I always included a short devotional in each lesson and was working through the Lord's Prayer. When we came to the section about forgiving others, Mary interrupted, saying, "I could never do that." I talked with her after the lesson and she told me her story.

"I was living in a village in Sudan. One day the Sudanese army from the north attacked our village. They began killing the men as we women stood looking on in horror. One, with a very cruel face, saw me cradling my baby boy. He snatched it from me, threw it up in the air, caught it on the end of his bayonet and then sliced it into two. I can never forgive this man. I hate them with such hatred that it is eating me up."

I listened with horror and a deep compassion for this dear suffering lady, and wondered how I would have reacted. After much prayer, I spoke to her again, explaining that unless we forgive others, Jesus says he cannot forgive us. She was still adamant. However over the next few days something was happening in her heart. I believe that the Holy Spirit was working in her, helping her, softening her. I asked her, "Mary, if you don't forgive, who is that hurting? Is it hurting that nameless man, or is it hurting you?" She looked thoughtful and went home.

The next day she came into class looking radiant. I at once guessed what had happened. She told me that she could never forget what had happened, but was carrying a burden that was too heavy for her, so she had prayed for strength to forgive. What a difference that made. I understand that later she became one of the leaders in her church.

TEACHING ABOUT HIV/AIDS

In the 1990s HIV-AIDS was rife in eastern Africa. I was told that in Uganda one in six young people would die because of AIDS. It was nearly as bad in Kenya, but it was not yet so common in Sudan. We were therefore asked to teach a course about how to prevent it.

John Chaplin of AIM had developed a very good programme, complete with textbooks for the participants, an excellent teaching book for the leader with a number of real life stories about AIDS, together with large pictures. The leader could hold up the picture and tell the story. Nobody else seemed to be free to teach in the refugee camps, so rather reluctantly I agreed to go.

Before going to do this, I received an urgent invitation to teach about AIDS in Sudan, so I agreed to go there first. I took time to study the materials and with a colleague off we went. Yet again the bus journey was pretty terrible, but we got there in the end and after a day's rest were about to begin.

The very next day, wonder of wonders, a vehicle arrived and out stepped a retired AIM missionary couple, Doug and Gill Reitsma, the couple who had first talked to me about Sudan. They had retired recently and were making a return visit, hoping that in some way they might be able to get into Sudan and help. I was also delighted to see them for another reason – Doug was a doctor and he agreed to help with the course. So whenever difficult questions were asked, he was there to answer them. God certainly moves in wonderful ways.

When I finally went into other camps to teach the course, I felt very well prepared.

KIRYANDONGO

Kiryandongo was another refugee camp in Uganda. I was again accompanied by Doug and Gill Reitsma. The people there had been having a terrible time because of the LRA. In their previous camp the LRA had dropped leaflets telling the people they must get out within 24 hours or they would be killed. They all fled, carrying what they could with them and leaving all the rest behind. They arrived in a traumatised state, some with only the clothes they were standing up in. We knew about this before we travelled, so with money from some of my supporters in the UK we were able to take some materials such as blankets, jerry cans (to carry water) cooking pots, etc.

After the course was over, the Reitsmas and I embarked upon yet another dreadful journey. We were travelling in a matatu and seemed to be doing very well, until a huge tropical storm arose. We were forced to stop as the driver could see nothing. When it was over, we resumed our journey. However when we were approaching Kampala our fortunes changed. The whole city was grid-locked. The city lies amongst seven hills, with the main roads and roundabouts in the valleys, so the roads were totally flooded and we ground to a halt. We had two big problems. One was that Doug was getting on for 90 years old and really needed to be taken to the AIM guest house to rest, and secondly I had a flight booked from Entebbe airport. We had allowed plenty of time for the journey, so at first we were not too concerned, but as the time passed and we were only able to inch forward, our concern grew.

The driver understood our predicament and told us to hold on tight. He then drove on to the railway track! We bumped along, swaying wildly and he then shot off into a maze of mud roads and amazingly got the Reitsmas to the Guest House. By then I was very nervous about my flight. It was leaving in about half an hour. The driver finally got us on to the main road to the airport and I arrived extremely hot and bothered, literally in the nick of time. However, I need not have worried, for all the planes were delayed because of the storm. How thankful I was when I finally fell into my seat on the plane. What a relief! "Thank you, Lord," I prayed. "But please couldn't I have some smoother journeys, just sometimes!"

This prayer was answered in a very special way on my next return flight to the UK. I was travelling with a small airline that has since gone out of business. During the long flight, the captain

190

used to hand over to his co-pilot and stretch his legs down the aisle. When he passed, I tentatively asked him if I might go into the flight-deck. As I had expected, I received a negative reply. However, he stopped to have a chat and I told him about some of my journeys and mentioned flying on Missionary Aviation Fellowship planes. He at once showed interest, explaining that his church supported MAF and he then invited me into the flight deck after all! I was thrilled. I was strapped into a seat and was able to see an amazing view from the nose of the plane. I could see so many other planes and asked how it was that they did not collide. He explained that each plane has its own number and is controlled from Heathrow. He turned on the Intercom so I could hear. There was a steady voice, calling different numbers and telling them their new direction. Our number was called and the pilot followed the instructions.

Suddenly a red light began flashing, with a message, 'trailing left flap'. He and the co-pilot got out a thick book to look up the details. He then sent a radio message to Heathrow to prepare a long runway, in case we could not stop on a short one. I just sat and prayed – perhaps that was why I was there? After a few minutes, the red light went off and we all relaxed. Not wishing to out-stay my welcome, I said I should return to my seat. The captain then asked if I would like to come back to see him land the plane. I said I would be delighted, so he promised to come for me.

As we were nearing Heathrow, he came and fetched me. This time there was a thick mist, with no visibility whatsoever. I wondered how he would find the runway, but then the voice came through giving instructions. As we descended, we were suddenly out of the mist and there directly in front of us lay the runway.

TEACHING ABOUT AIDS IN KAKUMA

I received another invitation to teach about HIV/AIDS, this time in Kakuma Refugee Camp Kenya – the place where I had been in the shooting incident. Trusting God for my safety this time, I agreed to go. At that time, an American lady called Sally

191

was living with us. She had brought quite a lot of money to distribute amongst the churches but also had plenty of time on her hands. She realised that what she was doing was mostly with other American or British expatriates or high officials in the churches and decided that she would like a real 'Africa experience'. She asked if she could accompany me to Kakuma. I warned her that Kakuma was a very tough and depressing place, but she was adamant. She had had some teaching experience, so with the help of the very good manual, I felt she would be able to relieve me of some of the teaching.

We managed to get a free flight direct to Loki, with Lutheran World Relief, rested at the ACROSS compound and then took a matatu to Kakuma. This was Sally's first 'Africa experience'. Eighteen of us were squeezed into a 14-seater van, as well as two babies and an incredible array or bags and bundles. We rattled and shook for two and a half hours. We were stopped at two police posts where everybody and everything was spilled out for inspection.

On arrival we had to go through a vetting process, carried out by the Kenyan UN staff. Here we came face to face with Kenyan beaurocracy. Three of them interviewed us and they were clearly not too pleased that we had come.

"Why have you come?" they enquired, rather forcefully. We explained that we had come to lead a course about HIV/AIDS.

"We teach such courses ourselves," they said. "Your course is not needed." So we explained that we were just teaching people from Africa Inland Church.

"You should not be confining yourself to one denomination," they told us. Fortunately we had invited two people from each of the other major Sudanese denominations. We showed them our text books and they grudgingly said that we could stay for the night and they would review our case in the morning.

With some difficulty we found the AIC church compound, where we were welcomed warmly, but little provision had been made for us. Finally they made us beds by putting four of the church benches side by side, with a mattress perched on top.

Kakuma is in the middle of a desert area, so it is extremely hot, dry and dusty. There are various dry river beds with one really wide one running right through the centre of the camp. As it only rains hard about once every two or three years, this does not usually present any problems.

We settled down as best we could on our makeshift beds and dozed, but were then alarmed by the sounds of a tremendous storm and of tropical rain falling in sheets. When we looked out of our tukul next morning, we found that we were on an island, with deep muddy and extremely smelly water flowing around us. The rain had been so heavy that the latrines had filled and overflowed. "Sally is definitely getting her Africa experience," I thought wryly to myself.

We waded into the main building and met the others. Then a visitor appeared – It was one of the three who had interviewed us the day before. While the other two had been totally negative towards us, this man had been much more open. He told us that his name was Baraka, meaning blessed in Arabic. He asked us whether we wanted to obey God or the whims of the UN staff. We had no doubt that we wanted to obey God, thinking of a verse in the book of the Acts where Peter says, *It is better to obey God rather than man*. Baraka's advice was that we should go ahead with the course, particularly as the UN staff would be overwhelmed with work because of the floods and the threat of cholera in the camp.

Gradually some students trickled in, and even though a number were stranded on the other side of the river, the course began. It went well, with an eager class of church workers. As their assignment each evening, the students were to mingle with the people in the camp and ask questions about what they knew about AIDS, where it came from etc. They used the Questionnaire that was printed in their textbooks.

As two of them were interviewing a young man, one of the two UN staff passed by and recognised the bright green textbook

193

which we had shown them during our interview. Realising that we were still in Kakuma, they came at once to the compound telling us that we must leave at once. We were to report to the UN building next morning with all our luggage and we would be taken out. Happily we had almost reached the end of the course and the certificates were all written out. One of the AIC staff was able to finish teaching the course the next day.

Sally was delighted to be given the opportunity to leave. She had been growing more and more unhappy, looking for any form of transport to get her home to civilisation! We rather wearily dragged our luggage to the UN compound and were put in a room to wait. So we waited and waited and waited, feeling very discouraged. Then a door opened and a man called out, "There is a visitor for Jan King." I followed him, wondering who on earth it could be, as nobody knew we were there.

On our way in, we had rested at the ACROSS compound. Douglas, the compound manager was rather concerned for us, in view of the flooding. Two Austrian ladies used to go to Kakuma once a week to lead a Bible Study, so Douglas had asked them to check if I was alright. The Austrians could not teach their course, as most of their students were on the other side of the river, so they offered to take us back to Loki. We very gratefully accepted their offer. They had a big four-wheel drive vehicle, which was just as well as much of the road was under water. In that area there were things called 'Irish bridges' across some of the dry river beds. The joke was that instead of a bridge, there was a sharp slope down, a rough passage over the river bed and a sharp slope back up again to the road level. When we came to one, we found it full of fast flowing water. The ladies were not too concerned, so we waited for about half an hour until the level was low enough for us to cross.

After we had negotiated several of these fords we came to yet another and this was different. It was very wide with a real torrent flowing down, carrying whole trees that had been uprooted. We stopped near the edge and surveyed the scene with some dismay. More and more vehicles lined up behind us, waiting to cross. The real problem lay on the other side. On the slope down to the river, an enormous tanker lorry was stuck with its wheels submerged in the sand, thus blocking the only way to the crossing. There was another very long line of vehicles behind it. The drivers and passengers all got out and we stood together on our side wondering what to do next. Kakuma was a long way behind us, and the riverbeds were all filling up more and more. We suspected that we would be spending the night in our vehicles.

After two or three hours, a local man from the Masai tribe decided to wade across. He removed his only garment, slung it over his shoulder and waded in. He could not make it and rather shame-facedly returned. After another hour or so, a very large four-wheel drive vehicle on the other side, came down the side of the slope, knocking down a couple of small trees and plunged into the water. We watched with bated breath and a great sigh of relief when he made it across. A few other brave souls also crossed. Our lady drivers were rather nervous, so when a kind Kenyan man offered to drive us across, they accepted gratefully.

It was a weary but exceedingly happy group that thankfully drove into the ACROSS compound, with the luxury of a shower and a proper bed. Had we not come out on that day, we would have been stuck there for a further two weeks. Then it would not only have been Sally who felt she had had enough of an Africa experience. The next chapter tells of some of the other particularly uncomfortable problems we had to face.

CHAPTER 14   LATRINES I HAVE KNOWN!

When you next sit on your shiny throne, with you luxurious quilted toilet paper, when you press the silver handle which releases a cascade of slightly medicated water - think of those who have never known such an experience! Tribal customs can be very different. There was a tribe in Sudan, where the husband must leave as big a pile as possible of his excreta on the ground by the fence, to prove to his mother-in-law how well his wife feeds him!

When various friends encouraged me to write this book, I told them that one chapter would be 'Latrines I have known' – so here it is. I'll also tell of some of the other hazards.

One of the greatest challenges facing westerners who come to parts of Africa is the sanitary arrangements. One English friend of mine was working in the comfortable Across office, but felt that she really must venture into Sudan to get the 'atmosphere'. And that is exactly what she got. She took one look into the latrine and immediately came out again. She said she could not use it so she could not stay. But of course she had to, until a plane could come to take her out. So for some days she refused to eat or drink, to avoid having to go into the latrine. So it was a very poorly, dehydrated lady who finally returned to Kenya.

I did rather better on the whole. I guess it was partly my early experience in family camping where we dug our own latrine and with the same sort of thing in Guide camp. Added to this was a strong determination to cope, whatever the situation.

It was always a moment of regret when I used my nice Nairobi toilet for the last time and ventured into the unknown. The first location where I stayed in Sudan was called Yomciir (pronounced yom cheer). I was to teach English to the Bible School students. They were all men – and so were the tutors. I was the only lady on the site (except for the cooks)

There was just one pit-latrine for all of the Bible School, both students and tutors – and it had a broken door. It consisted of a rather smelly hole in the ground. The men popped in and out, without worrying about what could be seen from outside, but that was certainly not the case for me. So I had the challenge of trying to prop the door up with one hand, while 'performing' down the hole. As you can imagine, this was extremely difficult. Happily one of the tutors realised my predicament, so he set some men digging. They dug a huge hole, nearly 2 metres deep, then put on a thick covering of mud and left it all to dry. As you can imagine, I watched all this with very great interest. When it was dry, they dug two holes – not one, about 2 metres apart. Well, I thought to myself, is it to be used by two people at once rather like the Romans who went in for communal latrines? Next they took some very long grass and began to put up walls around the whole area. Much to my relief, they divided it into two cubicles. Next morning when I got up, there it was, with little labels MEN TUTORS on one entrance and LADY TUTORS on the other. So I had my own hole to myself. What a relief!

The latrine in Ikotos had a concrete floor, with a keyhole shaped hole, which was not too bad. However, it was kept locked, so I had to take a tour round the compound to see who had the key. Any hope for nice British privacy was a forlorn one. The other forlorn hope was for toilet paper, so it was a cardinal rule always to carry some. Of course there might be a cardboard carton, from which you could tear off a piece, but was usually decorated with finger marks from the previous users.

In another location, the pit had a cover, which was a flat piece of wood with a long handle. The technique there was to remove the cover and stand back, watching a huge cloud of blue bottles as they swarmed out. Then it was important to perform quickly

(before they came back), put back the lid and beat a hasty retreat.

The cubicles for washing were not too bad. There was a solid line of cubicles, with grass walls and L-shaped entrances, for

197

privacy. We were each given a washing up bowl and a plastic mug. We could fill the bowl from petrol drums, one with cold water and one with a fire lit below it to produce hot water. Inside the cubicle was a sort of gadget made of sticks tied together (like we used to make at Guide camp). You rested the bowl on the gadget, then scooped up the water in the mug and threw it at yourself. It was extremely refreshing, after a long hot day. But woe betide  anyone who came after about 5.30 pm for that was the time when the mosquitoes arrived, often in clouds. They love water, so they settled on your body, to have a little of drink of water – and a little of your blood to finish off.

I found cubicles like these in most locations. Some were more 'private' than others. The very worst one I had to cope with had a broken door and was overgrown with creepers. But even the better made ones had a constant problem with the flooring – or the non-existence of any flooring. Nobody was able to make wooden duck boards, as wood was in short supply. Some of the tutors dragged in pieces of mortar or unused bricks, to try to make a platform to stand on. Balancing on one leg, while washing the other could be disastrous and I sometimes emerged with dirty feet and had to wash them all over again.

This lack of stones first struck me when I was teaching basic maths to a group of teachers. I was teaching tens and units, so I told them to go out and collect 10 pebbles.

"What is a pebble?" someone asked.

"A small stone," I replied.

"But what is a stone?" was their rejoinder. I was absolutely amazed to realise that in their areas, there were no stones, rocks or even pebbles. They lived on a flat plain made of exceedingly fertile black cotton soil, which could be up to 20 metres in depth.

So I quickly changed my request and asked for 10 small sticks instead.

Back to the latrines. As you can well imagine, crouching over a hole is not easy, particularly for someone who is not as young as she was and has one metal knee, which could not bend very far. It was often a case of 'hit or miss'. It also meant that I was not able to spend long enough in that position so, along with so many other westerners, I often suffered from constipation. Even now, when some missionaries get together, we find ourselves talking about our bowels!

When I returned the following year to Yomchiir, I found that they had very kindly made a sort of box for poor Mama Jan, which was so kind of them – but raw wood is not very comfortable to sit on! Later on, at another location, someone had actually carved a circular seat, which was a huge improvement. They called it my 'throne' – a nice joke on my surname, King.

Some time later, there was a fire that swept through the Bible School. I was not there at the time, but received an email saying, *Dear Mama Jan, we are sorry to tell you that your throne has perished in the fire.* So it was with some misgivings that I returned some months later, wondering what I should find. This time they had really excelled themselves. Some bright spark had actually procured a white toilet seat! The only trouble was that they had laid it on the ground. I regarded it with interest, but then asked myself, "How will I get down? – and even more important,

199

how on earth will I ever get up again?"
So the wonderful toilet seat was
abandoned, and it was back to the hole
in the ground.

In Nyal the latrine was also very
challenging. This was because they had
placed a large box over the long drop,
surmounted by a large flat piece of wood
with a hole in the centre. The problem
was that the board was so big, that if I managed to sit over the
hole, my legs had to stick straight out, rather than hanging down.
On first glancing at it, I thought I could probably manage alright.
However on second glance I realised that it was filthy dirty. I
realised that the Sudanese village people are so used to squatting
over the hole, that they had climbed up on to the board so they
could squat on top of it, as usual. They were not always very
accurate, hence the mess on it. This now presented an
extraordinary challenge. Having a stiff knee, I knew I could not
climb up and try to squat. Instead I had to find bits of paper or
cardboard to put round the hole, then I could sit on it with my legs
sticking out! In the end I had to tell James about my problem and
happily he showed me another long drop I could use.

Something similar happened in Emmanuel Christian
Training Centre. In 2008 they were upgrading the whole centre,
so they decided to put flush toilets in for the students. Again, the
students from the villages tried to squat on the toilet seats,
breaking some. In a depressingly short time, all these toilets were
broken.

In Paluer, a lady had to visit the latrine at night and noticed a
cat that seemed to be playing with something. It was a cobra! The
lady and the cat managed to finish off the cobra together. I was
adamant that I was never going to use the latrine at night, so I
always brought with me a certain blue plastic bucket with a
tightly fitting lid. It went with me everywhere I went.

SNAKES, SCORPIONS AND OTHER CREEPY CRAWLIES

Let me add a few more snake and scorpion stories. One evening the staff was sitting around in the cool of the evening. We were sitting on white plastic chairs, the type that can easily be stacked. Pat looked down and saw a very large black mamba slithering between her feet. She froze and the Sudanese soon dealt with it. Thereafter we would sit sideways in our chairs, with our legs hanging over one of the armrests!

The other snake story is about a pastor. As he was walking in a fairly open area, he heard an Antonov bomber and knew he must jump into a hole. He rushed towards a hole, but there was a very poisonous snake in it. So he tore along and just managed to get into another hole. He heard the bomb coming down, but he was safe. On emerging he realised that the bomb had fallen in the first hole and killed the snake. He had been saved by the snake!

Ants in Sudan are not like ours back in the UK. Some are very big, particularly soldier ants. They travel in large groups in straight lines. They can march into a tukul or granary and do terrible damage. I only had one encounter with them and managed to re-route them before they entered my tukul. Termites are another scourge as they can eat away the wooden poles on buildings until they become unsafe. Once I was sitting on a bench made of poles and saw smoke coming out of the woodwork. I jumped up in alarm, but my friends laughed at me. "It's only the termites inside," they informed me. Other termites are so industrious that they heap up the unwanted soil from their underground passages. This soil becomes termite poles, some of which are taller than I am!

Flying ants (termites) are much loved by the Sudanese, as they make a very tasty snack. At a certain time in very hot weather when thunder is in the air, the people rush out with empty sacks and gather them up in handfuls. The wings fall off very easily. Some people fry them and eat them. They are not too bad, but one or two were enough for me! The main plan is to make them into a thick paste, which to them is highly delicious. Here is a favourite story:

Deng loved termite paste, so when his wife made some, he put it away, out of sight. When he wanted to eat some, he would call his grandson. He would then tie a long string to his big toe and tell the boy to take the other end and go and sit on the path to the house. If he saw a visitor coming, he was to pull on the string. This would give Deng time to hide the paste away, so he did not have to share it!

I'm not sure of the truth of this, as the Sudanese are very generous in their hospitality – but it's a good tale.

Scorpions are greatly feared. I have seen a man shuddering with pain, with a blanket over his head for two days. I have heard of babies who die as their bodies just cannot take the level of pain. I always carried a special venom extractor. It looks like a very large syringe, but rather than injecting something into the skin, it draws out any poison. A Canadian friend was stung on his thumb but we rushed for the extractor. He said that he felt a burning pain travelling up his arm, but we were able to stop it going further. If it reaches the armpit, it causes almost unbearable pain.

A more amusing story (well, it is amusing to relate, but not really so funny at the time) comes from a time when we were staying in a so-called hotel in a small town in Uganda, close to a very large Refugee Camp, where we were working. We had previously stayed in a different hotel, which had been adequate for our needs, but that one was full, so we had to look elsewhere. We entered the New Hope Hotel, with our hopes on hold. Would it be suitable for our group of westerners to stay for three weeks? We were shown the bedrooms, which seemed clean and reasonably comfortable. Then I asked to be shown the toilets. They proudly showed us some concrete cubicles, with toilets with makeshift seats, which was also quite acceptable, until I looked up. Now, I know it is rather bad for a missionary in Africa to be afraid of spiders, but such is my lot. I really cannot bear them.

From the ceiling there were hanging festoons of spiders in a tangle of webs. I came out of the cubicle rather quickly and explained my problem to our guide. He said it would be no problem as the cleaners were all armed with Doom. Doom is the common insecticide spray used throughout East Africa, with it wonderful promise – 'DOOM KILLS DUDUS DEAD'.

So we agreed to stay in the New Hope and settled into our rooms. As we were eating our supper in the open-air area of the hotel, I noticed a cockroach crawling by, from the direction of the toilets – then another and another. We all leapt to our feet, grabbed some newspapers and began whacking them. As fast as we cleared some, others appeared. They were climbing up the walls and trying to get into our bedrooms! We kept on with our good work until they had all been dealt with. There was a great heap of them – I even counted them – 72 in total. It transpired that the cleaners had been so zealous with the Doom, that they not only sprayed the roof, but also sprayed down the holes, thus evicting the cockroaches. Before getting into bed that night, we all had a very good look round our rooms and pulled back the sheets, to make sure we had no unwelcome visitors.

As you can imagine, one of the particular joys of getting back home was having flush toilets and running water on tap and not a snake or scorpion in sight. Actually that is not quite true, as my grandson Peter often managed to find very lifelike plastic snakes and scorpions to hide in my bed or under my chair!

KNEE PROBLEM

As I have explained, the latrine posed a particular problem because of my stiff knee. Reading through my old letters, I find I am constantly making references to the pain in my left knee. In 1998 things came to a head and I found I could only walk with the help of a stick. I wrote an urgent prayer letter home explaining that I urgently needed a knee-replacement. At that time there was about a two-year waiting list for such an operation. My friend Pat's daughter was at that time the administrator for the orthopaedic unit at Guy's Hospital. She mentioned the problem to the knee surgeon, outlining a little about my situation and my having occasionally to run to safety. He was touched and agreed to do it as soon as I returned. What a great blessing from God, who had promised right at the start, in Isaiah 58:11 that He would 'strengthen my frame'.

I came home in November 1998 but was a little concerned about the fact that I was queue-barging, whilst others had been waiting for two years. What happened next was amazing. My surgeon worked in the knee operating theatre on Tuesdays and Thursdays and his colleague had the other days. In November, the 13th fell on a Friday and the colleague was very superstitious and refused to operate on Friday the 13th. Because of this, my specialist had an extra session, so I did not hold back any of the others who had been waiting, but went as an extra. The operation went very well, but the recovery was very painful. My leg was stiff, so I had to force it to bend, degree by degree until I reached 110 degrees, which is as far as my prosthesis will go. I persevered as I was determined to have the very best possible amount of mobility – so I could manage in the latrines. But everywhere I went, I always brought with me the small, faithful blue bucket, with its tightly fitting lid!

While I was at home for the operation, I did not always find England easy, as life moved on so quickly. I was staying with my daughter Alison who gave birth to her second son, Peter. He was very small and needed a hat, so I used a knitting pattern for an egg cosy and just made it a bit bigger – and it fitted snugly on his little head.

One evening Alison and David were going out, so I was left with Peter. Just as they were leaving, my son Murray arrived with Matthew, then aged two months and asked if I could look after him too. I was very happy and they left me cradling one baby on each arm. Soon Peter was in obvious need of a clean nappy. The first problem was how to get up out of my chair while holding two babies, with my very stiff, sore knee. I carefully laid first one baby, then the other on the floor and managed to get up and carefully put them near the middle of the double bed, so they could not roll off. Then came the greatest challenge of all. I had been left a mysterious package called a disposable nappy. I undid it and worked out which way round I thought it should go for a boy, but how could I fasten it? After some fumbling, when neither Peter nor I were enjoying the experience, I went and found some sellotape and fixed the nappy with that. You can imagine the hilarity when the parents came home again!

Three months after the operation I was well enough to return to Africa, so in February 1999 off I went again. I enjoyed being taken through Gatwick on an electric buggy, but was met in Nairobi by a rather rickety wheelchair. I was soon able to return to SLC and to resume my work there.

CHAPTER 15   GIRLS AND WOMEN

Training the girls is very important, as a dowry system is in place. A young man cannot marry until he and his family have paid a very large dowry to the girl's parents. This is decided after lengthy discussions between the two families and their representatives. The parents of the girls can often be extremely greedy and very demanding. However when Christian young people are getting married, it was not unusual in recent years for the bride's parents to demand a lower sum, as they are very concerned that their daughter should have a good-living and believing husband.

In most cases the groom is only allowed to marry after a fairly substantial down-payment, together with the promise of regular payments over the next months or more usually years. It is only after this down-payment has been handed over that they can they marry, but with only a civil ceremony. The churches, however, will not celebrate a marriage ceremony until the whole amount has been paid.

Here is another account written by one of our students,. As well as telling how the war affected him, it also shows the impact of the dowry system on his life.

HOW THE WAR AFFECTED MY LIFE by Peter Kuol

I began primary school in 1981 but in 1984 the enemy came and attacked the school compound and looted all the property. They abducted some children and wounded others. I escaped, but the people closed the school because of fear. So my father took me home as a cattle keeper, but in 1986 they raided our village and took all our cows. They killed many people including my uncle and his family. It happened at midnight. As I was hungry, I decided to leave my parents and look for safety in Ethiopia. I was sick and nobody came for me, I was alone, only a boy.

When we arrived in Ethiopia, I was taken to the military for training. At the end, we received guns and were sent to fight with the enemy. I fought on the front line for five years. Lastly I was wounded and was sent to Kenya for hospital treatment. I did not go back but went to Kakuma Refugee Camp to try to continue my studies. Since 1986, I have had no communication with my parents.

I decided to take a wife, so I confronted her parents. They agreed with me how much dowry I must pay. As I had no communication with my parents, they agreed to wait for the dowry. Now I have been married for five years and God has blessed us with two daughters.

In 2000 I became a preacher in the church. The church elders sent me to visit my home area, including my village. When I arrived, I found that all my relatives had been killed. There were no cattle. Only my mother had survived and she was suffering with nobody to support her.

When I went to my village, my in-laws were happy, because I would get money for my dowry. When I came back, my brother-in-law came to ask for the dowry. I told them I had nothing in my hand, that the cows were raided and the relatives were killed. They said, "Then we must take our daughter and the children back." So that is what they did.

Summary: The war stopped my education and killed my relatives. The cattle were taken, which led to my wife being taken by her parents, because of the dowry.

NOTE I was able to help Peter with money for his dowry, so his wife and daughters were returned to him. This sort of thing happens all too often.

It is because of the dowry system that some parents are still not interested in letting their girls 'waste their time' by going to school. I heard of one family who were offered a lower amount for their daughter because she had been educated! The men fear that if their wives go to school, they will not be willing to cook food for them! Therefore the girls only have to be trained to be good wives and mothers, who will also be obedient to their

207

husbands. I have seen this taken to its extreme when wives are expected to approach their husbands on their knees! One woman started to approach me on her knees, but I was horrified and rushed to pull her to her feet.

From their earliest years, girls are put to work. When a mother goes to collect water with her jerry can, the girl will be given a small jar and taught to carry it on her head. As she grows, the jar will increase in size until she too can carry a full jerry can. One day I decided to try out a jerry can and found that I could barely lift it from the ground, let alone carry it. I was amazed at the strength that the women developed. When writing about adjectives in one of my books, I enjoyed putting in the sentence, 'African women have strong arms'.

Collecting water is a tremendous chore for the women. In many areas they still have to collect it from the river or various pools, but these are often infected with bacteria of all sorts, including guinea worm. The UN and other NGOs (Non-Government Organisations) have dug a good number of wells, where water can be drawn using a simple pump called a 'donkey'. The women line up their jerry cans and then wait to take their turn, waiting in the hot sun. Some NGOs thought they should install more efficient but also more complex pumps but in a very short time the mechanisms failed and the pumps were no longer usable. Thankfully the 'donkey' is a simple mechanism, so it can be serviced by local people.

As well as carrying water, the girls have to collect firewood, tend the fire and also learn to cook, taking more and more of the responsibility as they mature. One of the tasks that always

208

falls to the older girls – and sometimes the boys too, is to care for their younger siblings. The baby will be strapped to the child's back and stay there for most of the day, while the mother works. The girls hand them back for breast-feeding, then resume their duties. If there are toddlers, the older children will also have to care for them. This means that during their childhood they can never run around and play or have fun. Some of the reading books I was using with the women's literacy classes often used the word *fun*. They would ask what it meant and I was hard put to it to find an explanation that they could understand.

As there are no pushchairs, babies have to be carried everywhere. In one area we saw women carrying their baby in a basket balanced on their heads, often without holding on!

The life of the pastor's wife is even more circumscribed. As well as doing all the above tasks, they had to clean the church, entertain visitors and organise the cultivation of the church plot of land, as well as their own.

While teaching in a Bible School in southern Sudan, we had the joy of helping our students to have fun. Each year we held a sports day for the women. We told them we were going to have fun so they must come prepared to run around. At first they were very hesitant and we had a tough job getting them to come to the field. Finally they appeared in dribs and drabs, looking apprehensive. We began by my teaching them how to do the Hokey-Cokey. They found it hilarious and begged to do it again. This was followed by a variety of races, including a needle-threading relay and a three-legged race.

Another sad result of the dowry system is that many husbands see their wives as their own possessions that they have bought. They therefore expect them to be obedient and hard-working, and wife-beating is far too common. In some tribes, particularly in the areas further from the Uganda and Kenya border, polygamy is still common. I realised this very clearly on one of my first teacher-training trips. When I was asking some students what was their ambition and one cheerfully said, "My ambition is to have ten wives and at least forty children." I was left almost speechless and soon found out that this aspiration was very wide-spread.

In later years, when working with the pastors and church leaders, I found that a different attitude was shown by most of the pastors. They often quoted to me the passage in Paul's letter to the young pastor Timothy where it says that *a pastor shall be the husband of one wife.* This could lead to thorny problems when a man had more than one wife before he became a Christian and also a church leader. Had this happened in the very early days of mission, the man would be told that he must send away all but his first wife, which had devastating effects on the other wives and their families. However things are different now and the man is usually allowed to keep all his wives, but in some cases only one is allowed to take Holy Communion. Thankfully, as the Christian message is being taught much more widely, the practice of polygamy is becoming much less common.

WOMEN'S EDUCATION

As I indicated earlier, in the last century few girls went to school. They were needed by their mothers to help with her heavy work load. It was not considered worthwhile for them to be educated, as they would be of greater value if they had become good housewives. Those who were lucky enough to be allowed to go to school rarely lasted as far as the top primary class. This was because as soon as they reached puberty, they were considered to be marriageable and their dowry would help their parents financially. Consequently the women's literacy rate was extremely low. It was thought that about 90% of women could not read. This led to a sense of low-esteem amongst the women. Happily attitudes are changing and more girls are getting a good education.

There is a real distinction between literacy and education. Many of the NGOs who were working in Sudan were staffed by highly literate, educated Kenyan or Ugandan women, as well as men. Those who had grown up in refugee camps had also encountered well educated women. This gave the Sudanese women a very low sense of self-esteem, as they could not read and write. In actual fact, many women were highly educated within their own culture. They could guide the young, lead groups of women within the church and carry on trade by barter or with money. Many of them were very skilled in a variety of crafts and others had an extensive knowledge of the uses of medicinal plants and herbs. Their disadvantage was only illiteracy. I remember Martha, the wife of one of the Sudanese Bishops, who was an excellent leader, although she could not read and write. Conversely there are people in the west who can read and write, but show little of the wisdom and maturity of these educated Sudanese women.

However, as time goes on, the Sudanese women are themselves realising the importance of literacy and are crying out for classes where they can learn to read and write. I had the great privilege of teaching many of them.

WEDDINGS

When I was chatting one evening with some of the pastors, I asked about their weddings. There was an uncomfortable silence and then Pastor John enlightened me. All the pastors had had a civil marriage, but not one of them had had a church wedding. According to their customs, nobody was allowed to marry in church until they had finished paying their dowry. The dowry has usually consisted of cattle. In Dinka areas, the prospective in-laws might demand two or three hundred cows! Poorer families would ask for fewer, but it is often a crippling debt. As none of the pastors I was teaching received any salary, none of them was able to pay off the debt. I could see the sadness in their faces as they explained this to me.

211

In my next prayer letter home, I asked people to 'Sponsor a Wedding'. Money flowed in, in a thrilling way and soon there was enough to pay off ten dowries, and also hold ten weddings. It could also cover the cost of the feast that would be needed, including roasting a bullock.

The next problem was that as none of these couples had been married in church, there was no-one to perform the ceremony. We contacted Rev John Moi of AIC-S, who had been married before the war and he was delighted to officiate. It is difficult to describe the great day. About one thousand people attended in the grounds of a local school. Shelters were erected to shade people from the sun and benches were put all round the sports field. I told the pastors very firmly that there was no need for a white dress for their wives, just nice African clothes.

The ten couples lined up outside the field and slowly filed in, to the accompaniment of drums and lots of ululating (shrill cries) by the women. When I said 'slowly' I really meant it. They took two steps forward and one step back and then paused before taking the next step. Their entry took nearly twenty-five minutes. Then a reverent hush fell over the crowd as the couples entered.

I was to be the registrar, but the problem was that we had no idea how to register the marriages. Someone unearthed a very old book, listing previous weddings. It recorded the occupation of most of the men as *peasant*. So all I could do was to invent some forms to be filled in and signed and also to produce some really fancy certificates.

One by one the couples came forward and made their vows. Putting on the ring was very important, so they managed it with their hands raised as high as they could, so everyone could witness the fact. When all the couples had been married, it was time for the giving of the wedding presents. People came dancing forward carrying their gifts – or leading in some rather reluctant goats. They received mattresses, cooking pots, washing up bowls and a great variety of other items. The celebrations and singing

and dancing went on for hours until finally we all stumbled back to our homes, exhausted but elated.

Our Sudanese brothers and sisters have suffered untold misery, but they know the presence and the joy of the Lord deep in their hearts and lives. Given a celebration such as this, there pours out from them a joy in the event itself, which mingled with their joy in the Lord produces a joy that must nearly be equal to the joy of the saints in heaven!

One of the pastors wrote an account of the great day. He and his wife were included next time.

A DAY TO REMEMBER BY Pastor Gama Joseph

September 7th 2002 was a great day in my life, when ten Africa Inland Church-Sudan pastors and elders celebrated their weddings. Since I came to Uganda as a refugee, I have never seen such a wedding. More than 1000 people attended the function. What a colourful day!

Do you know who organised the great day? I was dear Jan King, with the support of her friends in UK and Australia. I could not believe that it would be successful, due to the incursion of the Lord's Resistance Army in the area. Indeed, when we were fellowshipping, the rebels attacked and burned down houses

only eight kilometres away. Secondly, the amount of money used for the weddings was beyond the capacity

of the pastors and elders. They could not have done it without the support from friends. So God is great and lovely. Therefore, through Christ Jesus all things

213

were possible. The pastors could not believe that they would wed in church, as they still owed dowry money to their in-laws. This was all covered. If there can be another celebration like this one, my wife and I hope to be included.

The following year, more money came in so we were able to host nine more weddings.

I have previously mentioned Pastor William whose wife and children were taken by her parents. He has a very unusual testimony of how he became a Christian. He joined the army when 18 and was in charge of a small platoon. One day an old man was captured and the Commander thought he was a spy, so he ordered William to take the old man out and shoot him. William really did not want to do this, but was under orders. When he told him he had to shoot him, the old man asked if he could first read from the Bible and pray. Although William was not a Christian, he gladly agreed. The man read, *'Happy are those who die in the Lord'*. William was very moved by this, so taking a great risk he told the man to hide, and asked him where he would go when it became dark. The man mentioned a place, then William shot up into the air, for the Commander to hear.

That evening William was still very puzzled and went to find the man to ask how he could be so calm in the face of death and even happy to die. The man told William about Jesus, how he had died for him, so he too could know peace with God.

William ended his story saying, "I accepted Jesus then and there and now I am a pastor, showing other people how to find Jesus for themselves."

CHAPTER 16 NAIROBI AGAIN

POSTAL SERVICE

Living in Nairobi had its ups and downs. One of the 'downs' was the postal service. Coming from England, I was used to the postman dropping my post through my letter box, once or twice a day. In Nairobi it was very different. There were no postmen and no letter boxes. Instead everyone had a numbered Post Office Box and a key to access it. In the post offices there were rows of steel boxes, each carefully numbered. The clerk inside would place any letters inside the individual boxes and we could come along and open our box and extract the letters. This was not too much of a problem.

Collecting parcels or packages was an entirely different matter. To obtain them, we had to go into the centre of the city, to the central Post Office. The road leading to it was invariably blocked – sometimes the whole area was grid-locked, with nobody willing to let any other car into the traffic flow or even to go across to take a different exit. The drivers, getting more and more heated, would pretty well sit on their car horns, so the racket was ear-shattering. This could last up to an hour or more. Having negotiated the jam, there came the problem of finding a parking place. This also could take a long time.

So by the time you were actually in the building, the chances are that you were pretty hot and bothered. Then the fun began in earnest. You first had to register your presence, by presenting your notification of a package-to-collect to an official, who rubber-stamped the form. Next you had to register with the finance department, so that you could return there later to pay the fee for retrieving the package. At the other end of the hall was the counter where you queued up to get the package and open it under the eagle eye of an official. The contents would be inspected and a fee charged, with a new document stating the amount owing. Then it was back to the finance department to queue up to pay the charge and have the document rubber-stamped again, then back to the other counter to show the rubber stamp and collect the item. But that was not quite the end of it, for you had to report back to the first desk where you had registered, show all the documents and receive another rubber-stamp in order to be allowed to leave the building. Then back to your car, back to the traffic jam and finally home. It took on average two to two and a half hours to carry out the whole process!

One Christmas my friend Valerie had sent a parcel with lots of little presents inside, including a packet of flower seeds for my garden. Kenya does not allow seeds to be imported, so the official took away the whole parcel, re-wrapped it and sent the whole lot back to England. I begged to have the other items, but she was adamant that everything had to be returned. Having suffered the traffic jams and spent time queuing up for nothing, I went home very disappointed.

FOOD

As I have already explained, all the basic necessities could be bought at the local kiosks, while many western foods were available at the big shopping malls. Uchumi was our local supermarket. In the early years I used to bring items such as Marmite out with me, but over the years the stocks increased and soon a much wider selection was available, including Marmite.

There were many eating places, some serving Kenyan food and others specialising in foreign foods. When celebrating a birthday we usually went to the local Chinese restaurant, run by Chinese and serving delicious food that was not too expensive.

There were also very expensive restaurants, serving the wealthy Kenyans as well as the rich visitors from the west. The most exotic place, according to me, was the Carnivore. There was no way I could possibly afford to go there, but I was fortunate to have been invited there as guest, on two occasions. The Carnivore lives up to its name, for it specialises in meats of all kind. After we were seated, the waiter put up a small flag in the centre of the table. When I asked my host what it was for, he told me to wait and see. After ordering drinks, a waiter appeared with a large joint of beef, which he held up for us to see. He then held it up over each of our plates and swiftly carved a lovely slice, which

216

arrived with a satisfying plop on our plates. He was followed by another, offering zebra, then another with crocodile, another with hartebeest, then ostrich. This went on and on!. When we reached the stage when we could eat no more, we lowered our flag, to show that we were finally defeated, so no more waiters appeared. What a meal it had been! I enjoyed the experience so much, but I could not help thinking of our staff eating their 'airburgers' for their lunch.

Another of the joys of living in Nairobi was that there was the Nairobi Game Park, a Giraffe Centre and an Elephant Orphanage all within easy reach. As well as looking after orphaned baby elephants, there was a young rhino and several warthogs.

Once I had my Work Permit, I could go into these lovely places free of charge. In the Game Park, we could drive our own vehicles, with the aid of a map. There was a good variety of game, but not as much as in Masai Mara. I made several visits, seeing a lovely variety of deer including beautiful, graceful gazelles, tall stately giraffes and small herds of zebra. We occasionally saw lions and cheetah, but in all my visits to game parks in Africa, I never managed to see a leopard.

It was very important to keep your car windows shut in the parks, as monkeys and baboons could be very troublesome. Some friends visited a park for the first time in a hired vehicle. They decided to have a picnic in one of the designated picnic spots. They opened the car doors and the parents and two older children got out, leaving the youngest in the boot, beside the picnic. Two baboons leapt in through the open doors to get at the picnic, with the poor child cowering in the boot, screaming. The father could not at first find the right key to open the boot. When he finally got it opened, he grabbed a bunch of bananas and hurled it into the bushes. Fortunately the baboons chased after it and he was able to rescue his terrified daughter. In fact, it was usually impossible to have a picnic even in these designated areas, as the monkeys and baboons were always hanging around waiting for treats. One day we wanted to eat our picnic, so I suggested we drove down to the shore of a lake and ate it in the car. The only problem was that the food was in the boot. We had been given firm instructions not to get out of your vehicle while in the park, so I looked round very carefully and seeing nothing amiss got out and went round to the boot. Just as I opened it, the 'log' we had parked beside, got up and – fortunately for me – slipped into the lake. It was a huge crocodile!

NAIROBI GIRAFFE PARK

Another attraction in Nairobi was the Giraffe Park. I went with a Kenyan friend and her two small children. It is only when you are near these amazing animals that you become aware of just how tall they are! The next thing you notice is the length of their tongues! We were given some pellets to feed them with. You hold the pellets in the flat of your hand and out flicks the tongue and grabs it! A very strange sensation!

Giraffes grow to between 16 – 20 feet (5-6 metres) and their footprints are between 8 and 12 inches. They are the only animal that is born with horns. They love the leaves of the prickly acacia tree and feed from the topmost branches. The male and female usually eat from different parts of any tree, so as to avoid competition!

SHELDRICK ELEPHANT ORPHANAGE

The slaughter of elephants for their ivory is still all too common. The poachers have no concern as to whether they kill males or females, with the sad result that many babies are left as orphans, with no hope of survival in the wild, as they are breast-fed by their mother for four to six years. Without their mothers they would also suffer from sunburn, particularly on their ears. They always walk beside their mothers, using her bulk to shade them from the sun, until their skin becomes thick enough to withstand it. Even adults have some problems and can often be seen dousing themselves with water or throwing dust on to their bodies, for protection.

Sir David Sheldrick was a great conservationist in Kenya and founded one of the Kenyan National Parks. In 1977 he was instrumental in starting an elephant orphanage on the outskirts of Nairobi. Sadly he died after 6 months, but his wife Daphne, now Dame Daphne continued the work. The centre has been instrumental in rescuing over 100 baby elephants.

Elephants are very emotional animals and show real deep signs of grief. When a baby is found, word is sent quickly to the Centre who make arrangements to collect the small grieving calf. It is then adopted by one of the keepers, who now becomes wholly responsible for the baby. They will bottle feed it, play with it, hold an umbrella over it in the hot sun and then sleep beside it. During the night the baby will often feel with its trunk to make sure 'mother' has not abandoned him.

The centre is a wonderful place to visit and I was able to go several times, taking different friends. There are set times when they can be seen at play. There are also other orphans including wart hogs, various varieties of deer and the occasional baby rhino. The elephants are provided with huge rubber rings to play with and pools where they can wallow. The work goes on and people can adopt an elephant, via the David Sheldrick Trust, which can be found on the internet.

A DARKER SIDE OF NAIROBI

Nairobi is not a very safe city, with an extraordinarily high crime rate. The villains are armed with more and more sophisticated weapons, so the police often hold back from confronting them. Pickpockets abound, particularly in the craft markets that are frequented by foreigners.

Cars are often targeted, either being broken into or having the wheels removed. However hot the weather, you do not drive with a window open. As I had no Air-Conditioning I would be sweltering inside, but knew not to open one. A young friend was sitting in her car at a traffic light, speaking on her mobile phone (a rare commodity in those days) when a man appeared, grabbed the phone and tore it out of her hands, along with a large tuft of hair, which left her with no phone and blood coming out of her head.

Another lady I knew was sitting in her car, when a well-dressed man tried to speak to her through the window. Once he had fully got her attention, his colleague quickly opened the passenger door and grabbed her handbag, which she had left in full view. I very quickly learned the art of survival!

SABA SABA – 7/7

As well as being the capital of Kenya, Nairobi is a very important city, as it has attracted many international groups. They have headquarters all over the city, as well as a large number of Embassies and High Commissions. (High Commissions are for any countries that are members of the Commonwealth. They have a High Commissioner, rather than an Ambassador.) It has therefore become an international target.

In East Africa, the 7th July is known as Saba Saba Day. It is a day of significance in Kenya, since 1990. It was then that there were pro-democracy protests against the authoritarian government, which led to much bloodshed. Since then, on Saba Saba Day the country is on edge against further trouble

On the 7th of July 1998 I was working in the office in Nairobi, getting on with some writing. It so happened that on that that very morning, one of the staff had brought in his television to show some pictures during Devotions and the set was still there. As I continued to write, I was aware of a dull roar and a very slight shaking. We all looked at one another, wondering what it might be. Then the phone rang and a friend told us that a bomb had gone off in the centre of the city. We rushed and turned on

220

the television and could see all the graphic images of the devastation in the area, with constant re-runs of the explosion itself.

All the staff became worried about the safety of family and friends who were working in the city that day. There followed a spate of phone calls, as people checked up on each other. Happily none of our staff had lost any loved ones. Afterwards we heard several stories of friends who had intended to be in that area of Nairobi, but for one reason or another, had changed their plans. One was a cancelled hair appointment; another had a phone call asking for a favour before going to the city centre.

As more news trickled out, we heard that the attack had been aimed at the American Embassy and had been organised by Osama bin Laden, as a revenge attack on USA. Credit for the attack was also claimed by a splinter group, part of Egyptian Islamic Jihad. The plan had been for a suicide bomber to drive a truck laden with explosives up to the main gate of the American Embassy. The driver was then to force the guard to open the gate, and then drive right into the compound. Bravely, the guard refused and was shot. Unable to get into the compound, the driver ran off, which was not what had been expected of him by the planners. The damage and loss of life was less than it would have been if the truck had driven through the gate.

The final count of casualties was that 212 people had been killed, only 12 of whom were Americans. The remainder were innocent passers-by and workers in neighbouring buildings. The Embassy has been rebuilt in a more open area and is heavily protected against the possibility of any future attack. Since that time, the 7th day of the 7th month has been regarded with some trepidation in East Africa.

It is also very interesting that there was an attack on London on 7th July, 2005. Three bombs went off at about 8.50am on underground trains just outside Liverpool Street and Edgware Road stations, and on another travelling between King's Cross and Russell Square. The final explosion was around an hour later

221

on a double-decker bus in Tavistock Square, not far from King's Cross. Fifty two people were killed and over 700 were injured.

As I contemplate my years in Africa, I often return with great thanksgiving to the original verse which God gave to me before I set out on my adventures – "The Lord will guide you continually; He will satisfy your needs ..."

HI-JACK ATTEMPT

I was yet again aware of God's protection on another scary journey. I had spent Christmas with some friends near Eldoret and was driving back to have New Year at the Brackenhurst Conference Centre. It was the day after the Kenyan elections and there was almost no traffic on the roads, which gave one a rather eerie feeling. After a while, I saw a large car parked at the side of the road, with its bonnet open and felt sorry for the two men, as all the garages were shut. However, some time later, the same car passed me at some speed. "Good," I thought to myself. "They have got the car going again." However it did not turn to be very good for me.

I was a driving along a very winding part of the road, which snaked down into a valley. As I came round one of the bends, there was the same car, parked right across the road, with the two men in bobble hats waving me down. I had no doubt what their intentions were – a single woman on a deserted road. I realised that I had my camera, my laptop, my passport, my binoculars and some money with me. A prime target! As I drew near, I saw that at the rear end of the car there was a small amount of tarmac still showing with some foliage beside it. Although I knew that roads often ended with a one-foot drop at the side, I did not have time to think it out. My sense of outrage – as well as the thought of losing all my precious items, took over. I headed straight for the car – and was rewarded by shocked looks on the faces of the men – then I swerved suddenly, just skirting the back bumper of the car. Wonder of wonders, there was no sudden drop and I was through.

So far I had scarcely had time to feel afraid, but now the fear set in. I was not sure if they would follow me and try again, but was not going to stay around to find out. I continued down and down the winding road as fast as I dared. After just a few minutes, a mist came down, which forced me to slow down. I realised it would also have had the same effect on the other car. Down in the valley I remembered that there was an AIM guesthouse called Sunrise Acres, I made straight for it and tumbled out of the car. The couple there took me into their house, calmed me down and gave me a more than welcome cup of tea. They prayed for me and after some time I was able to resume a more leisurely journey to Brackenhurst. There, the New Year Conference was a lovely time, so I returned to Nairobi ready to resume my work with ACROSS.

CHAPTER 17 1999 to 2003

I had been very happy working with ACROSS. I was allowed to take only three trips a year into Sudan, but managed to fit in some to refugee camps as well. I was fully occupied with writing the series of English text books for the schools, as well as editing other materials in English. Then I received a bombshell. I was told I must leave ACROSS. I was devastated and at first very angry. It turned out that another ACROSS member of my age had just died. He had been suffering from both typhoid and dysentery and would not stop work to get treatment. There was of course great distress and sorrow. It was therefore decided that ACROSS must introduce an age limit of 65. So as I was 66, I must go, although I would be allowed to stay until June 2000. I felt this was very unfair, as I was always careful to treat any illnesses as soon as they had been diagnosed.

As I prayed about it, the Lord gave me a sense of peace. I was actually working on the final English text book in the series, so would soon need to find another occupation. I told some of my Sudanese and expat friends. Within a few weeks I was invited to work at Literacy and Evangelism, but this would have been a desk job in Nairobi, so I did not feel it was right for me. My heart still lay in Sudan.

During my time at ACROSS I had met many pastors from Africa Inland Church-Sudan (AIC-S) and had just received an invitation to attend the 50th anniversary of the church. There was a mistake on the invitation, so instead of being mere 'Mrs.' King, I was designated 'Bishop'. This caused some hilarity among us. However, I was happy to accept and found that some leaders from AIM UK would also be attending. While I was there, we were able to have good discussions between AIM and AIC, which concluded with my being invited to work full time with AIC-S. I had thought that my divorce could have been a stumbling block, as there are much stricter rules about divorcees in many African churches. However the AIC-S leaders all agreed that it was not an issue. The other problem that arose was concerning baptism. I was baptised into the Anglican Church as a baby and believe that that put me into a covenant relation with the church and consequently a full member. AIC-S practised full immersion for believers, so the question arose as to whether I would need to be re-baptised in order to work with the church. I wrote home to my vicar asking for advice. He very wisely left the decision with me. In spite of some misgivings I had reached a point when I felt I could take the step if necessary, but happily the church leaders were able to overlook the problem and accept me as I was.

Once I knew I had been accepted, I had some mixed emotions. I had some moments of doubt. Could I really take up a new ministry at 67 years old? Could I organise courses, provide materials and make travel plans without the logistics provided by ACROSS? At that time I was reading a devotional book and this is what I read – God will never give you an order that He will not Himself release His power to make it happen. This was a real encouragement.

However my other emotion was that I was overjoyed. All along I had hoped to work more closely with the Sudanese, rather than with a western organisation. I realised that on my first arrival, I was far too ignorant of Sudanese life and culture. I still had a long way to go, but during the four years at ACROSS I had learned a lot. I really praised God for this new step and was again reminded of my special verse in Isaiah 58:11 The Lord will guide you continually.

The next hurdle I had to get over was the matter of where to live. I had been living in an ACROSS house, but when I left I would have to find somewhere else to live, but still in Nairobi. I began to pray about it and then I met Shirley. She was an American who was working at Literacy and Evangelism and heard of my dilemma. (I wrote about her being arrested in Chapter 6.) She bounced up to me and said, "I've just rented a house and one of the rooms has your name on it!" I was delighted, until she added. "I have a cat. I hope you like cats." Oh dear, I thought. For many years I had had a phobia towards cats. If they came too near, my hands would sweat and the hairs on the back of my neck would tingle. However I had been challenged about this back in Croydon and after prayer I was now able to tolerate them, but I was not too keen. So I told Shirley I would come and vet the house – and the cat – whose name was Tinker.

The house was very nice, in a secure compound, within walking distance of the Sudan Literature Centre (SLC). At that time AIC-S did not have a proper office, but they were looking for one in the same area. The room she had offered me was very pleasant and I immediately felt at home in the house. Tinker then appeared and eyed me suspiciously. I eyed Tinker suspiciously. Then he walked by, ignoring me. I felt we could tolerate each other, so the agreement was made that I would move in at the end of June. Shirley was pleased and was willing to wait.

I continued to work at SLC. Later I was invited to go and talk in more detail to Bishop Andrew and the other church leaders about my future.

MORE TERRIBLE JOURNEYS

I still had a reputation for having rather disastrous journeys and sadly this continued to be true.

Another of my many memorable trips was to a remote village called Lohutok. It was the area of Sudan where the first AIM missionaries worked in the 1950s. The United Nations decided to hold a Peace Workshop for the often troublesome tribes in the area. I was invited to go, so Klero, the man in charge of health development for AIC, said we could go together, using the rather elderly church vehicle. It was a long and arduous journey. We reached Loki without trouble and then travelled in a UN convoy, accompanied by several soldiers, to the border between Kenya and Sudan. There the armed guard turned back and we were on our own. At first we drove on fairly smoothly, although there were a good number of 'Irish bridges' as described in chapter 13, on our trip to Kakuma Refugee Camp.

After plunging down into some of these bridges and accelerating up the other side, disaster struck. As we struggled up the far side, there was a resounding crack! We all got out and it was soon apparent that the main spring that held up the chassis

226

had snapped. What a dilemma for all of us. We had seen no other vehicle all day. The passengers were not to be beaten, so they raised the vehicle with the jack, until the two sides of the broken spring were end to end. Next they cut down a small tree and carved two lengths of wood. Then they lashed these wooden splints to the springs, using strips of inner wheel rubber and tied it tightly. I looked on, feeling rather uncertain that it would work – but it did. As there were no garages in the area, we drove on for the next two days, with the splints still in place!

By this time it was getting dark, so we had to find somewhere to sleep. Klero had friends in a nearby village, so off we went, arriving in the dark. We were welcomed with typical Sudanese hospitality. Everyone was delighted to see long-lost friends and they talked – and talked and talked. After a couple of hours, I was feeling pretty weary and rather hungry. They finally produced a little food from their slender resources, then a couple of men appeared carrying rolled up palm leaf mats and laid them out on the ground. "Help!" I thought to myself. "Can I possibly sleep on the hard ground, among all these men?"

However, help was at hand! A man showed me to a tall, square, strongly -built building. He told me it had been built by the British in the 1980s. He led me inside and proudly showed me a bed, then closed the door and left me in total darkness. Happily I had my torch and had a look around. There was a homemade bed with a thin mattress, but no mosquito net and it was pitch dark. A mosquito net is essential, not only to keep out mosquitoes, but also any other flying or crawling creature that might like a taste of human blood – particularly from a white person whose skin is very thin. As there was no other option, I lay down, fully clothed with my sunhat over my face and prayed for protection. Before I had even finished my prayer, I was fast asleep. The next morning I awoke refreshed and without even one bite on my body. How I praised the Lord!

The local Commander had heard of our arrival. Visitors were always welcomed. with typical Sudanese hospitality, but also with a desire for news. It is hard to realise that in the villages there are no newspapers or magazines of any sort. Most people have radios and can hear CNN and BBC World News, but they know nothing of what is going on in other parts of their area. The Commander was a well-educated man, with good English. He offered to show me around his village and I willingly accepted. I had my video camera with me and so was able to get some good pictures. What I saw made me want to cry. With great sadness, he told me how the Sudan Army had attacked the village and I could see it for myself. There had been a good school and a hospital. Both had been pulled down and all the contents taken away. Houses had been burnt and one of the wells had been filled with rubble. He also told me that he had evidence that they had used chemicals in a bombing attack and offered to introduce me to some of the victims. There was no time for that, but I was overcome by the horror of it all, the senselessness of treating civilians in such a way. I went away with a heavy heart.

Later we were on our way again, with the temporary repair still in place. It would be some days before it could be repaired and the rubber strips still held it together. We arrived at Lohutok, where I was given a good bed and – thankfully – a mosquito net.

The Peace Conference was run by a group from the United Nations and was well-received. Most of it was translated into English, so I was able to follow it. In some ways the speakers were 'speaking to the converted', as the area had not been too much troubled by the war and all were keen for peace. The major issue was cattle-rustling. As soon as that topic was announced, the atmosphere changed dramatically, with the different groups immediately blaming the others. It was a sort of microcosm of the bigger issues. The major problems, as ever, were people with long memories of past conflicts and an inability to forgive.

The journey back was very different, as I was offered a place in the UN vehicle, accompanied by an armed guard, who followed our vehicle in their open sided truck.. All went well, until suddenly the guards jumped to their feet and pointed their guns into the undergrowth. We were all about to fling ourselves on the floor, when the driver realised that they had seen an antelope and were looking for a welcome addition to their evening meal.

228

FINAL TRIP WITH ACROSS

While I had been working with ACROSS, I was able to fly into distant areas to teach. However, I realised that once I was with AIC-S this would no longer be possible, as there were no funds to cover such trips. I would be confined to working in refugee camps or in locations that could be reached by a vehicle.

My last trip with ACROSS was good, with no threats and I enjoyed the teaching. Two things stood out. The first was a visit to a cattle camp. When children in the major tribes of cattle-keepers like the Dinka and Nuer grow up, they will spend some time in the cattle camp. They are sent at the age of five or six and have to learn to stand on their own feet. Each one is given a cow to look after. Every morning they take it out to look for pasture, which can be extremely challenging in the time of drought. During the day, they collect and dry the dung. In the evening they return to the camp. The cows know their own 'peg' where they will be tethered, and return there, without any problem. This is not true of the bull! The group then burn the dung on a slow fire, creating smoke, which keeps the mosquitoes and tsetse flies away. Then they sing wonderful cattle songs in the evening. Many of these children never return to their parents and never receive any education. However, I am told that things are changing and parents are realising the value to themselves in their old age, if their children are educated and can get good jobs.

The second excitement was a day of Wrestling. This was the national sport of the area and was a very special event. I asked the students to write an account of the day. Here is their version of the day's events.

On the afternoon of the Wrestling Match, about 2000 people came streaming into Panyagor from all directions. They came along, singing, dancing and beating drums. For next day was scheduled for a wrestling match.

Early next morning, some of the youth decorated their best bulls with pieces of coloured cloth, tied big bells around their necks and paraded them proudly around the arena. Each of the teams, with their supporters, ran

229

towards the church, carrying flags and waving cloths and branches. Inside the church, they prayed that they would wrestle fairly and keep the rules. They also prayed that the weather would be cool. As they prayed, a cloud came over the sun and it remained cool all day. The Area Commissioner was present, as well as the Commander and other guests. They were seated under an awning. The crowd was estimated to be about 6,000.

Here are three of our students, who took part in the wrestling, dressed in bright colours. They made a colourful picture, with ladies in bright  dresses and many people with coloured umbrellas they waved wildly when the owner's team won a round.

The first round was between two famous wrestlers from the past, each of them showing great strength. The round ended in a draw. Next came the first serious round, for heavy weights. Our man from Panyagor showed great skill and finally put down his opponent. All his supporters erupted with joy. They rushed on to the field singing, dancing and waving flags and umbrellas. Others were blowing very long cattle horns, while some older men ran round the edge of the field with pumpkin leaves around their shoulders and singing songs of victory. This was followed by rounds for different weights. By the end of the afternoon the scores were equal, so everyone went home feeling happy!

Among the spectators was a man who had stepped on a landmine and had had a leg amputated. He joined in all the fun, waving his yellow umbrella.

"I cannot be the best wrestler," he said, "but I can be the best supporter."

Here are the same three, who had taken part, back in class again next day.

MY NEW JOB WITH AIC-SUDAN

The church wanted me to do four jobs! I was to be the Bishop's assistant, be Information Officer, Training Officer and oversee Women's Work. I agreed to take on the first three, but not Women's Work, which was being handled by Anna Wawa, the Bishop's wife. I was also to write reports and project proposals. The latter was something I knew nothing about. 'To my great delight, a notice came round inviting personnel to a 2-day Workshop on writing reports and project proposals. Once again I could see God's hand in this.

Once I had settled in, I found I was to be a jack-of-all-trades. The job as Information Officer was the most interesting and the most demanding. I discovered that when the missionaries came out of Sudan in 1989, there were just ten AIC churches. My job was to try to find out how many there were in 2000. As there is no postal service and no telephone or email, this was a daunting task. I prepared a simple questionnaire, asking the name of the church, the number of believers, the name of the pastor, etc. and printed a large number – then I waited. The Lord was good, because we had a succession of visitors from all parts of the area. Each went away with some questionnaires and then came the long wait. It took several months, but finally the replies trickled in. We found there were 118 churches, 32 of which were in the Khartoum area. This was wonderful news.

231

In 2011, Sudan became two countries. As I write in 2015, almost all of the 32 churches in Sudan (in the North) have been bulldozed, burnt down or closed. However, those in South Sudan are flourishing, with many new ones opening. As there was at that time next to no communication between most of the churches, I produced a 'Newslink', with a message on the front from Bishop Andrew and lots of information on the other pages. These again were distributed by our visitors to the office.

Having left ACROSS, where everyone used Ventura Publisher, I was now on my own with a new laptop I had brought with me from the UK. Now I had to learn Microsoft Word. This proved to be much easier than Ventura. However, when I wanted to be more ambitious and make fancy Marriage Certificates, I needed to use MS Publisher, which was already installed. I managed reasonably well, but when I embarked on writing small booklets, I got myself into terrible muddles and lots of frustration. Then God sent Caroline!

A lady called Caroline had come from Australia, short term to help a project of CMS (Church Missionary Society). She moved in with our friend next door. When I asked her what she had been doing back in Australia, she told me that she used to teach Microsoft Word and Publisher. My heart began to sing! How I praised God. The next problem was when she could find time to come to the office to teach me. That was sorted out in a remarkable way. At that time we were suffering from power cuts in Nairobi. It was a matter of four hours on and four hours off. It so happened that when the CMS office was off, my office was on! So she helped me to get the scanner working and taught me a good deal about Word and Publisher. After Caroline went home, I managed pretty well and produced some small booklets for the Women of the Good News and a simple Newslink, but then I hit another seemingly impossible problem - and Caroline came back! I do praise God for so many such co-incidences, or I might call them God-instances.

The rest of my time was spent as a sort of personal assistant to Bishop Andrew, preparing project proposals, to raise money, creating certificates for Baptism and Marriage, translating simple handbooks for the women, with a helper. As I had a car, I was also employed as unofficial taxi-driver for the Bishop. This could pose problems. One day he had a very important appointment with a German NGO, hoping that they could help to finance one of our projects, so he asked me to drive him there. It had been raining for several days and the road was very rough. At one point there was a sort of ford, where the road dipped down steeply, across a small water course, with a steep drop on one side and then up the other side. As we approached, we could see that the water course had become a torrent. There were cars lined up on either side, hoping it would subside. We joined the queue. After some time a big vehicle managed to cross and later the middle-sized cars followed. Mine was a very small Toyota Starlet. I asked Bishop Andrew what to do. He told me to go. It was certainly exciting, with waves nearly up to the windows, but we made it.

I continued with the literacy work in Nairobi and travelled into Sudan or the refugee camps five or six times a year. I loved my work, apart from financial problems. Our endless flow of visitors mostly came with one need – money for their churches. Sadly, we had very little, so things got rather fraught at times. One day a young man called Edward came in demanding money to go to an expensive Bible School. There was no money. When he heard this, he threatened to lock us out of the office. Next morning we found he had done just that, and we couldn't enter, so we each had to work at home. This went on for four days, with Edward becoming more and more aggressive – not the typical Bible student! Somehow some money was raised and he went for training. As soon he had graduated, he disappeared and never fulfilled his role as pastor.

My worst financial nightmare came true when a German group sent $7000 US for a particular project. I had to give them my personal assurance that it would go to the correct project. Unfortunately, when the money arrived, I was away in a refugee camp,. As soon as I got back, as you may have guessed, most of the money had been used for other purposes – and with no receipts of any sort. I was frantic. Somehow we managed to raise

233

some other money and I used all of my own that I could spare, until I was able to send it to the correct location.

TRAINING COURSE IN ADJUMANI REFUGEE CAMP

I accepted the job as Training Officer for Africa Inland Church-Sudan with great pleasure. While with ACROSS, I could only make three trips a year, but now I was free to go more often. I was approached by Dr. Ron Holcomb, an American member of AIM. He was planning to hold training sessions for AIC-S pastors in Adjumani, the Refugee Camp where I had taught the Christian Writers' Workshop. He was looking for an English Teacher. I was more than happy to work with him. We went twice a year for the next few years.

Ron taught Theology and I taught English to the students and also invited other church members to come for English teaching. One joy was being able to take Devotions. One joyful memory concerned a student called Abraham. Most of our students came from smaller tribes, living towards the Uganda border, but Abraham was a Dinka, from the biggest and most warlike tribe. He was rather militaristic and often outspoken. In conversation we touched on homosexuality. I asked if it was common in his tribe. He assured me that it didn't exist, but then checked himself and said that there had been one case of it. I asked him how it was handled. "Oh, we killed them," he replied rather nonchalantly. I was appalled and left speechless, which from hindsight was just as well, as there are some topics that must be left alone by outsiders to any culture.

One morning I was leading Devotions and telling a story about Moses. When the people had sinned, God sent poisonous snakes into the camp. They prayed to God to help them, so He told Moses to set up a pole and fix a bronze snake on it. Whoever had the faith to look at the snake was healed. I showed a model of the pole with a snake on it. Then I compared it to Jesus, who was also put on a pole (I held up a cross). Anyone who has the faith to look to Jesus would be saved. Most of the students were Christians and had heard the story already. I noticed a rather pensive look on Abraham's face and he slipped out of the classroom. Once I had finished, I went to find him and had the great privilege of leading him to the Lord. He told me afterwards that he had been going to church for some years, but had never really heard that Jesus had died for him personally and that he had to respond personally.

During class one day, Pastor Gama received a message that his two-year old son was very sick. He hurried home, but before he arrived the elders had knocked out two teeth and made a two inch cut on his back, to let out the evil. He boy recovered, but this sort of thing was far too common, due to cultural rites.

On a lighter note, Bishop Andrew Wawa came with us to Adjumani, so on Sunday we managed to hire a vehicle so he could visit some of the AIC-S churches. At the first church the people were waiting outside the village and welcomed us enthusiastically, clinging on to the vehicle to get a free ride. Andrew preached a sermon and I greeted the church in my halting southern Arabic. They then insisted we should remain and eat with them. As there were three more churches to visit, we left as soon as we had eaten a fairly hearty meal. The people at the next church were also waiting eagerly so we repeated the same pattern as before – including eating yet another hearty meal. Time was getting on and we still had two churches to visit. At the next church, the people had been waiting for a very long time, so we had to repeat the same programme – including yet more food. It is rude not to eat what is given, but by then I had to slip a lot of my ugali (thick maize porridge) on to a friendly pastor's plate.

By then it was nearly dark, but we knew that there was still one more church to visit. I was wondering how on earth we could eat yet more food! Thankfully this church only produced tea and a piece of cake! We travelled back to our base with joyful hearts, having been so encouraged to see so many believers who had been so delighted to have a visit from the Bishop – and from a mzungu (white person).

My next visit to Adjumani started off very badly. It was a very special trip, as we were holding nine more weddings as well

235

as holding another course. Three days before I was to leave, I tripped over Tinker the cat as I was coming off the bottom stair and hurt my foot. I went off to the Office as usual, but was aware that the pain was getting worse. There is no Health Service of course, but there is an Imaging Services Centre, so off I went to have an X-ray. This is so easy, with no necessity of a note from the doctor, but just an X-ray on request. When it was developed it was obvious that I had a long crack, down the length of my fifth metatarsal. I asked the radiologist what I should do about it. He pointed out that there was an orthopaedic surgeon just across the road.

I was ushered straight in and we looked at the X-ray. "It is broken" he said, rather obviously. I agreed that it was indeed broken and asked what I could do, explaining that I was due to travel soon. He replied that I could have it plastered or just have it taped to the next toe and allow it to heal. He said that the second option would be more painful but was the better one if I could bear the pain. I realised that if I wanted to travel next day, I could not do it if I had a plaster, so he taped it up for me.

I prayed about the situation and decided I would still go. When I awoke next morning, I found it was a good bit better already, so off I went. The wedding went off with all the usual excitement and celebration. In my diary I wrote, "Yom ta farah!" (A day of joy) The course was to be held at a good distance from where we were staying. Although I had managed the journey and the weddings, my foot was still painful. So I had to travel boda-boda, side-saddle, very uncomfortably on the back of a bicycle, over bumpy roads. This is a means of transport I most certainly do not recommend. By the end of week I was thankfully able to walk far enough.

As Dr. Ron and I were walking one day, a long, slim snake passed between us, so quickly that it seemed to be flying. On another day, we saw the track of a snake in the dust – it was a good four inches (20 cms) across. A local driver told us his friend had been travelling with his window open and a huge cobra put its head through the window and tried to bite him! Happily we did not see any more, but we certainly went carefully and never put our hands into a drawer or cupboard without first having a good look! In my diary one day I wrote, 'Today Gama killed eight spiders in the latrine!'

BICYCLES

One of the main problems for the Sudanese living in Adjumani was travel. The camp was divided into four main areas, with dozens of villages in each. There were 19 different AIC-S churches spread widely throughout the area. Vehicles could be hired, but the cost was prohibitive for most refugees. Rev John, who was the District Chairman, hoped to visit each of the churches at least twice a year, but they could be 25 Km apart. At that time I had a video camera, so I recorded him explaining his problem. On returning to UK I was able to show the video to various groups. We soon had enough to buy a small motorbike, which was a tremendous blessing. Next I started a 'Bicycles for Pastors' programme and over the years was able to give over 20 bicycles. This was such a blessing to the churches.

In a country with very little in the way of transportation, there was always the danger of over loading the bicycles. People used them to carry huge bags of their harvest or two or even three jerry cans of water on them, putting them under too great a strain. Then there was the problem of punctures. I soon realised that when we gave a bicycle, we also had to give money for spare tyres and other spare parts.

HERESY

One of the saddest things that happened in Adjumani was the arrival of a heretical sect. A group arrived and infiltrated into the churches, explaining that they belonged to a different denomination, very similar to AIC. If any pastor decided to join them, they would receive $100 a month salary. As the pastors at that time were unpaid, it was a huge temptation. To add to this, they said they would give them a mobile phone. These had only recently appeared in the area. The temptation was just too great and fourteen of the pastors joined the sect. Some took their whole church with them. Others caused their churches to split. It was a

237

matter of great sadness for the Bishop and church leaders. Even Rev John, the District Chairman became a member and went around the camp on the motorbike we had given him, enlisting more members.

Needless to say, neither the phones nor the salaries appeared. It transpired that the sect was actually part of the Unification Church, or Moonies. Over the next two or three years almost all the churches came back to AIC. I was very moved to see how those who had remained faithful to AIC were very gracious in allowing them to come back as full members after a probation period. Only the District Chairman was refused membership, for leading so many people astray. However after I had retired, I heard that he had finally been forgiven, but stripped of his position.

I was struck by the way the churches behaved when there were problems. They were always keen to forgive when people had gone astray. However, they were just as ready to face people who were not living morally. The pastor would confront them and call them to repent. If they agreed, they would be disciplined by being excluded from the church for a set period and then would be warmly welcomed back 'into the fold'. They also took seriously Jesus' command not to take one another to court but to settle the matter amongst themselves. There was an openness we do not usually know in the west.

SHORT MEMORIES FROM MY DIARIES

A number of small things happened, which I would like to record:

"Today Beatrice found a snake in her tukul. She smoked it out and killed it. Rather her than me!"

"After weeks of negotiations and heavy import dues, our container of drugs arrived from America. Sadly many are very near their sell-by date and there is nothing for tropical diseases. What a disappointment."

"On our flight we were with a different airline. The pilot started to take oxygen, so we all became extremely nervous. Afterwards he told us that after so many hours, pilots must take oxygen as a matter of course. We wished he had told us first!"

"Today I had to have my finger prints taken to put on my 'Alien's Card! Am I really an alien?

"I've had an interview with our new AIM Unit Leader. He asked me what I was doing and was upset because I don't fit in with his paradigm. What's a paradigm?"

"An email came from Shirley asking me to take the cat to the vet. Help! I can't handle cats. Laura is staying with me, so she got the cat but could not put her in the cat-box. The cat went mad! Later Laura managed to pick it up again, so I held a pillow case open and she dropped it in and I tied it up with string! It squirmed all the way to the vet's. The vet was highly amused, treated the cat and popped it back in the cat-box without any trouble. I drove home, mightily relieved!"

"I've tried out a different anti-malarial called Larium. Now I feel nauseous and all my joints are swollen. Hopefully it will pass after a week. (The symptoms did go, but only after seven days.)"

Written while on holiday in Kakamega Rainforest: "We were bird-watching, trying to see the very rare Great Blue Turaco. The guide pointed out where to look. Caroline managed to see it. I was so excited I couldn't keep the binoculars still and missed it!"

"Today was a very difficult day. We suspected our house-girl was stealing things. I had left a pile of clothes belonging to a friend in the house and came home unexpectedly. I went straight

239

to the pile and as it was a good deal smaller than before, I asked her about it. As she stood up, something fell to her knees. She was wearing several items below her normal work clothes. I had no option but to sack her. She cried – and I nearly did, too, as I felt sorry for her."

"Today Noel left an upstairs window open in his study, with his door locked. It is a perfectly straight wall, but some monkeys somehow got in. Their house-girl heard the noise, but could not get it. She got the gate guard to bring a ladder and he chased them out. When Noel came back he saw a state of devastation. They had played with all his computer floppy discs. Some were OK, but they had bitten off all the labels. It was a good reminder to keep everything shut."

"On holiday in Mombasa, I left a sliding door slightly open. When we got back we found footprints of two baboons and lots of screwed up sweet papers on the floor – but no sweets! We were lucky, as it could have been a lot worse, particularly if the baboons were still there."

"More monkey business!. As we were having a cup of tea at the hotel, we saw a monkey grab the sliver sugar basin from the next table and scamper up on to the roof. There he shared it with his pals. They all had a good finger-licking time. Evidently the restaurant waiters have to go up on the roof regularly when they are running short of sugar basins. It is a great game for monkeys – but not so popular with the staff!"

Holidays are great, but there was always work waiting for me back in Nairobi and Sudan.

CHAPTER 18 EMMANUEL CHRISTIAN TRAINING CENTRE

My last few years in Sudan were centred on Emmanuel Christian Training Centre (ECTC). This was a project run by Open Doors. Open Doors is an international body working with Christians who are suffering from the effects of persecution. It has recently been handed over to the Sudanese staff.

In 2001, I was invited by George William of Open Doors to teach in a new college he was opening near Yei, in southern Sudan. I was very pleased to have been asked and readily accepted. George arranged to meet me in Arua, Northern Uganda and drive me to Yei, near the borders with Uganda and Democratic Republic of Congo. The flight to Arua was fine and next day George collected me as planned. The journey was pretty hair-raising. Once out of Uganda, the road, if it could be given such a name, deteriorated with every few miles we went. Some of

it was over sheer rock, but most of it meant negotiating thick red mud. There are two main ways of driving on these roads. The usual one is to go a little slowly, avoiding all the worst bumps and potholes. George belonged to the other school of thought, which was to go at great speed, over the top of all the obstacles. We bumped and bounced and swerved and spun for miles and miles. It took several hours, but you can imagine how relieved I was when we finally arrived in Yei.

Our accommodation was run by the Yei Women's Empowerment Group. This was started by some very enterprising women. They wanted to get on in life, so they began by shovelling gravel out of the river bed and selling it to Non-

Government Organisations (NGOs), who were busy building various structures. With their first profit they bought seeds and planted vegetables. It was a good harvest that year, so they made quite a lot of money. They were soon able to buy a plot of land. Gradually the plot was increased. Next they built a series of tukuls as a hotel. By the time we arrived, they had also built a large lecture hall.

As this was the first term for the college, there was only one year-group, of 22 pastors. The majority of them were from the Africa Inland Church-Sudan (AIC-S). This was because George William had previously been working with them in their villages. Rather than him travelling and teaching each group in their home areas, he decided to bring them together in Yei.

As it was a Bible School, most of the teaching was from the Bible, but they had one good session of English every day, which was where I fitted in. As this did not occupy me for the rest of the day, I quickly found a group of people wanting to improve their English, so we began daily lessons. For the rest of the time I had the privilege of attending the Bible teaching given by George William and Oliver Soma, a Sudanese pastor. I was greatly blessed by their teaching.

One other memory from that first course happened on a very hot and windy day. Someone in a nearby village had foolishly lit a fire. The wind had swept it through the village, just across the river. We watched with horror as it very quickly set fire to the thatched roofs of several tukuls, before it was finally put out. The local people at once went to find the culprit and might well have lynched him, had not the chief quickly stepped in. Fire was a very real danger, as I was later to find out

Open Doors was looking for a plot in Sudan, where they could develop the work. While George William was travelling from Maridi to Yei, he spotted some old, but well-built structures near the road side, and stopped to investigate. They turned out to be buildings built by ACROSS to house refugees from Uganda in the 1970s during the time of Idi Amin, the violent President of Uganda. George spoke to ACROSS, who were happy to have the buildings used for a Bible School. There then began lengthy negotiations with the local tribal Chief. After many meetings, the Chief made available a large tract of land, with space for the Bible School and also for a home farm, where vegetables could be grown to feed the students. Each student was also given a plot on their arrival. I was amazed to see that most of them had a good harvest of beans before the 12 week term ended.

In 2002 we were able to move into the new site, with just 4 tukuls for staff and eight for all of the students. Building went on steadily and by 2004 we had three year groups of students. The first graduation was in 2004 and was a tremendous time of celebration. All the local chiefs, commanders and commissioners were invited. Open Doors representatives came, some all the way from South Africa. George managed to obtain a set of splendid gowns for the 22 graduates. The Sudanese certainly know how to rejoice! Everyone waved flags or small branches. The men cheered and the women ululated, making their traditional sounds of joy. As each student came forward for his Diploma, any family members and friends rushed forward, cheering and dancing.

I again asked the men to write about their experiences during the war. Here is another moving story.

HOW THE WAR CHANGED MY LIFE by John Buol

Here is a brief history about how the war changed my life. The longest African war has dramatically changed my life in many ways. Since this war kicked off in 1983, the Sudan civil War has affected the lives of many.

I attended Primary School in 1983, but the onset of war forced me to seek safety back in my village. I was totally absorbed

243

and adapted to remote life. From 1983 until 1987 I spent time with my parents, but in that year I was taken to Ethiopia for reasons best known to my parents. On the way there, I covered many hundreds of miles on foot, from my homeland to Ethiopia. In this way I learned to cover long distances. It was during the rainy season, which made the journey so difficult because of the accumulation of mud on the clay soil. Many children I was walking with fell sick. As time went on, death took the upper hand, claiming many lives. For this reason, fear was created in me, causing many thoughts of what to do. But no matter how terrible it was, I continued my journey.

In November I reached a place called Panyudu in Ethiopia, where many of us were settled as refugees. It was a terrible situation, because there was no food. So I trained myself to feed from the leaves of edible trees. To make matters worse, I was attacked by measles, which was the cause of many deaths in the camp.

In the course of my suffering, I observed something missing in my life and that was the Word of God. Many of my age-mates told me to believe, but I was strongly rooted in my traditions. After many sufferings, I came to acknowledge Jesus Christ as my Saviour.

In 1999, when the government of Mengistu was overthrown, I escaped back to Sudan, covering many hundreds of miles. In the course of my movements, I walked bare-footed.

The most bitter part of the war in my life was the death of my parents in 1992 and 1993, which gave me home leadership at the earliest age.

I came to a refugee camp in Uganda in 1994, where I finally resumed my studies, after seven years of hardship.

TRAINING OF PASTORS' WIVES

This training was at first only for men. However things were going to change. The students had seen that I, a mere woman, was educated and able to teach. They had questioned me carefully about various issues, the main one being – "Did you still cook for your husband?" I realised that this was a big issue. If their wives were educated, would they still be good housewives? I assured

them that I did continue to cook for my husband and family. They talked among themselves and then came to a remarkably un-Sudanese conclusion. They asked if next year their wives could come for training. We were thrilled with their request and assured them that we could indeed accommodate their wives. They even agreed that they would stay at home while their wives were away and look after the family. This was yet another astonishing offer in spite of their normal culture.

Next year we received our first intake of pastors' wives. What a colourful picture they made! It was quite an achievement for them to leave their homes and travel without their husbands, often on the back of a lorry. Most of them had babies or toddlers with them, but somehow they made it. It took some time for them to settle down.

We offered several courses, such as Old Testament Study, New Testament Study, The Role of a Pastor's Wife, Health and Hygiene in the Home. This latter was extremely important as many people still had not dug a latrine, but just used the bushes around their compounds. They had no concept of water-borne diseases and often drank from bug-infested pools or streams. These courses were conducted in Juba Arabic, the local trade language.

Out of the first intake, only one lady was able to read. A few had a smattering of English, but the rest were totally illiterate. So here was my new task – teaching literacy. Happily I had been able to attend a course in Nairobi, but now I was faced with a big group of very mixed ability and a variety of languages. We began

245

with oral English and this was as far as many of them managed to achieve. We sang simple English songs and played simple games. I took out some jigsaws from the Early Learning Centre, which intrigued them. Some got the idea, whereas others just tried to push the pieces into any available space. When I next came home, I mentioned this to my young grandson Ben. He had been given a jigsaw book, with five jigsaws of Bible stories and insisted that I should take them with me the following year. I was able to bring him back a photo of the ladies working on them.

We worked on the alphabet, letter by letter, beginning with C. I had prepared a large number of flash cards, with clear pictures of a variety objects known to them. As I showed a picture of a cow, they would chant, C for cow two or three times, C for cat and so on.

Some of the ladies got the idea, but others just smiled happily and joined in where they could. It was slow work. After some time, I put three letters on the board, close to each other p o t. Most of them just stared at them, but one bright spark shouted out, "pot". I was thrilled and soon several of them got the idea. We also taught them how to write. I began with c, as it was the right shape to make into a then o then d and g.(We did not bother with q).

Several had never held a pencil, so it was yet another challenge. By the end of the course, each of them was able to write their own name, which to them was such an achievement. They could hold their heads up high because they could now sign a document, rather than a traditional X.

There was also a Peacemakers' Programme. In this, the women learned to honour God by making peace with one another, no matter which tribe they belonged to, and to love one another as sisters in the Lord. It was not always an easy lesson for some.

Health and Hygiene was a very important course for the women. We had touched on the importance of digging latrines with the men, but little was done. Once the women realised how crucial a latrine could be for health, they made sure that they were dug in their own compounds and then spread the word through women's groups. The same was true of the vital importance of clean drinking water. They were encouraged to boil their water and also taught other ways of filtering water before drinking. The result was a decrease in sickness and infant mortality in their families. The women continued to spread the word in their families and communities. It underlines the truth of the saying that is found both in the west and in Africa which states, "If you teach a man, you teach an individual. If you teach a woman, you teach a nation".

Reproduction and birth control was another topic that was taught. Heather, a midwife who was working in Uganda, was invited to run the course. At her first session, she put up some pictures to help her to explain. When the women saw the pictures, some of them fled out of the room, being unable even to look at them. She gradually got them back in and began to teach. Sex takes place in the dark and the subject is taboo in many tribes, so Heather had to teach very sensitively. Gradually she gained the women's confidence, particularly when she explained that they could have some sort of control over the number of children they produced. This was a matter of huge importance to them, as many of them give birth to children year after year and wear themselves out in the process. Heather explained about the monthly cycle and that some days in the cycle were safe, but on other days they were very fertile. They were delighted to realise that they might be able to have some control in the matter.

Meanwhile, the men had heard about this and they also wanted to know. This was a great encouragement. So Heather was invited to address all the men one morning. She was understandably rather nervous, but the unhappiest man of all was the one who would have to translate her talk. This meant that he would have to utter words that were never spoken in public, such as 'sex' and 'intercourse'. If very black people could blush he would certainly have done so!

The men were fascinated by the talk and wanted to hear more about it. It so happened that I was due to teach English to each of the year groups, so the English lesson turned out to be a lesson about birth control. They soon got the idea of the monthly cycle. Then I asked them about how their different tribes dealt with the subject. One man said that in his tribe, pregnant women were not allowed milk, in case the baby became too fat to be born. Another said that in his tribe, they were not allowed fish or eggs, another said they could not eat meat in case the baby looked like a bull. When I explained that the pregnant women needed these foods, they looked uncertain. On inquiring, I found that in the various tribes it is the grandmothers who are in control on childbirth and they doubted if anything that a man said would be accepted by them if it went against the tribal practices. It seems that the grandmothers wield great power. Female Genital Mutilation is rare in South Sudan, but where it does occur, it is again the grandmothers who are determined that it must be done. The hope is that when the current women who are being taught about these matters become grandmothers, things might change for the better.

In the afternoons the women had craft sessions, such as sewing, embroidery, crochet, bead-making and tie-dye. One of my most challenging afternoons was when the craft teacher was sick and I was asked to teach 18 women how to knit. None of them even knew how to cast on, so I was feverishly trying to get 18 items started and then show them the stitches. It was not easy, the results were pretty disastrous and I vowed never again to take on such a challenge!

At the beginning of the third year, the wives were taught how to run a small business. This could be a life-changing project for them. Most of the pastors whom I taught were very poor and lived by subsistence farming. If the crops failed, they might starve. If they were sick, they could not afford any medicines. So if the wives could earn money for their families, this could revolutionise their lives.

I had been given gifts of money to support this project. A tutor taught them about micro-finance and suggested various small businesses they might try. The ladies then had to write a project proposal, explaining their plan and showing how they might run it, using the small amount of money they would be given. As it can be imagined, this posed a great challenge for

248

these semi-literate ladies. However with the help of some of the men from their own tribes, they came up with their ideas. Some were clearly unworkable, like selling furniture. The most popular were rearing goats or chickens, selling small quantities of basic foodstuffs or setting up a roadside tea stall.

Off they went at the end of the term and we waited anxiously to hear how they had got on. Only a few had failed totally, due to some disaster, such as sickness among the goats, or from mismanagement. Most had managed to cover their costs and make a small profit. Much later, when we got news of some of these ladies, it was good to hear that these small beginnings had led to a complete turnaround in their lives. Their businesses had prospered and they could now afford to send their children to secondary school and pay for medical needs.

TRIBAL CONFLICTS

In the first and second year, the new students had come from among the smaller tribes, toward the Uganda and Kenya borders. Open Doors decided that they should widen the scope and invite participants from some of the other tribes. So it was decided to invite some from the Dinka tribe. Both the Dinka and Nuer tribes are regarded with fear and suspicion, because of their warlike behaviour. When the news came out, the ladies who were cooking pretty well went on strike! "We will never cook for Dinka men," they asserted.

Next term, the Dinka contingent arrived - tall, very black men with tribal markings on their foreheads. Some of the cooks had refused to come back, but replacements were easily found. I think we were all rather anxious about how this would work. When the women came forward tentatively to greet them, they responded with huge irresistible smiles, giving praise to God for bringing them safely. The women were amazed, thinking to themselves, "Are these really Dinka?" They were very polite and determined to fit in with the others and do well. This was a very important issue that had been addressed and it was a very healing

249

experience for some of the students who in years gone by had suffered at the hands of some of the Dinka.

THE DINKA

The Dinka tribe is both the biggest and strongest tribe in South Sudan. They constitute the heart of the South Sudan Resistance Army and are particularly proud and warlike. When the early missionaries entered their territory, there was practically no response from them. However, after many years of war, things began to change. A young pastor called Nathaniel Garang (later Bishop) walked through their area, preaching a gospel of peace. For people who had grown up under the constant threat of war, peace had a definite attraction. Nathaniel explained that although he could not give them peace from war, he could show them how to have peace in their hearts, by having a relationship with Jesus. They began to listen to his preaching and many of them felt the call to follow Christ. But there was still a problem.

In each of the Dinka's compounds there was a pole standing in the middle. This pole, or Jok, represented the spirits of their ancestors and other spiritual powers. On the pole they kept a cult object, usually a cow's hide or a spear, to ensure that their cattle (which even now represent their wealth) would flourish. Nathaniel told them that if they wished to become Christians, they must burn the Jok!

This caused a lot of consternation. They had not fully realised how much they relied on the Jok, so they did not dare burn it. One family decided that in spite of their initial fear, they would go through with it. All the villagers assembled in their compound and watched as they burnt the Jok. Then they waited in anticipation, expecting terrible disasters to fall on the family. To the contrary, they had a very good year, several male babies were born, their cows bore healthy calves and their harvests were better than usual.

After this experience, more and more families decided to burn the Jok and become Christians. But when something as important as the Jok is taken away, something is needed to

250

replace it. So instead of the Jok they put up a cross, and some villages erected a tall cross outside their village. They also made small crosses, which they took to church with them. In 1999 I was in a Dinka church along with 600 Dinka worshippers. They had written their own hymns and songs, with their special haunting melodies. As they sang, they lifted their small crosses up and down in time to the music. It was a very moving experience. The cross in the picture is 18 feet tall and stands outside the village, telling everyone that this is a Christian village.

It was in this church that I saw some bundles hanging from the ends of the poles that held up the roof. When looked more closely, I realised that each of the bundles actually had a baby inside!

On reflection, it was a very wise decision taken by Nathaniel Garang to tell the people that they must burn the jok.. When people become Christians, they often carry a great deal of 'baggage' with them, from their previous lives. Much of Africa is steeped in witch-craft and spirit worship. From childhood people are taught to revere and also to fear the spirits. Babies are often given amulets to wear to ward off any evil. These will be carried into adulthood. Syncretism is rife in many African churches. This means taking on the new religion but also retaining some of the old religion. Syncretism actually shows that the new Christian does not have sufficient faith to throw off all of their old ways. The amulet or other cult object is kept to fall back on, in case Christianity proves itself unable to protect the new believer. It takes great courage as well as faith to break completely with the old traditions. Making such a break may well cause deep unhappiness or even aggression from family members who feel that the new Christian is abandoning the old and loved traditions and casting a slur on the family as a whole.

DINKA AND NUER

As I have already mentioned, the Dinka and Nuer have been enemies for centuries. Each tribe has suffered at the hands of the other in large areas of the country. The main grievances concern land possession and cattle rustling. The problem is that they seem unable to forget or forgive. Parents and grandparents tell the stories to the children and so the hurts are passed from generation to generation. One year, there was a peace conference arranged by a group trained in reconciliation. On day one, only the Dinka were allowed to speak, while the Nuer had to remain silent. So the Dinka poured out their grievances, telling how their families had suffered over the centuries at the hands of the Nuer. The Nuer had to sit and listen. On Day 2, it was the turn of the Nuer, who poured out theirs. As each group listened, they began to realise that they had all had the same experiences.

The leader gently helped them to understand the futility of their enmity. He encouraged them to forgive one another. I was not present at this meeting, but by all accounts there was a wonderful and very emotional coming together of the two tribes, with many tears. Much later we heard that although the problems went on in other areas, the peace that had been established held for some time.

We had a similar experience in the Bible School. Once the Dinka had been accepted, Open Doors decided to invite some Nuer students for the following year. Again there was a certain

amount of apprehension. On the Sunday, George William preached a strong and emotional sermon about reconciliation. There followed a time of exuberant worship that lifted us up into the very courts of heaven. At the end of the service, there was an amazing time of reconciliation as the Dinka and Nuer students jumped up and began to hug one another and once more there were many tears of joy. One of my students wrote about it, saying, "My heart was so gladful that it nearly bursted with joy!" I had my camera with me and took a picture of three Nuer and two Dinka showing how they were 'all one in Christ Jesus'.

The other students, from the smaller tribes, looked on with pleasure. A couple of years later, some Murle students were invited. As mentioned above, the Murle have a history of stealing children from other tribes. This time, all the other students were suspicious. At first they were ostracised by most of the others, but as the term went on they again began to say, "They are just like us – and they are Christians." So once again, there was a time of reconciliation.

This experience led me to write a poem about freedom.

> We cannot escape our past,
> Satan, the skilful spider laughs
>
> It envelops us like a garment,
>
> To see us caught, enmeshed in his web,
>
> Like the tentacles of a great sea monster,

A prisoner to our past.

Clinging, cloying, claiming us for its own.
We, unlike God, cannot choose to forget,

The blueprints of our past,

Our past, like the poor is always with us,

The imprints of your family line

One component in our personality.

Are carved in the depth of our being,

Written large on every page

BUT, for Christians –

"Stand fast in the freedom where Christ has set you free!"
Freedom from the past – can it be? Even for me?
"My chains fell off, my heart was free."
Can this be true, for you, for me?
The blueprints, the imprints are graven deep,
But Christ the great Eraser, the Liberator can set us free.
His mighty power can break the bond,
Snap the links, cut through the chains.
The clinging web can lose its grip.

So throw back your head, lift up your eyes
And shout to the one who would keep you enslaved,
"In Christ I have freedom, he has the victory!"
For "He has broken chains that bound me,
He has set this captive free."

CHAPTER 19 THE END – AND LOOKING BACK

In 2003, when I was 70, AIM felt that it was time I returned home and settled back into my home. The following year, I reclaimed my house, but continued to make journeys to Sudan twice a year for six weeks at a time. Admittedly, the journey was becoming a bit more challenging, but in my pride I thought I could go on until I was 80. That however was not to be.

In 2009, as I lay in my bed one night I began to feel my heartbeat becoming a little irregular. It occurred more and more often, so I started taking my pulse and felt four beats, then miss one, three beats, miss one, eight beats, miss one – or two. At first I tried to ignore it, until it began to trouble my sleep, so I gave in and visited the doctor. After a few tests it turned out that I was suffering from arrhythmia, so was given some pills.

This occurred in September and I was booked to go back to Sudan in October. When I applied for my travel insurance, I was horrified to see that the cost had increased by £800. This was quite outside my budget, but I was still determined to travel. So I decided to go without insurance! As I wrote earlier, my mission had labelled me as a risk-taker – and here I was taking yet another risk.

I arrived safely and settled in happily. I have to admit that I felt a little guilty at being there without any insurance, so I decided I should confess. I called on George and Maretha, the South African couple who were leading the work and told them of my position. They were not very happy!

In my pride, I had felt sure that I would be one of those seasoned missionaries, going on into my eighties. I began to realise that the three-day journey to and from the UK and the tough conditions had recently become a bigger challenge physically.

After much prayer and discussion with George and Maretha, I came to the conclusion that this was to be my last trip to Sudan.

It was not an easy decision, yet once taken, I began to have a deep feeling of peace.

I had a good time once again with my students and really enjoyed not only the teaching, but the relationships. I enjoyed good times with the other tutors, who of course were very sorry to see me go. When a member of a team retires, it may leave a big gap. However for the last couple of years I had been accompanied by Chris Doust, a retired AIM missionary, who shared both the English teaching and Devotions. She was also called upon to teach some of the theology. So it was a big comfort to Ruth Kwani, who was leading the women's courses, to know that Chris would be returning the following year.

I had a wonderful send-off from both students and staff. The staff party took place outside, with all of us sitting around in a big circle. There was singing and worship and then various tributes, which really touched my heart, and some very generous gifts. One of these gifts was two lengths of cotton material, with a typical African pattern of large flowers on a bright blue background. It was very pretty, but I somehow did not feel it would fit into my life back in South Croydon. However, I accepted it with real gratitude for the generosity of these people. I brought it home with me and put it away. The following year, my home church of Emmanuel was hosting the Africa Inland Mission Conference. This was my last Conference as a mission partner, so I was able to give my final report and explain about my retirement. I had decided to take the material with me to see if anyone would like to have it. At that time, a young couple, Owen and Miriam were preparing to go out to Tanzania, so I offered Miriam the fabric. She was thrilled, as she would be able to make a really nice African dress before she went. Later that evening I had an email from Miriam. She was thrilled to have the material, but even more so as she saw in it a deeper significance. In the Bible, when the old prophet Elijah finally retired, he gave his mantle to the young prophet who was going to take his place. So she felt that as I was retiring, I was passing on my mantle to her.

After all the farewells to my friends in Sudan, I set out for my final three-day trip back home. It was a moment of very mixed emotions. There was real sadness at leaving the students and my dear friends on the staff. There was also great sadness at leaving my beloved Sudan. However there was also a sense of relief that this was to be the last journey I would take. But deep down there was a real sense of peace. I knew that God had sent me out and now I just as surely believed that He was the one who had said, "Enough". I became even more sure of this when I revisited the Cardiologist. He could find nothing wrong with my heart. It had settled down again to a perfectly normal rhythm and has remained so until this day. God has ways and means of guidance. Some people are able to hear the 'still small voice' of God, but others like me needed more like a trumpet blast!

On returning to Nairobi I had the challenge of packing up for the last time. It was a time of multiple decisions – what to take with me, what to send by post and what to sell or give away. I had a yard sale at extremely generous prices and was delighted to see some of my belongings going to good homes where I knew they would be of use. I had the joy of giving away a lot of items to friends. Finally, with all the precious items I wished to take with me, I was ready for the last journey home.

Was it the same woman who had undertaken that first journey when my son Murray had seen me off? He had said that he had watched me go, a small, lonely figure gradually disappearing up the ramp into the departure lounge. Now I was returning as a seasoned traveller, but I was clearly not the same sort of woman who was returning 15 years later. As I seek to answer this question, I need to reflect on many of my experiences. I have had the privilege of speaking to a variety of groups about my time abroad. My presentation is called 'Sudan, its Joys and Sorrows', so now I am thinking back to some of my own joys and sorrows.

My ongoing sorrow is for the fighting that is still going on in Sudan. Here is another account written by one of the students, who is also longing for peace.

HOW THE WAR HAS AFFECTED MY LIFE

by Alemin Komi

In 1983 the war broke out in Sudan. We used to listen to the radio to know what was going on. When we heard that the Sudan People's Liberation Army had conquered any area, we felt excited, even though we were not politicians. In 1989 the SPLA advanced towards our area, in the Nuba Mountains, but the situation became more difficult. Next, the Khartoum forces invaded the area, but they did not differentiate between the civilians and the army. They started to burn down houses and churches. Many civilians became victims of war, some killed and others arrested.

After two more years, that was 1991, the conditions became worse and worse. Do you know what happened? All the people in the region were threatened by famine and insecurity for some years. People began eating only leaves and some animals' meat because we could not grow any crops. There was no humanitarian aid.

As the situation was getting even worse, the civilians could not endure it any longer, so they scattered and dispersed from their homes. Some fled and surrendered themselves to the Khartoum government. Some ran to the areas around. Those who surrendered they killed or tortured and others were imprisoned.

The war crisis was very critical and we who stayed were in miserable conditions. We were disturbed by Arab militias, killing people and looting our cattle and so on. As for me myself, I was attacked during the night by the militia, but God is great and he rescued me from danger.

During the war, Christianity in Nuba was very strong. The remnant from the war started to plant new churches in the areas they ran to. In all these difficulties God was with his people and made them strong. When the ceasefire was signed, the people could be at rest.

NOTE Sadly the 'rest' did not last long. The Agreement in 2005 left the Nuba Mountains area to be decided later by ballot. This has not yet taken place. The Christian majority want to belong to the south. As I write in 2015, the north is still bombing the area and the people are once more living in caves and

258

suffering hunger and insecurity. However, we hear that the churches remain strong.

In 2011 South Sudan gained its independence, but inter-tribal fighting continues, mainly between the Dinka and Nuer. Thousands are in refuge, hundreds have died, including two of 'my' pastors. It is heartbreaking that this country, created with such hope, is still being torn apart. As ever, it is the ordinary people who have been suffering most. The Sudanese have a proverb that aptly fits this scenario – When elephants fight, it is the grass that gets trampled.

Some NGOs are daring to come and help to rebuild the country, but most stand at the sidelines, waiting for peace to reign, so that all the original hopes for a prosperous country will be fulfilled. I pray that that may be soon.

JOYS AND SORROWS OVER MONEY MATTERS

Corruption is rife in many parts of Africa (as well as all over the world). I remember the sense of outrage when the $7000 I had promised for a particular project 'disappeared' while I was in Sudan. I remember how Edward locked us out of the office until we paid his College fees. These sorts of occasions were rather frequent and became one of my chief sorrows.

However, as far as my own finances were concerned, I was greatly blessed. As I mentioned, AIM is a 'faith' mission, so we are expected to 'pray in the money', and for me this was very easily accomplished, with so many friends and personal contacts. I have kept lists of those who gave money for me to take to Sudan. There are over 130 on the list. Many of these were people who 'adopted' one of the pastors' wives. This was a lovely programme. After interviewing each of the new wives, I took their photo. On my return I found people willing to become a 'friend' of one of these ladies. When I returned again to Sudan, they gave me a photo of themselves, a simply-written letter and a present of £25. Even more importantly, they promised to pray for each other.

Here is the story told to me by Kabina:

259

I was living in a fertile valley in the Nuba Mountains. The war had not come to area, so life was good. Then one day we heard gunfire and saw smoke rising from another village. We knew that the army would soon be here. I decided to take my children up into the mountains to hide. I had a baby, a toddler and I was heavily pregnant. I tied the baby round my neck, tied the toddler on my back and struggled up into the mountains to hide. It was a very hot day. I finally found a cave and sat down thankfully to rest. We were very thirsty, so I prayed to God then crept out to look for water. And there, just nearby was a small pool. I scooped up the water in my hands to drink and then carried some in for the children. Then we sat down to wait, listening to sounds of war and of people screaming. It became very cold at night.

Meanwhile, my husband, who was teaching a few miles away, saw the smoke and realised what was happening, so he ran back. When he neared our home, he knew he must not enter the village, as the army would kill all the men, take the women and girls as slaves and force the boys into the Quranic schools, to make them become Muslims. He guessed that I would have gone up into the mountains, so he set off to look for me. At midnight he found us and we sat together, trying to keep warm. Next morning we were able to find berries and other fruits to eat.

I asked Kabina how long they stayed up in the mountains. "Twelve years," she replied, "and that is why I cannot read or write." However Kabina was one of our best students and by the time she left she was able both to read and write. The sad thing is that war is still raging in her area, so she must once again be living up in the mountains.

Each time I went out to Africa, I carried with me all the money given to me for the ladies and the pastors. It was usually between £5000 and £7000. It was quite legal, of course, but rather scary, as I carried it in cash in various small bags around my body. I know many people prayed especially for me each time that it would arrive safely – and it did. The next excitement was exchanging it for Uganda shillings. (Southern Sudan did not have its own currency at that time. Now they have dinars.) As one pound was worth about 3250 Uganda shillings, I very quickly became a multi-millionaire!

Next there came the joy of giving out the money. But it was also a tremendous challenge and responsibility to know who was genuinely in need. I have kept dozens of receipts from various recipients. The three biggest needs were 'family needs', health problems and secondary school fees. I would have loved to have been able to give something to every pastor in the Bible School, but there just was not enough. I realised the main denominations like the Baptists, Anglicans, Presbyterians etc had a 'mother church' in the west and were able to receive funds from them. However Africa Inland Church-Sudan is an indigenous church and so receives nothing from the west, so I limited my giving to pastors from AIC, with whom I had been working. Looking through the receipts I found several other categories of gifts: bicycles for pastors, Bible School fees, printing costs, Sunday School materials, clerical collars, materials for teaching AIDS awareness, song books, church building. Then there were the major projects I have described, such as the weddings, including paying off the dowries and the micro-projects for the pastors' wives.

I have only now realised that if I carried several thousand pounds each year, for fifteen years, that is a great deal of money. What generous hearts people back home had for me to be able to distribute such life-changing gifts. As I write in 2015, I am still able to send about £1,500 twice a year, the majority coming from our church's financial giving with about £500 I have raised, mostly from gifts as I visit different groups to talk about my work. Also my daughter Alison holds cake sales from time to

261

time to raise money. This has reminded me of a time when my grandson James, who was about 10 years old, organised a toy sale, to raise money for 'Gran' to take out!

So, in weighing up my 'Joys and 'Sorrows', as far as money was concerned, there were far, far more joys than sorrows.

MY WORK

As far as my work was concerned, it has been a great joy. My working life had been quite narrow. I was a school teacher from 1956 to 1995, with a break for child bearing. My subjects were Religious Education, Classical Studies and a bit of junior Latin. I was very confident in front of a class, but if asked to give a vote of thanks or short speech, I was very nervous, with sweaty hands. My life revolved around family, school and church. There was nothing else on the horizon. At the age of 62 all this was to change dramatically. I went out to Africa expecting to expand my activities by editing materials for Sudanese churches and schools. Within the first year, I found myself teaching teachers and to my absolute amazement writing English books. This English 'failure' at school, found that God had put gifts into me which He was drawing out, to enable me to meet new demands. I firmly believe that each of us has gifts which God has planted within us, which He can draw out when the need occurs. So if we are asked to do

 something which we feel we are not capable of, if it is God's will, He will provide the ability. This is a pretty challenging thought.

Over the next years I again found myself doing things I would not have thought possible. I had the privilege of teaching AIDS Awareness, which may have stopped many young people from contracting this terrible scourge. I had the joy of teaching illiterate women how to read – and of providing the books and materials. I love this picture. It shows two previously illiterate women sitting in the long grass and reading one of my textbooks. It somehow encapsulates my joy in being able to help in this way.

Would I ever have dreamed that I would be instrumental in paying off the dowries for nineteen pastors and then hosting their weddings? Or that I would be able to provide bicycles and even a motor bike for some of the pastors?

Was it Jan King who did all this? No, it was a generous and caring God, working through a home team of generous and caring people, through an unworthy woman who dared to hear God's call and answer it.

OTHER SORROWS

So far in this chapter, I have dwelt on the joys of my work. But there were also many sorrows. My greatest sadness was to see how so many of the Sudanese live in the thrall of witchcraft. It permeates their lives, leaving them full of fears and fantasies. Often problems or set-backs are attributed to the spirits. When I was teaching AIDS, there was the funeral of one of the local sub-chiefs. We decided to go to watch the proceedings. Several of the men, who I presume were witch-doctors, were dressed in skins and feathers and were dancing and chanting. At a given signal, all the women began to race out of the area, shouting and screaming. It was horrible. I asked what was going on and was told that they were chasing away the evil spirits that were trying to attack the dead man. I was very aware of a heaviness in my spirit, of the power of evil. Back in our tukuls, we could hear the women running and screaming, far into the night.

I came across several instances of people poisoning Christians. In Adjumani, John, the District Chairman was at a celebration. A man he did not know came with a drink for him and was very pressing, encouraging him to drink it. As soon as the man left, John poured it onto the ground where is fizzed and hissed. A very strange thing happened to Pastor Sam's wife, Rose. There had been opposition to the church from the local witch doctor. When Rose sat on a particular chair, she could not

263

get up. It was as if she had been glued to it. Sam came to try to help her up, but it was impossible. Then the witch doctor appeared and said he would release her, but they must pay him. Either Rose would have to become another wife for him, or Sam must build him a new tukul, or he must pay a large sum of money. Sam chose the third option, so he released Rose, but then said she must come and live in his compound until the money was paid. Fortunately a number of AIM personnel and others were there, so we clubbed together and raised the money. Rose was released, but it left us with a new and frightening insight into the power of evil.

Another sorrow was the existence of the Lord's Resistance Army, which rampaged in the south east of the country and on into Congo and Central Africa Republic. I heard of so many instances of crops being stolen or burned, of people being caught and having their noses or ears cut off, of young boys being abducted and forced into their ranks. This is yet another reason why so many people live in fear.

Their other fear is the fear of illness and the presence of venomous snakes, scorpions and the ever-present mosquito. It seems strange that in the UK we have none of these things, whereas they are a constant threat to the Sudanese. So many children die from tropical diseases, malaria in particular. I have heard of organisations pledged to rid Africa of malaria and can only say, 'Amen, let it be soon'. As I consider all these sorrows, I begin to realise what a privileged person I am, living in a safe and comfortable home in our temperate climate. It is very easy to take it for granted and to forget the sufferings of other peoples throughout the world.

Quite a different sorrow was that of missing a lot of my grandchildren's early years. Sammy (Val's daughter) and James (Alison's son) were both born before I left. Sammy's sister Annie arrived next, while I was in Africa. Two years later Murray's eldest, Matthew was born, followed two months later by Peter, a brother for James. Finally Matthew's brother Ben arrived. Occasionally I received cassettes from the families, and it was a great joy to hear their voices. I missed over ten years of their early development, but whenever I was home I tried to catch up with all of them. When visiting Val once, I found that the girls had chosen to have their bedroom decorated in an African style with jungle curtains and a waste-basket in the shape of a giraffe! Every term I sent the grandchildren lovely postcards, which were cut out in the shape of different animal. These also had a place on their walls. The six of them are now in their teens and early twenties, growing up to be super young people.

HELPING OR HINDERING?

There are a large number of organisations working in Sudan, trying to help the people after their devastating years of civil war. This is generally a real blessing, but it can back-fire. One kind hearted group decided that what the Sudanese needed was good metal hoes, so that they could cultivate better. Unfortunately they sent them to an area where everyone kept cattle and were not interested in agriculture. The hoes, however, were not wasted. The Sudanese do their cooking by resting their pots on three stones, which were sometimes unstable, so three identical hoes did a far better job! I had to smile when I saw this, but felt sad. If only the group had asked what the people would really need and would appreciate, their money would have been so much better spent.

Another problem stemming from all the outside help is dependency. Some people soon realised that if there was an organisation that was giving out aid of one sort or the other, they just had to wait for their turn and not make any effort themselves. One of the saddest remarks I heard over the years was spoken by an older man. "My people have forgotten how to dig," he told me. "Instead they are just lazy and wait for hand-outs." He said this with tears in his eyes, as he was a man who had worked hard both in the church and the community all of his life.

On the other hand, having westerners in their midst can present people with a good role model. I read recently of an American priest who was overseeing a project, with a good team

265

of workers. Although he was the boss, he would roll up his sleeves and work with the team. A pastor was watching and afterwards spoke to him. "In my culture, the boss just gives out the orders and then sits back and watches the work." The priest explained that Jesus has called us to be servants. This would have been a big challenge to the pastor. I have not heard what happened next.

The theme of service was taken up by pastor Samson, when we were teaching in a refugee camp. In his sermon he told us a story. The church compound was in urgent need of repair, so he asked his people to come at a certain time and get the work done. The day dawned, but nobody turned up. He decided to pray about it and had an idea. Next week, he gave out the same message, and still nobody came. So he got his tools and started to work together with his wife. Some of the neighbours saw what was going on. "Look," they said, "Our pastor is working. Let's join him." Soon there was a good team of church members and also of other neighbours and the work was finished. He ended his sermon with a challenge for the entire group, including himself. "My brothers, if you have come for training so that you can return to your churches to gain high positions, you are on the wrong course. We are here to learn to be servants of our Lord Jesus Christ," What a privilege it was for me to have experienced this and seen how the people were gradually becoming more Christ-like in their lives.

Another issue which affects many Sudanese is their status, as was illustrated in the story above and can take other forms. Some students come to a course to learn, for themselves. Their certificate gives them a certain status in their community. Therefore it is quite common for them not to share their newly-found knowledge, but keep it to themselves, so putting them in a higher category compared to those without such knowledge. For the same reason, some pastors refused to share their knowledge even with their own wives. This could occur among our male students, but not so with our women. As soon as they had learned something, they were all too eager to share it with their communities.

Another sorrow struck me when I was teaching church leaders at the Writers' Workshop. I had realised that the AIC pastors were busy preaching the gospel and opening new churches, but this was not so with the Anglican clergy. On enquiring why this was, I was told that they could not open a new church as they had no clerical robes for the clergy. It seemed that to them the status of wearing robes was more important than evangelising and planting new churches.

Once I was home for good, I weighed up the joys and sorrows. It was quite clear that the joys easily outweigh the sorrows I experienced so many blessings which I would never have known, had I remained in the UK.

FINAL FAREWELLS

Having had such a good send off in Sudan, I had another in Nairobi. Rhondda (being Australian) wrote a song to the tune of Waltzing Matilda, with its refrain,

Venture with Grandma, venture with Grandma, Who'll come and look for adventures with me

I was very moved by the letter of appreciation when I left ACROSS, saying, We are grateful for all achieved you in your time with us. We are thankful that you were sent to us and know that you have touched many lives.

I was equally moved by one of the pastors who wrote, Mama Jan, I am highly appreciating your lovely time with us. My hands are hanging up greetings to you.

One of the wedding couples wrote, When Mama Jan came to us, my heart was so gladful that it nearly bursted for joy.

HOME FOR GOOD

I waved goodbye to my friends who came to see me off. There were so many who wanted to greet me that I nearly missed the plane. So it was with tears in my eyes that I set out for my last long flight from Africa. My arrival home was marred by the fact that my luggage did not arrive home with me. I was terribly upset,

267

as I had brought back all my most precious things, with many memories. However at 8.30 am the following morning, to my great relief, the bags were delivered to my door!

Settling back was not always easy. We are warned about culture shock, when going off to Africa. But reverse culture shock can be just as difficult. In my final prayer letter, I listed the things that I missed or were a challenge:

> I miss my dear Sudanese brothers and sisters, with their warm fellowship and deep trust in our mighty God, in spite of their problems.

> I miss going off happily to the office every morning. It seems strange to get up without an agenda for the day.

> Now I am just Jan King, rather than being part of a group and net-working with people often in high places. I guess that would be called loss of status.

> I have a problem of fitting into the Britain of today.

> Things are expensive here. In Africa we had house-help at 30p an hour. We did not throw things away but took them to a 'fundi' to be mended.

> It is so cold here. I went to the park to see the glorious autumn colours and nearly froze to death.

> I don't much like living alone, after sharing a home in Nairobi.

Quite soon after I returned, I decided to visit a new superstore near my home. On entering and seeing the rows and rows of luxuries that my Sudanese friends could never aspire to, I turned and fled. I came back a few days later, determined to overcome my problems and did quite well until I came to a long aisle containing 'luxury food for pets'. I could only think how the contents of some of those tins would have been a real feast for some of the poor. So once again I left, with the few items I had managed to take. Of course, this situation became easier and easier and is no longer an issue. However I am still horrified by the amount of food wasted. One day, I was being entertained by a couple, who served lovely chicken breasts. There was one left, so my hostess offered it to me. I quickly thought that it would have made a good meal for one of them the next day, so I politely refused – only to see her throw it into the waste bin!

My list of things I missed was written eleven years ago and now I actually find that I do like living alone and I have fitted happily back into British life. But I know that deep down I am not the same woman who set off alone in 1995. I have had the privilege of touching many lives for good, of experiencing a very deep fellowship with many Sudanese brothers and sisters and of being aware that God had his hand on me and has used me for his special purposes.

My life has been enriched by my experiences in ways that are very different from my friends back home. I have lived with Australians and Americans, I have worked under Sudanese, Kenyans and South Africans and at one time in the College, those of us on the staff came from nine different countries!

As I look back over the years, I can see how God has had His hand on me over the years. I first felt His call in 1955 and 40 years later I was finally able to respond. I realise that He had had His hand on me throughout my years in England but it was in a much more dramatic way in Africa.

I know that in spite of a number of sorrows, I have experienced joys I would never have dreamed of. Did I deserve all this? Certainly not, but God is a God of grace and it is this undeserved grace that has overwhelmed me in those amazing years of ministry with the Sudanese.

I can only end my story by saying, 'To God be the glory, great things He has done!'

Jan King is now 82 and lives in South Croydon, in a comfortable house with a garden that is her great joy. She has three adult children and six grandchildren. Jan is much involved in her local church, doing jobs that range from church cleaning, to leading a Home group and teaching new Testament Greek. She believes in keeping fit and attends a keep fit class, taking it sometimes when the leader is away. She is a member of the U3A – University of the 3rd Age and is learning Russian and studying Medieval history. She sings in a local choir and loves to keep busy.

If you have enjoyed this book please consider leaving a review on Amazon and I would love to hear your views or answer any questions the book may raise, you can contact me on: Janking36@yahoo.com

Bible Study/Book Club Questions?
1. It is often said that when God shuts a door, He opens a window. How has this been true in Jan's story?
2. What experiences in her early life were a preparation for her time in Sudan?
3. People new to most of Africa are warned about 'Culture Shock'. What were some of the problems she had to cope with in Kenya, before she went to Sudan?
4. 'I believe that we all have talents that we have never used'. How was this so for Jan? Could it be true for you?
5. Mary's story on page 188 talks of forgiveness. Why is it so important for us to forgive any who have hurt us?
6. Look at Jan's 'special verse' on page 10. In what ways did God keep the promises in this verse?
7. (for women) How would you have coped with being a woman, in Sudanese culture?
8. Just for fun – How many cows would your boyfriend pay for your dowry?
9. Jan was called in her 60s. How should we best spend our retirement?
10. How different might Jan's life be today if she had never been to Sudan?

Made in the USA
Charleston, SC
08 December 2015